Connotations of
Movement
in
Sport and Dance

BROWN

PHYSICAL EDUCATION SERIES

Edited by

AILEENE LOCKHART
University of Southern California
Los Angeles, California

Connotations of Movement in Sport and Dance

A Collection of Speeches
about Sport and Dance
as Significant Forms
of Human Behavior

by

Eleanor Metheny

Professor of Physical Education
University of Southern California

WM. C. BROWN COMPANY PUBLISHERS
135 SOUTH LOCUST STREET • DUBUQUE, IOWA 52003

Manufactured by WM. C. BROWN CO. INC., Dubuque, Iowa
Printed in U. S. A.

Preface

One way to explore an idea is to talk about it — preferably to an interested audience, hopefully to a critical one. The idea explorations now gathered together in this book were developed in this way. Through the years various organizations have invited me to speak in their meetings, sometimes on an assigned topic, sometimes under a title of my own choosing. Then, in accordance with professional custom, I would be asked to provide a written draft of my speech for inclusion in the Proceedings of the organization or for distribution in mimeographed form. And, on those happy occasions when what I had said seemed important to someone, requests for additional copies of these manuscripts have come in long after the initial presentation. During the past decade I have accumulated a file of these more frequently-requested speech manuscripts. The purpose of this book is to make them available in convenient and semipermanent form.

The speeches that make up the first section of this book have grown out of a long-term attempt to explore the relationships between characteristically human organizations of voluntary movement and the processes and functions of human thought. Taken as a group they suggest the outlines of a comprehensive theory about the significance of sport and dance as educationally meaningful forms of human experience. Taken separately, each speech is an attempt to deal with one aspect of that theory in some way that might be meaningful to a specific group of people within the limitations imposed by the speech-making situation.

Like any veteran speaker, I have often repeated myself. At times I have used material developed for one occasion to round out another speech presented before a different group of people, and I have frequently used certain speeches on several different occasions. In this collection I have made no attempt to weed out the repeated paragraphs, because this would destroy the structure of the speeches in which they occur. Neither have I attempted to list the several occasions on which a given speech may have been repeated. Rather, I have noted the pertinent information needed to suggest the setting in which each talk was first presented; and in those instances when the manuscript was eventually published in some generally available book or periodical, I have listed these bibliographical details.

It may also be noted that what I have said in later speeches is not always wholly consistent with what I said in earlier ones. If this were a formal book I might feel obliged to rework those earlier statements in an attempt to eliminate all trace of these developmental differences in my own thinking. But this would destroy the identity of each speech as a reasonably coherent organization of ideas, put together for presentation to a given group of listeners. So rather than attempting to write a whole new set of speeches that might represent my present thinking, I have chosen to let each paper stand on whatever merit it had in its own time.

All of these comments are equally appropriate to the second group of papers dealing with women as participants in sport and as teachers of physical education. Here, too, I have repeated myself; here, too, I have occasionally contradicted myself. But so be it.

The final paper, however, is in a class by itself. "I Like Being a Teacher!" began as a spontaneous statement in a meeting of college teachers some fifteen years ago. Since that time it has gone through countless spoken versions and several written and tape-recorded ones. After fifteen years of circulation I am still getting requests for copies — so it seems to say something that is meaningful to many teachers. In this collection I have used a short version that appeared in the NEA *Journal.* Its appearance elicited many letters from teachers who were grateful to me because I had spoken out about the many rewards they, too, had found in our chosen profession.

Perhaps some day I shall do a companion piece called "I Like Being a Speaker!" For me, this extramural activity has been as rewarding as teaching — and for many of the same reasons. But here let me say only that I am grateful to the countless program chairmen, audiences, welcoming committees, and new-found friends who made these rewards possible. And at this moment I am particularly grateful to those who gave me occasion to make the speeches that are recorded in this book.

I am also deeply grateful to Alfred A. Knopf, Inc., for permission to use several extended quotations from the published works of the poet Wallace Stevens, whose insight into the nature of symbolic forms has made many contributions to my own growing understanding of the significance of sport and dance.

Some measure of my debt to Lois Ellfeldt, my colleague at the University of Southern California, is acknowledged in listing her as coauthor of several of the papers included in this collection. My greater debt, however, must be measured in terms of many years of collaboration in the development of the major ideas expressed in these speeches. For that happy collaboration between a maker of dances and a maker of speeches, I am also deeply grateful.

ELEANOR METHENY

University of Southern California
Los Angeles, California
March, 1965

Acknowledgments:

As noted in the text, certain speeches and articles included in this book have been published initially by the American Association of Health, Physical Education and Recreation, The Athletic Institute, The Physical Educator, The American Journal of Occupational Therapy, and The NEA Journal. I am indebted to these organizations and publications for permission to reprint these articles in this collection.

I am also grateful to Alfred A. Knopf, Inc., the publishers of the poetry of Wallace Stevens, for permitting me to reprint material from the Copyrighted edition: THE COLLECTED POEMS OF WALLACE STEVENS, New York, 1954. The poems from which the reprinted lines have been taken are indicated in the appropriate sections of the text.

ELEANOR METHENY

Contents

Part I

On Significance
in Sport and Dance

How Do They Learn?

Southern District Association for Health, Physical Education and Recreation — Jacksonville, Florida — March, 1964

The idea of physical education is as old as the idea of sending children to school so they may learn whatever their parents want them to know. In the early schools of Athens and Sparta, the palestra and gymnasium were the center of the school plant. Children were required to spend much time in these facilities, and the taxpayers of Greece prized the learning that went on during these periods. Boys who excelled in the arts of running, throwing, wrestling, and dancing were greatly admired — and often richly rewarded by their communities. And many of them became public officials and senators because the people respected them for their athletic achievements.

But the philosophers who conducted their academic classes on the shaded porches of these facilities were not wholly in accord with this public evaluation. They recognized that skill and strength would be needed in time of war, and so they encouraged young men to participate in these vigorous activities; but they could see no connection between what was occurring in the gymnasium and their own lectures and debates about the nature of human knowledge.

Today we find this same pattern of educational interpretation in our own country. Whenever the taxpayers build a new junior or senior high school, they spend at least one-fifth of the building fund on facilities for a full-scale program of physical education. They pass laws requiring every pupil to spend a major share of his school time in these costly facilities; and the abilities developed in them are highly prized within the community — and often richly rewarded. Boys who excel in these arts are sought out by business men who wish to employ them — and on occasion they may be elected to high public office because of these abilities.

Thus it would seem that taxpayers, parents, and educators attach much significance to this part of the over-all educational process — but when we turn to the educational ledgers in which units of learning are accredited, we find a quite different story. Here the learnings of the gymnasium rank far below the learnings of the class room — so far below that registrars may not even bother to translate this learning into units of credit or evaluative grades.

And how do the parents really evaluate this learning? Let us listen in on a dinner-table conversation in a more-or-less typical American home as father turns to Junior with the age-old parental question: "What did you learn in school today?"

Junior says enthusiastically: "I learned to hit a target; I learned to skip-to-my-Lou-my-darling." At this reply, father smiles indulgently. He says: "That's good! Your body needs some exercise, and I hope you will be a good ball player some day. But I'm not asking what you did with your *body*, son. I'm asking about how you used your *mind*. So tell me, what did you learn in your regular classes — like arithmetic, reading, and geography."

Junior knows what his father is talking about — but he is puzzled by the inference that he uses his mind in some classes and not in others. Didn't he pay attention in his physical education class? Didn't he listen, look, and touch? Didn't he think about what he heard, saw, and felt? Didn't he try to "get the idea" the physical education teacher was explaining in the same way he tried to "get the idea" conveyed by his arithmetic teacher? And didn't he do the same things in all of his classes when he tried to "make these ideas work" by trying to do what the teacher asked him to do?

The modern answer to Junior's question is: Yes, Junior. You did behave in the same ways in all of your classes — because you really are *the whole child* we have been talking about in our educational conferences for some forty years — the fully-integrated thinking and acting whole child who functions as a fully-integrated whole. We believe that this whole child does pay attention to what he perceives in all of his classes. We believe that he does try "to get the idea" of ball-throwing in the same way that he tries "to get the idea" of multiplication, because there is only one fundamental process of idea-getting. And we believe that the whole child uses these ideas to structure his own attempts to do whatever he tries to do. (And what is more, Junior, we believe that there is only one kind of learning — but many ways in which learning may be expressed.)

Having said this, however, we must also add: Please be patient with your father, Junior — and with us, your teachers. We have been talking about this whole child for forty years, but we have not yet quite "gotten the idea" represented by this phrase, because adults always find it difficult to give up old ideas they learned from their ancestors, even when they are convinced that those ideas no longer work.

The old idea that Junior can be treated as a learning mind and a behaving body was formulated by the Greek philosophers who sat on the shaded porches of the gymnasiums some twenty-five hundred years ago. It has been the central idea in man's evaluation of himself during all the intervening centuries. Every traditional theory of learning rests on it, and practically all of our educational methodology still revolves around it. So we must not be harsh with Junior's parents for their inability to recognize the *real* learning that was going on as Junior attempted to hit the target and skip-to-my-Lou-my-darling. (Neither must we be too harsh with our educational colleagues who refuse to give him credit for what he has learned. But we may well be harsh with ourselves if we refuse to explore the implications of our own forty-year-old belief in the functional integrity of the whole child. No area of education has more to gain than we do from the recognition that Junior develops his understanding of *ideas* by putting them to work in other ways than word-saying; and no area of education has more to lose by refusing to modernize its own interpretation of the nature of human learning.

This is neither the time nor the place to examine the mounting stock of evidence that supports our belief in the fully-integrated nature of the learning process. Rather, let us explore some of the implications of this evidence by asking what Junior means when he says: "I try to get the idea; and then I try to make the idea work."

Many of our older theories of learning are based on experiments that recall the familiar story of the ape, banana, and stick. You will remember that the ape was in a cage and the banana was hanging outside just beyond his reach. The experimenter called the ape's attention to a stick placed in the cage, but the ape did not immediately recognize the connection between his arm, the stick, and the banana. However, as he brandished the stick about, he pushed it through the bars of the cage in the direction of the banana, and discovered that it could be used to extend his arm to banana-reaching length. Thus, he established an association between sticks and faraway bananas, and on subsequent days he used this association to get other bananas.

But our newer theories of learning place more emphasis on the second chapter of this story. One day the experimenter hid the familiar stick and replaced it with a green, uneatable banana. The experimenter knew that green bananas make very good "reach extenders," but the ape did not detect this important resemblance between green banana and stick. So again he had to go through the whole trial-and-error process. He had discovered that a stick could be used as a "reach extender," but he could not go beyond that point. He could not abstract the *idea* of reach-extending objects from his perception of the concrete stick. And so he could not use this *idea* to compare the green banana with the stick on the basis of the characteristics that made it a reach-extender.

By the time human children are three years old they can do what apes can never learn to do. They can deal with *ideas* about how certain aspects of reality seem to be organized. For example, they can abstract the idea of "what a circle is like" from their perception of a specific circle that is made of a small bit of green paper. If the experimenter shows them such a small, green circle, they can choose all of the objects that are like it from an array of many objects of different shapes, colors, materials, or sizes. It may be many years before they will be able to explain that they chose these circular objects because all of them were bounded by a continuous line on which every point was equidistant from a point within, called the center. It may be even longer before they will be able to describe these circular relationships in terms of 2-pi-r or pi-r-squared. But as soon as a child "gets the idea" of what a circle is like, he can put that idea to work in many different ways.

He may draw his understanding of this idea on paper with his crayons. He may mold this idea with his modelling clay. He may construct it with his blocks by pushing them around in a ring. He may describe the idea in space by moving his fingers, his hand, or his whole body around in a circle; or he may make this idea work by running around on a circular path or rotating around his own vertical axis until he gets dizzy.

As soon as he is aware of this general idea of "what circles are like" he also begins to discover circles in many areas of his experience. He finds roundness in his playmates — and his first attempt to draw a "little boy" shows a round head with two round eyes and a round mouth, all mounted on a circular body with a row of round buttons down the front. He sees a round sun, a circular lamp, and round plates on a circular table. He also discovers that he can make circles with his mouth — some say OH, some say OO, some blow bubbles, and some "make a kiss." He sees his father make a circle as he whistles. He sees circles in the wheels of his toys, and hears them in the whirrings of their inner mechanisms. He also feels them in his hands as he winds up those toys, and discovers the difference between clockwise and counterclockwise circles.

And when he starts to school, he will make a great many discoveries about what circles are like and how circles work in his physical education classes — as the elementary teachers among us will most certainly testify.

In all of these experiences with the *idea* of a circle, he discovers that many happenings within his small universe seem to be organized in the same way. And he is discovering that he can use this idea about how the universe is organized to "make things happen" of his own volition. In time he will learn that this organizational principle can be represented by the word-sound *circle,* and by related words like *wheel, round, rotation, turning.* But this idea does not become meaningful because it is now represented by a word-sound; rather the word-sounds are meaningful because he already had a good working idea of "what circles are like," "how circles work," and what he can *do* with this understanding.

This is not to deny the value of words. The words, as such, will be used in many ways — including explaining to his parents what he learned in his geometry class, his art class, and perhaps in his studies of the social circles that structure the larger patterns of human life. They will also be very useful to him as he tries to sort out his own ideas and diagram the relationships among them. But today we know that he will also deal with many ideas that can not be put into words; and we know that many of his most important ideas about how the universe is organized, how it works, and how he can work effectively within it, will fall in this nonverbal category.

Today we know that the central process of human learning must be described in terms of an ongoing attempt to formulate *ideas.* In pursuit of those ideas, the children of men do not behave as the ape did. Rather they decide for themselves what they will pay attention to, and then they subject every chosen unit of perception to the process of determining "what is it like?" How does this resemble or seem to be related to my ideas about other events I have perceived? How is it related to my current ideas about myself? Then, when they have decided what they think this event *means* — or how it fits into the larger pattern of their present ideas — they attempt to *do* whatever this interpretation means to them.

This is why many experimental psychologists prefer to work with rats. In any given experimental situation the experimenter can usually induce the rat to pay attention to the stimulus, — and he can usually condition the rat to respond to that stimulus in reasonably predictable ways. Not so with children — as every teacher knows.

When thirty children of the same age are confronted with the same teacher-chosen stimulus, each one will screen his perceptions of it through his own current network of attention-centered ideas, and then he will make his own decision about what the stimulus means to him at that moment. Then he will *do* or *try to do* whatever he thinks this stimulus means to him. One child may choose to ignore it; another may sit motionless, either "lost in thought" or paralyzed by indecision; another may stand up and salute the flag; a fourth child may laugh; a fifth may write some words in his notebook; a sixth may throw a spitball; and so on through the whole range of possible human behaviors. And the next day, in a similar situation, each child may do something quite different.

But in his own way, each child is trying to do something that neither the rat nor the ape can do. He is trying to *make sense* out of what he has perceived by trying to incorporate this new unit of perception into the larger pattern of his ideas about how the realities of his life are organized, how reality works, and how he functions within this working organization.

Today we have some reasonably good explanations of how this idea-formulating process is implemented by the neutral structures of the human brain; but the child has no need for this neurophysiological explanation. Rather, he incorporates his perceptions into the idea-patterns represented by the excitation of these complexly organized neural elements as naturally as he breathes. Or we may say, he thinks in this human way because he is an idea-organizing human being.

As he incorporates his interpretation of "what the teacher means" into his own idea structure, he may or may not be motivated to try to test that idea by attempting to "make it work." If the idea he finds in it is only mildly interesting to him, he may tuck it away in his thoughts for future consideration — or he may forget it entirely. But if he finds the idea interesting, he will focus his attention on it in every way possible, and this will involve him in an attempt to test the workability of the idea by trying to act out his understanding of it.

Again, we have some reasonably good explanations about how this idea-structure is transferred from the afferently-governed neurons of conscious thought to the efferent or motor nerves of bodily action. But, again, the child has no need for this explanation. He is no more concerned than the ape was with the intricacies of muscle contraction. Rather he does what the ape does — he simply *tries to do* whatever this idea means to him. The movements of his body may greatly resemble the movements of the ape's body in many ways, but if we examine them closely we will see that they differ from animal movements in that they are directed toward the accomplishment of objectives that animals do not seem to understand. They are directed toward an attempt to "make an idea work."

Thus, today we know that children do not develop skill in ball-throwing and skipping-to-my-Lou-my-darling by being pushed and pulled mechanically through appropriate movement patterns. Rather, they learn to "hit the target" by getting the idea of what target-hitting is like, and then trying to test their understanding of that idea by attempting to make it work. In this process they may utilize the process of trial-and-error, as they discover that this idea works better than that one. But with the help of a good teacher, they can clarify their ideas much more rapidly and effectively. The teacher may suggest that it would be a good idea to "try to keep your eye on the target" or to try to "start the throw from the ankles rather than from the shoulder" or to try to "point your fingers at the target as you release the ball."

As the child gets the meaning of these new bits and pieces of ideas, he incorporates them into his whole idea of "how to hit a target," and the teacher can observe the extent of this incorporation in the child's next attempt. And as teachers, we all know to the minute precisely when all parts of the idea fall into place, and the whole idea *makes sense* to Junior. So does he. From then on he can use that idea as readily as he uses a familiar word, because he knows what it means.

He can recall it at will; think about it; and use it any situation where it seems to be appropriate — even in situations that seem to have nothing to do with either a ball or a painted target. As he uses it, he may continue the process of clarifying his understanding of it; and in doing this he may relate it to many other ideas. In time, he may become a physical education teacher, or he may write a book about the kinesiological principles involved in imparting velocity and direction to a round ball or an oval-shaped one. Or he may write about the physiological changes that occur during and after repeated attempts to describe a curved path with the arm. In time, he may even reduce his understanding of ball-throwing to a formula for the curve produced by the effect of gravity on balls thrown at different angles — a formula much more complex than 2-pi-r or pi-r-squared. Or perhaps he may become a sportswriter and invest his whole life in the process of telling other people about men who throw balls, hit them, field them, and run around bases in an attempt to elude other ball throwers. And who knows, he may even be appointed to a high post in the national government because of his proficiency in ball-throwing.

No human idea is ever confined to a one-to-one connection between sticks and banana-getting. Like Junior's idea of "what a circle is like," every idea is linked to many other ideas that seem to be analogous with it in some way. This human ability to discover "likeness" in many concretely different events carried Junior's first idea of "what a circle is like" from the green paper to the tray of objects, to the little round boy with round buttons down before, to circle games, and on to the larger circles men form in their attempts to work together. So, too, as anyone who works with children knows, Junior's interest in ball-throwing is not confined to one round rubber ball and one circle painted on the wall of the gymnasium.

As he throws, he may well be thinking about rocks and tigers, about spitballs and teachers, about rockets and the moon. He may in fancy see himself in the center of some vast arena, throwing his ball at human targets, while other men cheer his success and boo his failures — and while sportswriters fill the pages of their newspapers with words of praise or blame.

As we all know from our own experience, the very phrase "hitting the target" may symbolize success in any form of human endeavour. No one knows precisely what ideas Junior is dealing with by extension as he performs the specific act of ball-throwing in his physical education class, but from our own personal experience we can guess that they center around the feeling of personal competence represented by the idea that *I can do something* with my own personal powers.

Every game, every sport, every gymnastic, aquatic, and track or field event that men have ever devised has been born of man's need to demonstrate his own ability to "make things happen." As we recognize this, we recognize why we all have such a large emotional investment in these events — both as participants and as spectators. And perhaps we can better understand why hard-working men spend their leisure time sitting in the hot sun and yelling: "Kill da bums!"

So, too, the ideas represented by skip-to-my-Lou-my-darling go far beyond the making of step and floor patterns. This simple dance ties us to our own history in the same way that "Wagon Train" and "Gun Smoke" do, by re-enacting the drama of human emotions that was played out many times as the wagon trains moved West, — the same drama that is still played today whenever boy meets girl.

Many — in fact, most — of the ideas developed within the context of sports and dance cannot be readily translated into words. Like the ideas developed in the laboratories of science — or in the laboratory situations of the classes in art, music, shop, home economics, and engineering — the physical education kind of ideas about "how men make things happen" are best symbolized by the act of *doing* what the idea means. But today we know that this human kind of *doing* involves the human ability to deal with ideas — which is also evidenced in the ability to translate ideas into words.

And so today we know that the Greek philosophers who sat on the shady perches of the gymnasium were only partially right in their conclusions. They were right in assuming that the ability to deal with words is the hallmark of human intelligence. But they valued these words for the wrong reason. They valued them because they seemed to distinguish man from his four-footed animal companions. And so they do. But the philosophers failed to note that dogs that cannot speak words can not play baseball, either. Neither can apes dramatize the history of human emotions in dances called skip-to-my-Lou-my-darling. These man-made forms of bodily behavior are not constructed out of the ability to associate one stick with one banana. They are born of man's human ability to deal with *ideas* about how the universe is organized, how it works, and how men may make their own man-made kinds of events happen within it. These sports and dances that men prize so highly are symbolic formulations of these ideas; and in their own right they are as meaningful as the words that issue from men's mouths and fingers.

And so we may conclude that the taxpayers are right in their insistence that a major share of the school budget be devoted to the building of gymnasiums, pools, arenas, and dance studios. But like the ancient Greek philosophers, they may be right for the wrong reason. Unquestionably the attributes called physical fitness may be developed in these facilities; and unquestionably they make an important contribution to personal and national welfare. But the larger reasons of education are centered on the target called *learning*. And as yet we have not made it clear that a lot of *"real"* learning goes on in those facilities — "real" learning that is fully worthy of being accredited on the ledgers and report cards of the schools.

In educational circles, we physical educators have long been described as *doers*. Perhaps, in the most private recesses of our own thoughts, we have never been quite certain that we also deserved recognition as *thinkers*. But now, as all educational theories are beginning to converge in the belief that *thinking* and *doing* are both implemented by the same brain and nervous system, perhaps we may well recognize that we have done a lot more thinking than we have given ourselves credit for. And perhaps we — who have so much to gain from modernization of educational theory and practice — can now demonstrate that we really are effective *doers* by updating our colleague's understanding of the fully-integrated process by which the whole child does his learning.

But What Do They Learn?

Convention Luncheon Session — American Association for Health, Physical Education and Recreation — Cincinnati, Ohio — April, 1962

In these closing hours of the convention we may well empathize with children at the end of a school day — not only because we are tired and restless, but because we know that we, too, must soon find the words to answer our colleague's form of the oft-repeated parental question: "What happened in school today?"

There are many words a child may use to describe these educational happenings. If he says: "I heard the teacher say that $1 + 1 = 2$, and that water is composed of oxygen and hydrogen," the parents will nod in approval. Their child is really learning; he is learning something about how the universe is put together and how it works. If he says: "The teacher told us that all men are created equal," his parents may or may not agree with this concept about certain relationships among human beings, but they will agree that he has learned something that is either true or false.

But what happens when the child says: "I drew a picture; I beat drums; I ran; I threw a ball; I skipped with a partner." Are the parents equally agreed that he has learned something worth knowing? Or will they say: "So you drew, and beat, and ran, and threw, and skipped — that's good. But what did you *learn?*"

The child knows that he *did* learn something. He can show his parents what he learned. He can draw a picture for them; he can beat on the table with his knife to demonstrate his understanding of two-four time. He can run around the table; he can pick up a dinner roll and throw it toward his father's hands; he can teach his mother to skip by showing her how skipping is done. He can act out what he has learned — but he can not explain it in words.

Years later he may be able to say: "As I drew the picture I discovered something about the relationships within and among visually perceivable forms. As I beat the drum I discovered something about the rhythmic structure of the universe and my own relationship to it." Artists and musicians say these things; but children seldom do. And — unfortunately — neither do we.

I think we should. I think we should be able to say: "As I ran and threw and skipped with my partner I discovered something about how gravity pulls on people and objects; I learned more about how I can use the forces in my muscles to resist gravity, to counteract its pull, to defy it, to assist it; and these learnings served to make my awareness of myself and my relationships within the universe more articulate." I think we can say much more than this about the wordless learnings of movement that are so much like the nonverbal learnings of music and the graphic arts; but let's start from there.

Learning has been defined in many ways, but essentially we may describe all learning as a process of making *sense* out of what we see, hear, touch, taste, smell, and feel. Whatever we may learn, whatever we may come to know, is derived from data initially provided by our senses. Within the human nervous system, these data are sorted out, compared, classified, and reorganized. Thus, learning may be described as a process of discovering how various kinds of sensory data are related to each other.

Of all these primary sensory data, none are more complex, more intimate, or more necessary for our own survival than the kinesthetic data provided by the proprioceptors. From these data we derive our awareness of our own identity as a self that has the power to move about in the universe, to change its relationship to its environment, and to interact in consequential ways with the elements in that environment. If we were to be deprived of these kinesthetic data — as we are sometimes deprived of awareness of the movements being made by a foot that has "gone to sleep" — we would be helpless, because we could not create the precise movements that enable us to act constructively on our own behalf.

We know that we make some kind of sense out of all of the many kinds of sensory data that we perceive. We do this by discovering how one set of data seems to be related to another set of data. When we discover such a connection between two sets of data, we *know* something about them that we did not know before.

We have a concept about their *relevance* — which is another word for relatedness. These concepts are meaningful to us because they give us some idea about how the universe is put together, how it operates, and how we are related to this universal pattern. A universe that exhibits relevant patterns of organization is no longer a chaotic whirling of dust in space. It takes on some semblance of purpose or order; and we can begin to make some *sense* out of our chaotic awareness of it.

This is what learning is all about. It is our ongoing attempt to find order in the seemingly chaotic — to find out how A is related to B — how Y influences and interacts with Z. It is the process by which we discover

> *What we know in what we see,*
> *What we feel in what we hear,*
> *And what we are. . .*
> *And what we think. . .*
> *A breathing like the wind,*
> *A moving part of motion,*
> *A discovery,*
> *Part of a discovery. . .*
> *Too much like thinking to be less than thought.*

When I read these lines by Wallace Stevens, my spine tingled. Could we ask for a more lucid description of what movement means to man? To comprehend the motions of the universe by being a part of them. A process of discovery — part of a discovery — too much like thinking to be less than thought.

To know what a wave is by sharing its motion as you ride its crest on your surf-board. To become speed incarnate as you fly down the ski slope. To feel a breathing like the wind as you race the wind for a measured mile. To pivot about your own axis with the earth as it revolves about its pole. To whirl with the whirling stars. To know what force is by being a force that hits and kicks and twists and throws your solid body against space — or against another body.

I need not try to list them all, because you, too, know what it is to be a moving part of motion — you, too, have made these discoveries that are too much like thinking to be less than thought.

We make these discoveries in all of the materials we perceive through our senses, but we have not yet found a way to express any of them in "pure" form. Thoughts are private or subjective; they can be made public only by transforming them into objective or perceivable forms. We do not communicate directly with each other; we communicate in code by shaping the perceivable materials of the universe into cryptograms that contain our thoughts. By using the tiny muscle fibers that are so beautifully arranged within our bodies, we shape vibrations of air into words; we shape pigment into letters and designs; we shape chemicals into new forms; and we shape our own lives into social organizations. Because we can control the movements created by these tiny muscle fibers, we can speak to each other about consequential things; we can sing, play violins, paint pictures, write poetry, solve algebraic equations, isolate chemical elements, write books about our own history, send astronauts into space, and go to the polls and cast our vote for the history of the future.

By directing the contractions of their own muscle fibers with their own meaningful thoughts, men have created many man-made forms to express their man-made thoughts. They have created speech and writing; they have created music and sculpture; they have created religion and science; they have created history and government. (They have also created their man-made sports and dances by using their own powerful movements in ways that have no counterpart in the stereotyped movement patterns exhibited by animals.)

Whatever materials we may use to create our symbolic cryptograms, all man-made forms have one thing in common. They are created to "act out" the meanings men find in their man-made thoughts.

The child "acted out" what he had learned in school when he told his parents about the relationship among oxygen, hydrogen, and water, and the relationships among 1, 1, and 2. He acted out his new-found knowledge by creating little puffs of air that his parents understood because they had gone through a long process of learning to relate these vocalized sounds to their comprehension of certain perceived relationships.

In the same way, the child "acted out" what he had learned about spatial, temporal, and gravitational relationships by drawing a picture, beating on the table, and skipping around the room. He was doing what all men do when they try to express their thoughts; he was using his muscles to make his silent thoughts articulate.

The words he spoke to his parents were no more *meaningful* to the parents than the picture, the rhythmic beating, or the running, throwing, and skipping. They only conveyed an element of meaning in a different kind of objective or perceivable form.

Words are such useful formulations of meaning that we create them endlessly. We use them to sort out our thoughts; we arrange them in sentences that serve to (diagram the connections between certain concepts.) This process of diagramming the connections between concepts serves to make our thoughts more articulate — because this is what becoming more articulate means. In anatomy, an articulation is a joint or connection between two bones; it is the perceivable relationship that exists between them. When a speaker arranges his words in such a way that we can clearly perceive how each concept is connected to the next concept, we say that he is articulate, because we can identify these articulations or connections or relationships. Thus, speech helps to make thoughts more articulate because we must identify the relationships among concepts before we can arrange them in syntactical order. However, the fact that we must diagram the connections within our thoughts before we can put words together in sentences imposes many limitations on speech as a form of expression and communication.

Much of what life means to us cannot be neatly diagrammed and stated in serial order. The experience of living is too complex to be sorted out, classified, and put into neatly organized categories. Much of the sense this experience makes to us is only "part of a discovery"; and much that we know we comprehend only vaguely as a tangled network of relationships. We can not untangle this network and put it into words, but we must still "act out" those amorphous thoughts in some way, because action is the end-product of the process of sensory stimulation that produced them.

One of the most complex concepts with which human beings deal is the concept of "love." Millions of pages have been inked with words about love — and most of us have inked a few ourselves — but somehow the words never quite convey what we think love really means. We cannot dissect it and expose all of its articulations, and so we try to convey its meaning by using analogies. We write "my love is like a red, red rose that's newly sprung in June; my love is like a melody that's sweetly played in tune."

Because Robert Burns was a poet, he stated his analogies in words, but he might equally well have sent his beloved a picture of a perfect red rose with the dew still sparkling on its petals, or — if he had been a musician — he might have composed a symphony of melodies all sweetly played in tune. Knowing that he could never spell out all of the intricate relationships within his love, he might have tried to make them more articulate by suggesting their nature in color or sound. This is the purpose served by picture-making, music-making, and the making of all kinds of nonverbal or wordless forms.

These nonverbal forms do not diagram the relationships they represent; they make them more articulate by suggesting that they are
analogous with other perceivable sets of relationships. A musical march,
like "The Stars and Stripes Forever," is analogous with the experience of walking because it is constructed out of similar time intervals,
with sound used to accent the rhythmic recurrence of these intervals.
We might say that the composer took a fuzzy, half-formed kind of sense
and sharpened its outlines so we could more readily perceive the relationships within it. The effect of making this idea about walking more
articulate can be seen by comparing the behavior of men shuffling
along in disordered ranks and men marching to the music of the band.

Picture-making serves to make vaguely perceived relationships more
articulate by showing their analogs in color and design. This is the
basis of the Rorschach Ink-Blot Test; it is also the basis of pictures
by Rembrandt and Picasso.

These nonverbal forms are not always clearly understood. The re-
cipient of the red, red rose may not get the message the lover intended
to convey. She may be allergic to roses; she may see only the thorns on
the stem and see them as analogous with a dagger. (It may be re-
marked, however, that many lover's quarrels have also sprung from
differing interpretations of a sentence.) But to the extent that the
analogies conveyed by nonverbal forms are comprehended, these forms
serve to make our thoughts more articulate by giving identity to some
of the vague meanings we find in the sense life makes to us. Thus, they
contribute to our ongoing attempt to identify orderly relationships
within a seemingly chaotic universe, and they make our human lives
more meaningful — or more full of meaning.

What kinds of meanings do we find in our man-made forms of
movement — the forms we call sports and dance?

Not long ago I happened to be visiting some friends when their
first-grader returned from school. Adult-like, I asked the inevitable
question: "What did you learn in school today?" His face was suf-
fused with excitement as he told me: "I learned to walk on my tip-
toes — like this." Then he taught me how to do it, too, and we had a
wonderful time tiptoeing around the living room.

A short time later, at a performance given by the Leningrad ballet
group, I watched the ballerina rise to one toe-tip and revolve over
that tiny base more than twenty times without losing her balance — and
with apparent ease. The audience gave her a tremendous ovation, and
I joined in their applause.

In Rome, in 1960, I watched John Thomas approach the high bar,
lift one leg into the air, rise on the toes of the other foot, and go flying

into space. As he cleared the bar, I shared something of the joy he must have found in demonstrating his personal ability to defy the pull of gravity for that one brief instant.

What had the tiptoeing child, the ballerina, and the high jumper learned as they performed these man-made feats? They had all learned something about their personal relationship to the gravitational forces that seem to hold the universe together. They had learned how they could interact with those insistent forces in such a way as to partially or momentarily resist, defy, overcome, or use them. And they were expressing that knowledge about their relationship to the forces of the universe by shaping their living bodies into dynamic forms that exhibited those relationships; just as the sculptor might use his muscles to shape a lump of clay into the form of a discus-thrower.

All forms of sports and dance are man-made forms created out of the forces that men are able to control — the forces of voluntary muscle contraction in their own bodies. The dynamic forms they create with their own bodies are the resultant of interactions between these human forces and the nonhuman gravitational forces of the universe. Or we might say, sports and dances are created out of the interaction between the powers *in* man and the forces that act *on* him. Too much like thinking to be less than thought, they make more articulate man's awareness of his own identity as a powerful person who is able to interact with the forces in the universe in consequential ways.

Taken in their most literal form, they make more articulate the sense of physical interaction with physical forces — the ability to achieve human objectives by moving with, against, and in interaction with the motions of the universe. But the meanings men find in the relationships they perceive among the forces they feel in their lives operate at many levels. So sports and dances may make the sense of many relationships more articulate by exhibiting them in analogous patterns of movement behavior.

The power movement has to symbolize many kinds of human relationships is perhaps most clearly shown in dance, but if I start talking about dance, either as an art form or as a folk form, we shall be here all afternoon. So I shall talk only about sports, because the metaphors of sport have received much less attention.

If we identify any sport as the resultant of the interaction between the forces man senses as his own powers and the forces in the universe that seem to act on him, the analogies we can find between games and "life" are beyond counting. As I suggest a few that seem meaningful to me, however, I must remind you that the lover and his beloved did not necessarily find the same meanings in the red, red rose. The

human search for meaning is a private search — and every man's ana-
olgies are his own. But here are a few of the meanings that make sports
meaningful to me.

Gymnasts deal with the action of gravitational forces on their own
bodies. Every stunt or event in gymnastics is both a literal and a metaphorical re-enactment of the drama of man using his own powers to
overcome the forces that act on him. By deliberately putting himself
in situations where he will be acted on by forces greater than those he
encounters in daily life and then (demonstrating his ability to overcome those forces, the gymnast makes more articulate his sense of
himself as a powerful being that can conquer opposing forces) Little
wonder that I shuddered every time the iron-curtain gymnasts in Rome
demonstrated on the rings the movements called "the iron cross."

In individual sports, as exemplified by golf, men pit their personal
forces against objects, and again and again they act out the symbolic
drama of human powers pitted against the forces in things. A perfect
drive is like a melody that's sweetly played in tune — a symphony of
human powers at their harmonious best — that makes man's sense of
himself as a powerful being more articulate. And — alas — every dubbed
shot is a discord that clarifies his awareness of his human limitations.

But golf is essentially a private game; it does not fill the bleachers
with a mob of spectators yelling, "Kill da Bums." Baseball involves
more than the forces in things; it involves the forces in other men who
oppose the batter. As one man, armed only with a bat, pits his personal powers against the powers of nine other men who will do their
utmost to keep him from achieving his objectives, the crowd goes wild
with excitement in seeing one man do, in fact, what all of them feel
that they are continually trying to do. Small wonder that Maris and
Mantle are national heroes. A man who gets only to first base gets
less applause. It may take almost superhuman power to get that far
in the face of overwhelming opposition — but the base runner must
depend on the aid of other men to reach home plate — and everyone
knows that the aid we get from other men is, at best, unpredictable.

In the annals of American literature there are few poems more
tragic than "Casey at the Bat." Casey tried; he tried as all men must
try to do more than they can; and every man in Mudville was standing in the box trying with him. But he failed; the ball went through
his bat. And you will recall the communal sadness of that final line:
"There was no joy in Mudville; Mighty Casey had struck out."

In games like basketball, the opposing forces are equalized, but
men must work with other men as well as against them. Thus, they

make more articulate man's sense of interdependence with other men. The Greeks, who gave us our track and field events, were superb athletes; but many historians believe that Athens fell because the Athenians were not able to make articulate the sense we find in team-play.

We must not lose sight, however, of the difference between what men do in the game situation and what they do to prepare for it. A player developing skill in basket-shooting is as intent as any physicist might be on analyzing the interaction between his own forces and the forces represented by the ball. As he experiments with various combinations of his own forces until he finds the relationships that produce the desired effect, he is trying to sort out his sensory awareness of his complex ability to create force; he is trying to clarify the relationships within it and make them more articulate. In the game, he will use what he has learned about his own powers of muscle contraction "without thinking about it," — just as I am using what I have learned about controlling the muscles of my throat and face in many practice sessions with words. In the game he will use these learnings to accomplish his human objectives — but first he must learn them by experimenting with the sensory data provided by his proprioceptors.

I must not linger longer on these analogies. For my purpose today it is enough to suggest that sports and dance are meaningful to men in the same way that all man-made forms of behavior are meaningful. We create our man-made forms of movement to make the sense that life makes to us more articulate, and in doing this we enlarge the store of meanings we find in the experience we call life.

"So you ran and threw and skipped — that's good. But what did you *learn?*" The child learned what we all have learned in sports and dance — "what we are, and what we think. A breathing like the wind, a moving part of motion, a discovery, part of a discovery . . . too much like thinking to be less than thought."

Perhaps it will take us many years to explain these thoughts to parents, to other educators, and to ourselves because — again quoting from Stevens —

The squirming facts exceed the squamous mind,
If one may say so. And yet relation appears,
A small relation expanding like the shade
Of cloud on sand, a shape on the side of the hill.

I think we know enough about the shape of this relation between movement and meaning to begin to describe its outlines. Personally,

I am committed to trying to make our awareness of those outlines more articulate — and I hope that you will join me in that effort.

Note: The lines of poetry quoted in this paper are taken from *The Collected Poems of Wallace Stevens*. New York: Alfred A. Knopf, 1954. The first quotation is from "Looking Across the Fields and Watching the Birds Fly," and the second is from "Connoisseur of Chaos."

Meaning, Movement, and the Conative Domain

Philosophy Section of the Physical Education Division — American Association for Health, Physical Education, and Recreation — Washington, D. C. — May, 1964

Before I start talking about *meaning, movement,* and *the conative domain,* I must admit that I cannot offer you a concise dictionary definition of any of these terms. In this, I am not alone. Philosophers have been wrestling with the definition of *meaning* for some two thousand years, but they have not yet pinned it down. Our own professional struggle with *movement* has gone fewer rounds, but to date every bout has ended in a standoff. However, the philosophers are dealing with an abstraction, while we are talking about something concrete. So when words fail *us,* we can make a *concrete model* of our concept. Since all physical educators know that one good demonstration can be more definitive than a thousand words, I shall move on to the *conative domain.*

As most of you know, the general term *domain* was introduced into education some years ago in an attempt to classify the *behaviors* of the whole child. In 1956, one committee presented a taxonomy or classification of educational objectives related to behaviors in *the cognitive domain* — which includes reasoning, remembering and problem-solving. Another group is now exploring the *affective domain,* which includes the behaviors identified with emotion and feeling; and a similar study of *the psychomotor domain* has been projected.

The words *cognitive* and *affective* are well-established in the literature, and I have no wish to tamper with them; but *psychomotor* does not belong in this group of terms. *Affective* is derived from *afferent;* and the proper mate for *afferent* is *efferent,* rather than *motor.* Accordingly, the counterpart of *affective* is *effective.* So, in the interests of consistency, we might better call this third category *the effective domain.*

But what about *psycho-*? This prefix implies that the *psyche* or mind influences some motor-effective behaviors; but, by inference, it also serves to exclude the *non-psycho-* behaviors from the classification system. We may bring them into the picture with the prefix *somato,* which is derived from *soma* or body. Thus, we may subdivide the *effective domain* into *psycho-effective* and *somato-effective* categories.

This distinction between *psyche* and *soma* is also meaningful in *the domain of affect* or feeling. "I feel sad" refers the feeling to the psyche; "I feel sick" refers it to the soma. These two states may well be related, but we do make certain important behavioral distinctions between them. So we may also subdivide *the domain of affect* into *psycho-affective* and *somato-affective* categories.

These terms may be jawbreaking, but in accordance with custom they may be reduced to alphabetical form. *Psycho-affective* and *somato-affective* may be written PA and SA; while *psycho-effective* and *somato-effective* become PE and SE — with the happy coincidence that PE also suggests the field called *physical education.* (Unfortunately, SE does not equally suggest *physical fitness,* except perhaps in terms of the idea of *self-energizing.*)

For convenient reference, then, we may classify the several domains of human behavior as follows.

CA   THE *COGNITIVE* DOMAIN of awareness, knowing, reasoning and problem-analysis

PA   THE *PSYCHO-AFFECTIVE* DOMAIN of awareness of emotions and feelings that are identified with the *psyche* or mind

SA   THE *SOMATO-AFFECTIVE* DOMAIN of awareness of feelings that are identified with the *soma* or body

CE   The *CONATIVE* DOMAIN of conscious personal attempt to effectuate an idea

PE   THE *PSYCHO-EFFECTIVE* DOMAIN of bodily movements that are structured by the intentions of the *psyche* or mind

SE THE *SOMATO-EFFECTIVE* DOMAIN of muscle contractions, glandular secretions, and biochemical changes that are autonomically structured by the *soma*

Now, lest we be tempted to subdivide *the whole child* rather than his behaviors, let me emphasize that he can behave only as a fully-integrated whole person. However, in his ongoing attempts to define the *meaning* of that whole existence, he may focus his attention on each of the several behavioral domains in turn. So we may do likewise in our attempt to identify the several facets of meaning he discovers in that search.

To afford ourselves the advantages of concreteness, let me make a model of a potentially meaningful event. Like this: (It may be noted here that the speaker picked up an object and then made an overarm throwing movement.) For convenience in talking about this model, let us call it "X."

As I made the event that is now symbolized by X, my behavior was in the PE or psycho-effective domain. But let us begin our analysis of the meaning of X with *your* several behaviors as you asked the question: What does X *mean?*

In *the cognitive domain,* you began by focussing your *attention* on X. If you did not do this, our analysis is pointless because you have no knowledge of X. If you did *attend* to X, you recognized it (or re-cognized it) as an organized whole, rather than as a cluster of discrete dots of visual sensation. You were not aware of every detail within the dynamic structure of X; rather, as you perceived it, you had a *conception* of a general *form* or pattern. Then you scanned your mental storage files for other conceptions that seemed to be similar to it, or analogous with it, in some way. In this first scanning, you probably identifed it with the category of events called *arm movements* or *throwing movements.*

You then began to wonder how this throwing movement was related to the situation in which it occurred. Again you scanned your recollections for clues. If you found none, you may have concluded that X was *irrelevant,* or unrelated to the situation, and accordingly it seemed to be *meaningless.* But if it seemed to be *relevant* within the situation, you shifted your attention from the question of probable *causal* relationships to the question of predictable *consequences.* Is it likely that the arm movement will send an object flying through space? This raises the question of the probable *effect* of such consequences, and with it the question of *logical action* in relation to those possible effects. You may decide that it would be logical to erect a screen to protect audiences from the effects of flying objects. But this logical conclusion does not necessarily lead to overt action.

Fortunately, there was no need for this screen, because there was no flying object. But there might have been. If the object had, in fact, hit you on the nose, the questions of consequences and effects would have been answered; but the question of *intent* would still be debatable. Did the thrower *intend* to hit someone? Perhaps you? Again you would scan for clues that might suggest some *deliberate aim.* Finding none, you would probably dismiss the hit as accidental or *meaningless.*

This is not the only possible series of cognitive behaviors. As you re-cognized X, your attention may have been focused on some particular aspect of the general form. This subpattern may have suggested the categories *awkward, reaching, shoulder-joint, circle* — or possibly *baseball,* or *dance.* Any of these categories may be more interesting to you than the throwing movement, as such, and so your attention may have shifted to these more interesting ideas. By now, the baseball coach may be thinking *baseball,* which suggests *my team lost,* which suggests *I may lose my job;* or the dance teacher may be thinking *reaching, aspiring, pointing, pointing awkwardly,* and so on to themes which may be developed in many ways.

To summarize your behaviors in *the cognitive domain*: You attempted to establish a series of hypotheses about how X might be related to other events that may be symbolized by the letters A, B, C, D. Probably you concluded that X *denoted* the general category of events called *throwing,* or *intent to throw,* or *attempt to suggest an intent to throw.* But X also had other *connotations* for you. Its various subpatterns may have suggested anything from *awkwardness* to *baseball,* and these suggestions sent your hypotheses scurrying off in many directions. So what does the symbol X *mean* in your cognitive domain? It means whatever it has suggested to you.

Turning now to *the affective domain* of feeling and emotion. Here you were formulating your *personal* hypotheses about how the *self,* symbolized by "I," is or may be *affected by* X and A, B, C. D. This "I" is not hypothetical; it is concrete, immediate, personal, and more real to you than any cognized event can ever be. So your interest in X and its relationships was intensified as you asked the question: How am *I affected by* X? How may it *affect my life?*

As you considered these questions, your feelings and emotional tone fluctuated with every hypothesis about what X *denoted* and every *connotation* you found in its subpatterns. These feelings may have ranged from boredom to acute interest, from anger to joy, from disgust to approval; and each shift in feeling was accompanied by a shift in attention, which tended to dull or sharpen your cognitive wits. But if you focussed your cognitive forces on these feelings, you were able to modify them, either positively or negatively, quantitatively or qualitatively, with a little conscious effort. Conversely, they seemed to shift without effort on your part whenever you focussed your attention on a new discovery in the cognitive domain.

Similarly, your emotional state may be altered by a discovery in the *somato-affective domain*. If the object had, in fact, hit your nose, this painful *somatic affect* could have instantly commanded your attention, and pushed your feelings toward annoyance and anger. Conversely, if you were vitally interested in your cognitive thoughts, you might have been scarcely aware of this minor bump. Similarly, too, your concern for the *somato-affective* symptoms of internal pressures, tensions, and biochemical changes within the soma was either magnified or diminished by your preoccupation with your emotions and thoughts.

The interactions between the two kinds of feelings in *the affective domain,* and their joint interaction with the forces of *congnitive domain* are much too complex for verbal analysis. But the emotional resultant of this interaction is your *affective* answer to the personal question: What does X *mean to me?* Here, X means whatever you *feel* in connection with it.

Your personal involvement in those feelings makes the question of action more urgent. Your concern for "I" transforms the hypothetical question about logical courses of action into the personal question: What can *I* do about it? Or, more precisely, what *might* I *try* to do about it?

This question moves us toward the *domain of effective behavior,* but not necessarily into it — because the formulation of an *intention* does not necessarily lead to *effective action.* As we all know to our sorrow, we may store many of our best intentions away in our mental filing cabinet for years, or a lifetime, without making any realistic *attempt* to convert them into somatically effective forms. This distinction between *intent* and *attempt* brings us at long last to *the conative domain.*

Conative is defined as *attempting to perform an action.* In the dictionary it is listed as the teammate of *cognitive, affective, effective.* Unfortunately, it is seldom so listed in the literature of educational objectives — and for historically understandable reasons.

In the days when men believed that the *psyche* or mind existed as a separate entity that could be distinguished from the neural structure of the brain, they found it difficult, if not impossible, to establish any functional or operational connection between the thoughts or intentions of the *psyche* and the actions of the *soma*. Logically, they held themselves responsible for many of their own voluntary somatic actions — but in the laboratory they treated the soma or body as a mechanism governed by certain built-in connections in the nervous system. The basic mechanistic unit was described in terms of the reflex arc or some extension of it. In our time, all of us have drawn this familiar picture — a muscle dangling from a chain of axons, neurons, and synapses that bound it to a sense organ. Theoretically, when stimulus S nudged the sense organ, dots of neural impulse proceeded down this chain of neural elements to the muscle, eventually nudging it to contract in response R. Thus, in the laboratory, bodily movement was studied as a response to direct sensory stimulation, and in the absence of such stimulation it was presumed that the muscle rested. It was commonly agreed that this chain might pass through any or all of the higher levels of the brain; and it was agreed that its course might be changed by a process called conditioning. But in the absence of a theory that might identify the thoughts of the psyche with the neural structure of the brain, it was not possible to show how bodily actions might proceed from the realm of *ideas* or *intentions*.

Thus, these essentially mechanistic theories of bodily action, in which the brain was identified as a sort of telephone switchboard for establishing connections between S and R, served to account for movements elicited in the laboratory by direct sensory stimulation — but they provided no insight into the kinds of movement called *voluntary* — the complexly coordinated movements that are intentionally initiated by the thinking person, seemingly of his own volition. In other words, the older mechanistic theories bypassed the very questions implied by the concept of a *conative domain* of behavior in which the person *attempts* to act out some preconceived intention in some self-chosen way.

Today this laboratory and mechanistic interpretation of bodily movement has been largely abandoned, and explanations for the logical connection between thought and voluntary action are now being sought. In larger terms, it now seems impossible to conceive of the self called "I" as a biological robot, pushed and pulled about by stimuli that may impinge upon the sensory nerve endings. Rather, the modern image identifies man as a self-contained energy system capable of structuring much of his own overt behavior. By focusing his own attention, the self called "I" can choose to consider some stimulus events and ignore others. He can, and does, examine every chosen stimulus to determine what it seems to *mean* to him, how he feels about that meaning, and what he intends to do about it. Then he decides for himself whether or not he will *attempt* to transform that intent into effective behavior.

The neural structures that seem to govern this range of choices are now being traced within the brain and nervous system. The search for the connecting link between the behaviors of the *psyche* and the behaviors of the *soma* is now centered in three parts of the brain: *the reticular network of the brain stem, the hypothalamus,* and *the cortex.* It has been shown that functional *consciousness* is accompanied by an active interchange of neural impulses among these three structures. Concomitantly, it has been shown that this same active interchange occurs in conjunction with *the attempt to perform* an action that is construed as being intentional or *voluntary.*

The significance of this coincidence is enhanced by the fact that these three brain structures are all equipped with ascending and descending tracts, and in the reticular network these tracts are so tangled and twisted together that the afferent and efferent elements are scarcely distinguishable. It is also of interest that this tangled skein seems to play a major role in the function of *attention focusing.* And it may also be noted that every major branch of the central and autonomic nervous systems is in functional connection with these interacting brain structures.

Thus, these three structures seem to serve as a *coordinating center* in which the diverse components of *attention-focusing, cognitive, affective, conative,* and *effective* behaviors are brought together in one comprehensive, functional organization. Here *attention* may be *focused* on any set of behaviors; here thought and feeling may communicate with attempt and subsequent action; and here the consequences of the attempted action may be reviewed and integrated into the conceptions that may structure the next attempt to behave in an effective manner.

This concept of a coordinating center for human thought, feeling, and action is not yet supported by a full array of neurological details. This need not disturb us unduly, for neither could the stimulus-response theorists explain precisely how the stimulus energies of the eye were transformed into one specific set of muscle contractions. The more important question is: What is the factor that seems to transform certain bits of knowledge and intent into the bodily *attempt to act* on that hypothetical knowledge?

The critical factor seems to be *intensity of interest,* or the feeling of being *concretely, immediately,* and *personally involved* in the situation and in the outcomes of the intended course of action. This feeling of *concrete involvement* seems to focus attention on the *concrete somatic form* of the self; and in this shift of attention from the afferent psyche to the efferent soma, the *afferent* pattern of neural excitation seems to be transferred to the *efferent* nerve-endings within the coordinating center.

This transfer is experienced as a *feeling of personal bodily attempt* to *do* whatever is required to actualize the person's intentions. This is not a feeling of trying to organize specific patterns of muscle contractions; rather, it is an *effort to mobilize the soma as a whole* for the action needed to produce the desired *pattern of effective behavior.*

If the mover's primary intent is "to hit the target," this intention is clearly *denoted* by the somatic pattern, even though the target-hitter may report that he was scarcely aware of his own bodily movements as he used his body to make "the hit." Conversely, if the intent is to try to create a specific "pattern of movement," the mover's attention will be focused on his body, and the throwing movement will not impart velocity and direction to the ball.

In either instance, if the mover is afraid that he may fail to accomplish his intent, his fears and doubts will be evidenced in the somatic pattern, and they will obstruct his coordination. Conversely, if he is confident of his own success, or if he attaches no significance to success or failure in this situation, these *connotations,* too, are evident in the dynamic form of the somatic pattern.

If the initial conception of intent is a rather vague notion about "what I shall try to do," the somatic pattern will be blurred and indistinct, and many muscle fibers will contract in seemingly useless or obstructive patterns. Conversely, if the initiating conception is clearly defined, every muscle fiber will behave in an appropriate manner, and the somatic pattern will clearly display the nature of the intent.

In short, the self called "I" structures its own voluntary forms of somatic behavior by *knowing* what it *wants to do; wanting* it intensely; and then *attempting* to do it. The behavior called *knowing* belongs to *the cognitive domain;* the behavior called *wanting* or *desiring* falls in *the affective domain;* and the behavior of attempting defines *the conative domain* in which behaviors of *the effective domain* are *somatically* structured.

Returning now to the objectives of education. Historically, education has been concerned with the behaviors in *the cognitive domain* of knowing, remembering, reasoning, and problem-solving. More recently, some attention has been given to the behaviors in *the affective domains* of feeling and emotion. But an education focused wholly on academic hypotheses and possible intentions cannot hope to establish effective patterns of behavior or actually develop human potentialities.

Within the traditionally honored domains of cognition and effect, the children of men may theorize endlessly about the possible relationships among X, A, B, C, D, and "I." They may also theorize about their own human potentialities for dealing with these possible relationships in effective ways. They may also formulate their intentions to change themselves and the world at some future time; and they may pride themselves on these intentions, as well as on the belief that they will be able to actualize them when they get around to it.

But human potentialities are not developed by vague intentions; neither is the world greatly changed by theories about the probable effectiveness of this or that kind of behavior. Potentialities are actualized by *trying* to actualize them; and the world of men is changed by the *actual effectiveness* of *concrete somatic behavior.*

In *the conative domain,* the children of men can no longer juggle conflicting theories. Here they must commit themselves to one set of theories; and then they must submit themselves and their belief in those theories to the pragmatic test of attempted action. This *conative attempt* is intensely *meaningful,* because it is made with full awareness of the fact that the self called "I" must stand or fall on its own behavior — not only in its own judgment, but in the judgment of other men, and — in a larger sense — in the judgment of the non-personal universe. If the mover's theories are valid, his self-directed behavior will have the desired impact on the course of events in the universe. But if they are wrong, the self called "I" will be proven ineffectual, incompetent, and inconsequential within the structure of its own reality.

Thus, as the self mobilizes its concretely effective forces in the *conative domain,* it is seeking a realistic answer to the urgent human questions: What am I? Who am I? What does my personal existence *mean* to other men? What *meaning* does it have within the evolving designs of the enduring universe?

We who work in the PE domain of *physical education* deal directly with the implications of *the conative domain*. We may theorize about the relationships between boy, ball, and target, but this is mere prologue to inducing him to make a somatic *attempt* to hit the target with the ball. And as we evaluate his learning, we again deal directly with the *somatic model* of the event that symbolizes his understanding of these boy-ball-target relationships.

In other areas of education, the *concrete models* that symbolize what has been learned may be more readily divorced from the soma, as such. Here, the picture drawn by the somatic self, the musical sounds produced by it, the stuff that was mixed in the test tube, or the words traced on paper may serve as the immediate symbols of learning and understanding. But these tangible symbols are equally brought into being by *the conative* attempt to mobilize the forces of the soma, as a whole, to implement some form of human intention. Equally, they represent the *personal involvement* of the self in the hypotheses of learning; and equally they represent a realistic development of human potential in effective behaviors that can change the world.

Each area of education is directed toward the production of its own *kind* of forms; but all man-made forms are produced by the same self-motivated conative process. So there is little point in quibbling about the relative values attached to these various symbolic forms. Verbal educators must inevitably prize words; science educators must prize test tubes; music educators must prize songs; and art educators must prize pictures. So, too, must we prize the immediate and transient man-made symbols of somatic effort, as such.

And so we may return to our original question: What does X mean?

To you who observed it, it means whatever it suggested to you. It means whatever you think it *denoted*. More richly, it means whatever it symbolizes for you by virtue of the *connotations* you found in it. It means whatever *affect* those interpretations had on your feelings and emotions. It means whatever you were *motivated* to do about those feelings, whatever you *did do,* and whatever consequences stemmed from those actions.

To the boy who makes a model of a movement in the PE domain of physical education, X *means* all this, and more. To him it *denotes* a complex conception of his own ability to deal effectively with the realities of balls and targets. It also denotes his *personal involvement* in this conception, and his *willingness* to *attempt* to make that conception *work* within the world he shares with other men — and his willingness to be *judged* on the success or failure of that attempt.

The world of other men may not be greatly affected by one boy's ability to toss a rubber ball at a painted target. Neither, it would seem, are our educational colleagues. Neither, on occasion, are we — as evidenced by the fact that our professional passions are so often spent in proclaiming concomitant social learnings on one hand and self-energizing outcomes on the other. These concomitant values are important, and we should be the last to deny them. But our public emphasis on them may also blind us to the full *meaning* of each boy's *attempt* to hit a painted target with a rubber ball.

The conception of "my ability to hit the target" is not confined to the small realm of rubber balls and painted circles. It has *connotations* that extend it to the farthest limits of human aspirations — today, the moon, tomorrow the farthest stars. Thus, the X that *denotes* an attempt to hit a painted target may well *connote* a generalized conception of "my ability to make things happen." In this larger sense, the boy's immediate preoccupation with meaningless balls and painted circles becomes *intensely meaningful* as an attempt to define himself in concrete terms as an intelligent, self-directing, effective, and consequential force within the universe of his existence. It is one specific incident in his ongoing attempt to answer the question: What *value* is there in this *self* that was brought into being by an impersonal universe which will in time destroy its own handiwork?

Thus, the seemingly trivial act of tossing a ball at a target becomes an important part of each child's urgent *search for the meaning of his personal existence* within the existential scheme of reality-as-he-knows it. Accordingly, this attempt may be construed as a part of his ongoing search for satisfying answers to his most urgent questions: What am I? Who am I? What does my self-centered life *mean* to me? To other men? And to the enduring universe of my transient personal existence?

In our own immediate preoccupation with trivial balls, targets, patterns of movement, and the somato-energizing effects of these things, we may easily miss these larger connotations of the symbolic X. This paper is evidence of the verbal difficulties we may encounter as we attempt to translate these richer meanings into the educational coin of words. But in this attempt to interpret the full *meaning* of these *psycho-effective movements* that are structured in *the conative domain*, we may find a new measure of our own professional worth, and in that measure we may well find the larger *meaning* of our own movement-oriented professional existence.

REFERENCES

The ideas represented by this paper are now being dealt with by many writers in philosophy, psychology, and physiology. This list includes only those books from which a specific formulation of one of these ideas was abstracted for use in its original phrasing.

BLOOM, BENJAMIN S. (Editor) *Taxonomy of Educational Objectives: The Classification of Educational Goals; Handbook I: Cognitive Domain.* New York: David McKay Company, Inc., 1956.

CASSIRER, ERNST. *An Essay on Man.* (Originally published by Yale University Press, 1944) Now available in paperback edition as a Doubleday Anchor Book.

FRANKL, VIKTOR E. *Man's Search for Meaning.* Boston: Beacon Press, 1962. (Also available in paperback edition)

LANGER, SUSANNE K. *Philosophy in a New Key.* (Originally published by Harvard University Press, 1942) now available in paperback edition as a Mentor Book.

MURPHY, GARDNER. *Human Potentialities.* New York: Basic Books, 1958. (Paperback condensation also available)

SOLLEY, CHARLES M., AND GARDNER MURPHY. *Development of the Perceptual World.* New York: Basic Books, 1960.

TEILHARD DE CHARDIN. *The Phenomenon of Man.* New York: Harper and Brothers, 1959. (Also available in paperback edition as Harper Torchbook)

Symbolic Forms of Movement:
The Olympic Games

Adapted from paper presented in Fourth Session of the International
Olympic Academy — Olympia, Greece — August, 1964

Original text published in *Report of the Fourth Summer Session of the
International Olympic Academy*, Athens, Greece: 1964.

Text also available in Greek and French translation.

Today it is commonly conceded that men interpret their perceptions
of reality in three ways. They may attempt to describe a perceivable
form in terms of the composition of its substantial elements. They may
recognize it as a representative of a general category of forms, as denoted by the name commonly assigned to it. And they may interpret
it as a symbol or symbolic form that represents some meaningful conception of human interaction with the universe, other than that denoted
by the common name of the form. The present analysis of sports competition is patterned along these lines.

For the purposes of this analysis, *human behavior* is construed in
terms of interaction between a person and the universe. The term *personal behavior* is reserved for those forms of interaction that occur when
a person knowingly makes an attempt to organize his own behavior in
some self-chosen way. The concept denoted by the term *sports competition* is largely defined as participation in the Olympic Games.

35

I — The Characteristics of Sport Competition

In general terms, the characteristics common to all forms of *sports competition* may be described with reference to four principles: a personal attempt to overcome inertia, finite limits, nonconsequential effect, and human control.

The Principle of Overcoming Inertia: All forms of sports competition are structured by a personal attempt to overcome the inertia of some specific organization of mass. The human objective is stated in terms of causing the mass to move through space and time in some way determined by the person. Within this general structure, the contest may be organized in three different ways:

1. *The person attempts to overcome the inertia of his own body mass.*

In all forms of foot-racing, broad jumping, swimming, platform diving, and free exercise, the contestant organizes his personal forces into an attempt to move his own body about within his milieu. In the hurdle races, high jump, and gymnastic events, he introduces certain man-made obstacles into the situation. In the pole vault, he erects a man-made barrier, and then increases his own mechanical advantage by applying his personal forces through a man-made device. Similarly, in springboard diving, skiing, ice skating, cycling, canoeing and sculling, he utilizes man-made devices to support his body and to amplify his own propelling powers. The team forms of this type of contest are represented by the relays and the two-or-more-man aquatic events. In all of these events, however, the outcome of the contest is measured in units that describe the displacement of his own body in space and time.

2. *The person attempts to overcome the inertia of some external unit of mass.*

In the shot put, the discus throw, javelin throw, hammer throw, and weight-lifting, the person attempts to overcome the inertia of some external form of mass by direct application of force with his own body. In golf and bowling, which are not included in the Olympic list of events, the application of force is effected through a man-made implement. In the shooting events, including archery, the effective forces inhere in the man-made device, and the contest is structured as an attempt to utilize these man-made organizations of energy to overcome the inertia of another object. The team forms of this type of contest are represented by golf and bowling, in which teams of two or more persons make sequential attempts to achieve the objective, with each man performing individually within the sequence. However, in all of these events the outcome of the contest is measured in units that describe the displacement of the specified mass in space and time.

The equestrian events employ a nonhuman form of life as the inertial object, the outcome of the contest being determined by the extent to which the horse is induced to move in accordance with the rider's intent.

3. *Two persons, or two teams, designated as opponents, attempt to overcome the inertia in some external form of mass while opposing the efforts of the other.*

In wrestling, boxing, and judo, the specified mass is the body of the opponent, and the outcome is determined by the relative displacement of his body in space. In fencing, the specified mass is still the body of the opponent, but a spatial barrier is maintained between the opponents; an arm-extending device is used to bridge this barrier; and the outcome is determined by a physically inconsequential touch on some presumably vulnerable spot on the opponent's body. There are no team forms of these events in which the objective is to physically or symbolically subdue the opponent.

In handball, squash, badminton, and tennis, which are not included in the Olympic list, the inertial mass is a small object. The spatial barrier between the opponents is extended, and neither person intentionally touches the other's body or weapon. In handball, force is applied through the person's hand; in squash, badminton, and tennis, the force is applied through a light implement; and in badminton and tennis, the spatial barrier is maintained by a restraining net that serves to divide the playing area into two equal parts. The team forms of these events are organized as doubles, with the partners cooperating in the attempt to cause the inertial object to move through space in some specified way.

No new principles are introduced in the team sports, but the conception of cooperative effort is extended to teams of five or more persons. In all of these sports the team attempts to direct the movement of some relatively small and light object in space, either by applying force to it with some part of the player's body — as in basketball, soccer, water polo, and volleyball — or with the aid of a man-man device, as in field hockey and ice hockey. In all of these games, intentional body contact between players is prohibited by the rules. In volleyball, such contact is prevented by a restraining net. In American football, both body contact and an attempt to subdue the opponent physically are permitted and encouraged by the rules.

The Principle of Finite Limits: Within the infinite reaches of the universe, sports competition is intentionally confined to a small segment of reality, the limits of which are defined in finite terms, as follows:

Time: The circumstances which will determine the beginning and end of the sports competition, as such, are specified.

Space: The spatial boundaries of the area within which the sports competion, as such, may occur are clearly established, and other persons are excluded from this space during the appointed time.

Mass: The dimensions and substantial characteristics of all material objects utilized in the competition are specified.

Objective: The objective of the competition is defined in terms of the displacement of finite units of mass within the limits of time and space.

Outcome: Some way of quantifying relative degrees of achievement of this objective is designated.

The Principle of Nonconsequential Effect: When the sports competition is terminated by the finite limitations imposed on time, space, and mass, the contest area and all material objects in it are immediately restored to their precompetition state. The competitors leave the area. The contested inertial objects and all man-made devices used in the competition are taken away to be stored or discarded. The area is then made available for use by other persons. Thus, except for incidental deformation of the masses involved, no tangible evidence of the competitive effort remains, and the contest has no substantial continuing effect on the competitors, the spectators, or their environmental milieu.

The Principle of Human Control: The man-made rules that establish the finite limits of time, space, mass, objective, and outcome also impose certain limitations on the personal conduct of the competitors. Within the Olympic Games, the conditions imposed by these rules include:

Public Statement of Intent: Each competitor must publicly identify his personal intention to enter the sports competition. Additionally, he must testify that he has systematically prepared himself by practice, that he is entering the contest voluntarily and without coercion from other persons, and that he has no expectation of receiving any material reward for his efforts within the competition.

Personal Behavior within the Competition: Forms of personal conduct deemed appropriate within the limits of the competition are defined, and penalties for inappropriate behavior are designated.

Personification of Authority: Authority to enforce the man-made rules, to judge the appropriateness of personal behavior, and to penalize or punish personal transgression is vested in some person not involved in the contest, as such.

II. Sports Competition as a Symbolic Form

The category of personal behavior called *sports competition* has been characterized as an intentional personal effort to overcome the inertia of mass, conducted under man-made rules that serve to govern personal behavior within a finite segment of reality. This elaborately constructed form of personal interaction with the forces of the universe is essentially futile, in that no tangible or seemingly consequential effect is produced by it. Nonetheless, men attach great value to this seemingly futile effort. It would seem, therefore, that this behavioral form must symbolize some more significant conception of man's interaction with the universe of his existence.

One symbolic interpretation is suggested by the central theme of a contest between man and inertia. In its larger outlines, this contest must be waged continuously by all living organisms within the infinite dimensions of the universe.

Living organisms are brought into being by the action of universal forces. In order to survive within this life-giving universe, the organism must continuously organize its own lesser forces into an attempt to overcome the inertia of the organism's own body masses and the inertia of other forms of mass in its immediate milieu. The penalty for failure to overcome these forms of inertia is death. Thus, life may be construed as a contest between the forces *of* or *in* the living organism and the forces that act *on* it. Human life, as distinguished from animal life, is characterized by full awareness of the inevitability of eventually being destroyed by the forces that brought it into being. Thus the human question is: Why was I born? What is the significance of my life as a man? What consequential effect does my life have on the continuing structure of the universe?

In sports competition, men seem to be answering that question by staging a dramatic demonstration of the effect they *can* have on the universe, as denoted by their ability to overcome the inertial forces of its masses in accord with some human plan. This demonstration is planned on a stage set apart for this purpose, and the finite limits imposed on this time-space area clearly set it apart from the limitless reaches of space and time within which men must attempt to accomplish their significant human purposes. Every act performed within this finite area is ritualized by the imposition of man-made rules. The events enacted in this ritualistic situation resemble the actions men perform within their ongoing attempts to survive within the universe, but there is no expectation that the usual consequences will ensue from them.

It may be noted, however, that the performers are not play-acting. In drama, the performer asumes the role of a person other than himself, and hides his own identity within the illusion he is attempting to create. In sports, the performer calls attention to his own identity as a person as he, literally or figuratively, stands naked before his gods and other men to testify to the extent of his own personal powers. Then, within the ritualized context of the dramatic event, he makes a wholly realistic attempt to actually overcome the inertia of his own body and other real forms of mass.

All drama serves to call attention to some idea about the relationships between man and man within the context of their common relationship to the forces that structure the universe. In sports, this idea deals specifically with some conception of man's personal ability to "move the earth" — or, by extension, with some more comprehensive conception of the performer's power to cope with the physical forces that structure his own earthly existence, within the finite limits of his personal life.

This interpretation is suggested in Homer's description of the funeral games that were held to honor the fallen warrior Patroclus. His comrades had been wrestling with the Trojans for many years; they had thrown spears beyond counting and repeatedly performed every action represented by the games many times over. Nonetheless, in the truce that was called to honor Patroclus, they asked their gods to witness a demonstration of how the warrior had proved his manhood by mastering the forces of mass, space, and time during his all-too-brief life.

This interpretation is re-enforced by the parallels between a man's conception of "my work" and the sports forms he chooses. In Homeric Greece, no man was exempt from heavy manual labor. Even the master of many slaves worked the earth with his own muscular powers, and he used those powers directly in overcoming the forces in other men as he warred against them. These strength-oriented conceptions of human power are represented in all of the oldest events on the Olympic list: wrestling, boxing, the now-discarded pancratium, the foot races, the jumps, shot put, and the discus, javelin, and hammer throws. It may be noted, too, that the right to rule was centered in the strength of one powerful man — as suggested by the fact that none of the team sports were developed during this era.

The earliest forms of the team sports were developed by the peasants of feudal Europe, perhaps as an indication of some emerging sense of the power represented by a group of men, each of whom might be individually at the mercy of a strong ruler. These early team forms involved the inertia of large and heavy objects, and intentional body contact used to physically subdue the opponent. But as the concept of the team was adapted to suit the needs of the emerging class called gentlemen, the fact that these privileged persons did not labor with their strong muscles is suggested by their preference for smaller and lighter objects that might be manipulated with skillfully-designed implements. Thus, the elements of brute force and bodily contact with the opponent were eliminated from the gentlemanly team sports, and the objective of the contest was focussed on moving symbolic objects with skill rather than with strength.

Similarly, games like tennis, badminton, handball, and squash were developed by gentlemen who prided themselves on their intellectual powers rather than on their muscular strength. This sense of class distinction is associated with these sports as they are played today.

Turning now to the significance attached to the code of personal conduct, as prescribed by man-made rules and judged, rewarded, or punished by some personification of authority. Perhaps the earliest formulation of this code is represented by Hesiod's concept of "the good strife," in which men strive together in mutual respect as they attempt to improve their common human situation. In contrast, Hesiod identified "the bad strife" in which men strive against each other, attempting to establish mastery over the lives of other men even as they might establish personal mastery over the life of an animal. Thus, in "the good strife" men treat each other as partners in a common enterprise; in "the bad strife" they treat each other as animals or things.

The concept of "the good strife" is implicit in the word *competition,* as derived from *cum* and *petere* — literally, *to strive with* rather than *against.* The word *contest* has similar implications, being derived from *con* and *testare* — *to testify with another* rather than *against* him. The concept of "the bad strife" is implicit in the idea of "beating the opponent" as distinguished from "winning the contest."

In the larger context of Greek thought, the code that governs "the good strife" is denoted in the concept of *aidos*. In the English language, it is represented by the term *sportsmanship* or *sportsmanlike behavior*.

These interpretations suggest that sports competition may well symbolize some conception of a self-imposed code of behavior that marks the distinction between men and animals. It seems significant, too, that the earthly power to judge and punish men who violate that code is not vested in the gods, but in man, himself. Thus, men seem to be identifying their own sense of kinship with the gods, who have the ultimate power to judge, reward, and punish men and animals for their earthly behavior.

The concept of the athlete as a god-like being is well represented in the sculptured marble forms that have come down to us from ancient Greece. It is also expressed in the poetry of the period, as in Pindar's ode to the winner of a boys' wrestling match: "Thing of a day! such is man; a shadow in a dream. Yet when god-given splendor visits him, a bright radiance plays over him, and how sweet is life." The modern athlete's sense of kinship with his gods may be less explicit, but he may still be accorded well-nigh worshipful adoration as an exemplar of superhuman or extraordinary powers.

Thus it would seem that the forms of sports competition embodied in the modern Olympic Games may well symbolize man's conception of himself as a consequential force within the grand design of the universe, as well as each man's conception of his own ability to perform those functions that identify him as a man among men.

Symbolic Forms of Movement:
The Feminine Image in Sports

Adapted from paper presented in Fourth Session of the International
    Olympic Academy — Olympia, Greece — August, 1964
Original text published in *Report of the Fourth Summer Session of the
    International Olympic Academy*, Athens, Greece: 1964.
    Text also available in Greek and French translation.

The issues debated in this paper have a very long history. They were
raised as early as 776 B.C. by the custom of excluding women from the
sacred precincts of Olympia. They were raised in 1896 when women
were admitted to competition in some events in the modern Olympic
Games, but excluded from others. They are being argued around the
world today as every national Olympic Committee makes its own decisions about the inclusion of women in the lists of competitors. This
paper is not an attempt to resolve all of these long-standing issues;
rather it is an attempt to inquire into the underlying nature of these
controversies.

In an earlier paper — "Symbolic Forms of Movement: The Olympic
Games" — I have interpreted the Olympic events as symbolic formulations of man's conception of himself as a consequential force within
the universe of space, time, mass, and energy. In the present paper I
shall pursue that interpretation with reference to some conceptions of
roles appropriate for women.

43

I. The Biological Basis of the Female Role

At the biological level, arguments about appropriate roles for men and women must be pursued in terms of differences in anatomical structure and function. These sexually significant differences are too well known to need explication here. With reference to sports competition, the important question is: How are these differences related to the ability to overcome the inertia of mass?

In terms of averages, it is a truism that men are larger and stronger than women; but this generalization does not hold for individual representatives of the two sexes. Some women may be very large and strong, and their ability to overcome the inertia of mass may be far greater than that of the majority of men. Similarly, some men may be smaller and less muscular than many women, and in any contest with the inertia of mass they may make a very poor showing — and may, in fact, be bested by the majority of the opposite sex.

To some extent these relationships may be modified by pregnancy, the demands of infant care, and possibly menstruation; and all of these episodes may serve to limit a woman's interest in the kind of training men may undergo in preparation for international competition. But they do not vitiate the biological fact that women appear to be fully competent to engage in a contest with the inertia of mass. In terms of averages, women's achievements may be less spectacular than those of men; in terms of individual achievement, some women may well excel most of the male competitors in any athletic event.

It would seem then that the age-old arguments about whether or not women should be admitted to competition in the Olympic events can not be pursued in meaningful terms at the strictly biological level of anatomical structure and function.

II. The Mythological Image of the Female Role

In every culture, men and women play different roles within the social organization. In part, these roles are defined by the relative contribution each sex makes to the reproduction of the species — a biologically-determined contribution which is the same in all cultures. But in larger terms, these roles are established by some less well-defined set of factors not directly related to these biological differences, as evidenced by the fact that they differ from culture to culture. This complex of factors serves to determine the *masculine image* of behaviors appropriate to males and the corresponding *feminine image* of behaviors appropriate to females in each social group.

At the time of the early Olympic Festivals, which date back beyond the first recorded games of 776 B.C., the images of masculinity and femininity within the emerging culture of ancient Greece were clearly delineated. These early Greeks envisioned their gods as persons very like themselves, differing from human beings only in the extent of their personal powers over the natural forces of the universe. Thus, they assigned to their male gods all of the behaviors appropriate to their own image of supermasculinity, while the behaviors of superfemininity were assigned to the female goddesses. A brief review of the characteristics of these gods and goddesses may give us some insight into the fact that women were excluded from the sacred precincts of Olympia.

Among the male gods, Zeus, the hurler of thunderbolts, had dominion over all the forces of earth; and his messenger, Hermes, could overcome both space and time with winged feet. Poseidon, the earth-shaker, had similar dominion over the forces of the sea. Ares, the god of war, was a powerful destructive force; and Hephaestus, the god of the metal workers, could subdue the materials of earth with one powerful blow of his hammer and shape them into forms of his own choosing. Even Apollo, who epitomized the intellectual powers of reason and logic, was pictured as an athlete, well able to overcome the forces of earth by skillful use of his bodily strength as well as by his intellectual prowess.

What an Olympic team the gods would have been! How they would have excelled in every contest in the early Olympic Festivals! And it may be noted that the Olympic Games in which men strove to overcome the forces of the earth in symbolic contests were held in honor of Zeus, the all-powerful father of the gods.

In contrast, the image projected by the female goddesses is almost totally devoid of any suggestion of physical strength that might be used to overcome the forces of earth — or of men.

Demeter, the Earth Mother, is envisioned as the ground in which all life is bred and nurtured. Hera, the wife of Zeus, is pictured as his helpmate, whose own will must ever be subordinated to the desires of her husband. (It may be noted, however, that Hera is never wholly resigned to this role and at times she uses her own female resources to seduce Zeus into doing her will rather than his.) Aphrodite, born of the foam of the sea, has none of these homely virtues. She is the goddess of beauty, infinitely desirable to all men. But if she delights in arousing their sexual desires, she can also be cruel and treacherous. In return for her favors, she demands tribute from her admirers, and men may well be fearful of her vengeance when her need for adoration is not satisfied. We are told that she was an accomplished swimmer, but she appears to have used this skill largely to display her lovely body in attractive poses that lured men to their own destruction.

The fact that these early Greeks could not reconcile feminine desirability with athletic prowess is underlined in the legends of Artemis and Athena. Artemis, the beautiful goddess of the hunt, was fleet of foot, and none excelled her in the use of bow and arrow — but men did not find her lovely body desirable. Or perhaps it was the other way around. At any rate, legend relates that Artemis and her followers rejected the love of men and found delight in the companionship of women. Athena, goddess of wisdom, and of all goddesses the most respected, carried her own spear as she led men into battle, and her most famous statue shows her in full fighting array. But, alas, she too was denied the love of men, her perpetual virginity being commemorated in the Temple of the Maiden called the Parthenon.

Perhaps Artemis might have entered the foot races in the earliest games at Olympia; perhaps Athena might have thrown the javelin as well as the spear — and in fact there were some limited competitions of this type for maidens in some of the festivals attended by women. But even in Sparta, where young girls were encouraged to develop both strength and skill, marriage put an end to such competitive endeavours. For adult women, the virtues demanded were those of Demeter, Hera, and Aphrodite — and the strength, skill and intellect of Athena and Artemis did not fit in this image of feminine desirability.

These are the elements out of which the prototypes of masculinity and femininity were compounded by the early ancestors of Western civilization. But these images were never wholly static. As men learned increasingly to control the stuff of their universe with skill and intellect, rather than with sheer strength of muscle, the masculine image reflected this evolving interpretation of man's role as a consequential force within the grand design. So, too, the feminine image began to change — albeit much more slowly.

The shift from muscle to skill and intellect may be seen in the contrast between Heracles, the legendary hero of pre-Homeric Greece, and Theseus, the later hero who made Athens into the most powerful of all Greek cities.

Heracles, who is sometimes credited with founding the earliest form of the Olympic Games, was a man of incredible strength. Certainly he would have been a formidable competitor in all of the early Olympic events, for no man could excel him in size or in strength of muscle. In all truth, however, he was not very bright, and his great strength led him into all sorts of trouble. He suffered great pangs of remorse for the damage caused by his own ineptitude, but he did not seem to learn much from these destructive episodes.

Theseus, who comes along much later in the story of Greece, presents quite a different picture. He is smaller than Heracles, and he has less strength, but he uses that strength with far greater skill — and is more disposed to forethought than to remorse and vain regret. He is the first king to establish and maintain his right to rule largely by force of intellect, and in his story we find the first recognition of the virtues of cooperation among men and cities. Heracles might well have bested Theseus in the pancratium and other weight events in the Olympic arena, but Theseus would have excelled in any contest demanding skill and strategy in the use of the lighter implements, and probably in the team games — which were later to demand cooperation as well as competition.

In the time of Heracles, the feminine image projected by Demeter, Hera and Aphrodite was embodied in the legendary first woman, Pandora. She was lovely to behold, her name means "all joys," and she was welcomed as a helpmate — but, alas, she was really very stupid. Allowing her curiosity to overcome her caution, she opened the box that contained all the evils and sorrows of mankind, and let them loose in the world — where they plague men to this very day. But in her one display of good sense, she did slam the lid down just in time to preserve woman's greatest gift to man — the gift of hope.

In the picture of Pandora, there is little to suggest an interest in overcoming the inertia of mass. But Hippolyta, Queen of the Amazons, who won the enduring love of Theseus many centuries later, presents quite a different image.

As ruler of her own kingdom, Hippolyta was the equal of Theseus in intelligence and skill, although smaller in size and of lesser strength. As they confronted each other in mortal combat at their first meeting, her courage matched his, and she fought bravely and well, neither asking nor offering advantage. In the eyes of Theseus she was both beautiful and desirable, and when he had won her he found new joy in the sexual embrace, for her ardor and skill matched his own. In marriage, she was a faithful helpmate and a devoted mother, and equally she was a good companion, both at home and in the hunt. In the end, she proved her love for Theseus by offering up her own life to save his — and it is said that he mourned her unceasingly for the rest of his days.

The legendary Hippolyta seems to have combined in her own person the skill and intellect of Artemis and Athena, the homely virtues of Demeter and Hera, and the beauty and desirability of Aphrodite.

Surely, to Theseus, she was everything a man might hope to find in a woman. Had she been admitted to the lists of the Olympic Games, it seems likely that she would have earned her laurels proudly — not in the pancratium or weight-events, perhaps, but surely in the foot races and the javelin throw. And it seems likely that Theseus would have found pride in her achievements. But for the citizens of Athens, the time for recognition of such womanly feats had not yet come.

Hippolyta was cruelly rejected by the Athenians, both male and female. They could not reconcile intellect, skill and strength with their image of adult female sexuality. In her own life, however, Hippolyta proved them wrong — and they never forgave her for this. To this day, her name evokes suspicion in the minds of many men and women. Nonetheless, she left her own bright legend for future generations — the legend of a woman who delighted in using *all* of her own personal powers, a woman far ahead of her own time who won and held the love of the most eminent and farseeing man among the citizens of early Athens.

The gods and goddesses of ancient Greek myth have long departed from their old home on Mt. Olympus, but their images are still reflected in the connotations of the words *masculine* and *feminine* as we use them today. Historically, as men have moved forward on the path of skill and intellect pointed out by Theseus, they have tended to devalue the virtues of sheer muscular power — but the term *masculine* still suggests the image of Heracles. So, too, it is Pandora's image that is suggested by the term *feminine*. And many of the arguments about the appropriateness of sports competition for women hinge on those connotations.

However, when the modern Olympic Games were established in 1896, the image of Hippolyta was partially cleansed of the slurs that have tarnished it through the years, and women were at long last permitted to seek their own laurels in some events. Today the image of the feminine athlete is still somewhat blurred, but its modern outlines now seem to be emerging in currently sanctioned patterns of sports competition for women.

III. The Socially Sanctioned Image of Feminine Sport Competition

The socially sanctioned images of femininity and masculinity are always relative. They differ from era to era, from culture to culture, and from group to group within a given social organization. In broadest general terms, these socially sanctioned images may be described as a composite interpretation of what the members of either sex may be or do without impairing their opportunities for finding a mate within their own social classification.

The social sanctions indicated below were derived from attitudes expressed by college women in the United States. I am indebted to Dr. Laura Huelster of the University of Illinois and Miss Mabel Hart of the University of Southern California for many of the data used here. They must not, however, be held responsible for my interpretation of their findings nor for the extension of these data to international level or Olympic competition.

1. At the international level, some forms of competition appear to be *categorically unaceptable,* as indicated by the fact that women are excluded from Olympic competition in these events.

These forms include: Wrestling, judo, boxing, weight-lifting, hammer throw, pole vault, the longer foot races, high hurdles, and all forms of team games — with the recent exception of volleyball.

These forms appear to be characterized by one or more of the following principles:

An attempt to physically subdue the opponent by bodily contact
Direct application of bodily force to some heavy object
Attempt to project the body into or through space over long distances
Cooperative face-to-face opposition in situations in which some body contact may occur

It may be noted that the excluded team games are generally acceptable to college women in the United States at the level of intramural competition, and these games are popular during the years of adolescence. Some extramural competition is sponsored at the high school level, but this decreases in the college age group, and only a very limited number of college women continue their interest in team games during their adult years.

2. Some forms of competition are generally *not acceptable* to college women in the United States, although they *may be acceptable to a minority group* within the college population.

These forms include: Shot put, discus throw, javelin throw, the shorter foot races, low hurdles, long jump, gymnastics events, and free exercise.

These forms appear to be characterized by one or more of the following principles:

Direct application of bodily force to a moderately heavy object
Attempt to project the body into or through space over moderate
  distances
Display of strength in controlling bodily movements

Very few college women show any sustained interest in performance in these events, although some may have found them challenging during the early years of adolescence. Among the Olympic competitors from the United States, Negro women are disproportionately represented in the track and field events. In the gymnastic events, there is a preponderance of women of Germanic and Slavic ancestry, most of whom have developed their interests and abilities in ethnically-defined social and athletic clubs rather than in the college setting.

3. Some forms of individual competition are *generally acceptable* to the college women of the United States, and competence in these events does not appear to militate against social acceptance by males within the college population.

These forms include: Swimming diving, skiing, and figure skating, and such non-Olympic events as golf, archery, and bowling.

These forms appear to be characterized by one or more of the following principles:

Attempts to project the body into or through space in aesthetically
  pleasing patterns
Utilization of a manufactured device to facilitate bodily movement
Application of force through a light implement
Overcoming the resistance of a light object

In one way or another, all of these sports involve a considerable expenditure of time, money, or both; and participation is accordingly limited to women in the economically-favored groups. Bowling, which is the least expensive insofar as time is concerned, and in which a moderately heavy ball is used, finds greatest favor with middle-class groups. Success in the other events may contribute to upward social mobility in some instances.

4. Some forms of face-to-face competition are also *generally acceptable* to college women of the United States, with no implication of limited social acceptance for successful competitors.

These forms include: Fencing, such non-Olympic sports as squash, badminton, and tennis, and the team-game of volleyball.

These forms appear to be characterized by one or more of the following principles:

Application of force through a light implement
Overcoming the resistance of an essentially weightless object
Maintenance of a spatial barrier that prevents body contact with opponent

Fencing is not acceptable to certain religiously-defined groups, presumably because it symbolizes the destruction of human life. Adult competition in squash and badminton is largely limited to members of private clubs, but these groups include women from the middle as well as the higher socioeconomic levels. Tennis, which was once a private club game, is now commonly played by all groups having access to public facilities, but as yet only a few women from the darker-skinned minorities have reached the level of national competition. Volleyball is commonly played as a recreational game with mixed teams including both sexes.

It is of interest to note the difference between squash, which is socially acceptable for women in the upper economic levels, and handball, which is not. Here the distinction seems to rest on the use of a light implement to apply force in the one game and the use of the hand in the other. However, such resistance to hitting an object with the hand seems to be overcome in the growing popularity of volleyball.

Summarizing this analysis, it appears that the socially sanctioned image of feminine sports competition for college women in the United States may be derived from a few general principles:

1. It is *not appropriate* for women to engage in contests in which:
   the resistance of the *opponent* is overcome by bodily contact
   the resistance of a *heavy object* is overcome by direct application of bodily force
   the body is projected into or through space over long distances or for extended periods of time
2. It *may be appropriate* for women identified in the lower levels of socioeconomic status to engage in contests in which:
   the resistance of an *object of moderate weight* is overcome by direct application of bodily force
   the body is projected into or through space over moderate distances or for relatively short periods of time
3. It is *wholly appropriate* for women identified with the more favored levels of socioeconomic status to engage in contests in which:

  the resistance of a *light object* is overcome with a *light implement*

  the body is projected into or through space in aesthetically pleasing patterns

  the velocity and maneuverability of the body is increased by the use of some manufactured device

  a spatial barrier prevents bodily contact with the opponent in face-to-face forms of competition

IV. Sport as a Symbolic Formulation of Socially Sanctioned Female Roles

Within the context of the biological, mythological, and social interpretations of the nature of females, we may now examine the theory that the sports in which women compete serve to formulate some conception of the female's role as a consequential force within the universe of space, time, mass and energy.

At the international level, as represented by the Olympic Games, women are categorically prohibited from any attempt to overcome an opponent by direct application of bodily force. Since this prohibition cuts across all cultural lines, it would seem to be traceable to some biologically-defined difference common to the men and women of all social groups. The clue may lie in the differences between the ways in which males and females may use their own bodily forces in the mutual act of procreation.

For the male, the procreative act may be construed in terms of direct application of bodily forces subject to the male's control. Conversely, the female role must be construed in passive terms as the act of receiving and nurturing new life rather than creating it by personal intent expressed in terms of bodily force. Thus, the male may use his own muscular powers to coerce the female and force her to submit to his will, but the female can not similarly coerce the male. By extension, then, it may well seem biologically appropriate for the male to force another person to submit to his will by direct application of muscular powers through bodily contact; conversely, it would be biologically inappropriate for the female to coerce or subdue another person by use of the muscular powers of her own body.

This interpretation may be further extended in the roles assigned to men and women in the mortal combat of war. Here, men have long found it possible to justify their own attempts to coerce other men into submission by threat of death; but men have seldom permitted their women to engage in such direct forms of mortal combat. Athena may have carried her spear as she led men into battle, but, insofar as legend relates, she did not personally use her own body to wrestle with the enemy. Hippolyta and her Amazons did, on occasion, engage in hand-to-hand combat — but the most severe charge made against Hippolyta by the Athenians was that she had "fought like a man."

When the resistance to be overcome in a contest is centered in an *object*, rather than in the body of another *person*, the prohibitions against use of bodily force by women are stated in relative, rather than in categorical, terms. Here the issue seems to be: *How much force* may a woman appropriately apply to an object?

At the Olympic level, women are not permitted to lift heavy weights or to throw the hammer. They are, however, permitted to put the shot, hurl the discus, and throw the javelin. Similarly, they are barred from the pole vault, the high jump, the high hurdles, and the longer foot races, but they are permitted to compete in the long jump, the low hurdles, and the shorter races. They are also barred from the more strenuous team games, but in 1964 they were permitted to compete in the milder game of volleyball — the only team game in which there is no possibility of direct body contact between opponents.

The facets of biology provide no logical basis of support for these relative distinctions. The number of women competent to perform in the excluded events may be small — but so is the comparable number of men; and this is generally true for all of the events included on the women's list, with the numbers increasing as the events become less physically demanding.

Socially, however, there appears to be a relationship between participation in such strenuous events and the kinds of work commonly done by the performer's parents. Women from homes in which both the father and mother are commonly employed in some form of manual labor may seemingly use their own muscular forces in athletics without impairing their own marriageability. Here the old fallacy of associating displays of strength with sexual inadequacy seems to be greatly weakened — although it still can not be wholly dismissed as a factor in the determination of social approval. It must also be noted that even within the manual laborer group social approval tends to decrease as the muscular forces demanded by the events increase.

Within the category of fully-approved events in which the contestant attempts to overcome the resistance of an object, strength is generally far less important than skill. The contested objects in such games as golf, archery, tennis, badminton, and squash are essentially weightless, and the objective of the contest is to move these objects through space by manipulating a light instrument with skill and speed. (The heaviest such instrument is probably the bowling ball, which even

very small women can lift without difficulty.) This emphasis on in-
strumental manipulation is further emphasized in the face-to-face
games by either nets or rules that prohibit bodily contact. (Even in
fencing, in which the body of the opponent is touched by the instrument, the touch is symbolic rather than forceful.)

All of these games were developed in the later years of human
history by men called "gentle" — men whose personal status rested on
the presumption of superiority in intellect and skill rather than on their
muscular powers. But women did not participate in the early forms
of these games. Not until the Industrial Revolution had created new
forms of employment for women in industry, and not until women in
the more socially-favored classes had begun to claim some measure of
personal equality with their husbands, did women begin to participate
in these sports reserved for gentlemen.

Significantly, these sports pioneers seldom competed with men directly in any of these games, and there is still strong aversion to this
form of competition. Today, the socially-approved forms of competition
in tennis, for example, are still man-man, woman-woman, and mixed
doubles — in which the marriage relationship is symbolized by a partnership in which a man and woman combine their forces in a contest
with another partnership team. Today, styles in double play are changing — but the most common strategy still emphasizes the man's strength
of arm, while the woman uses her skill to support his efforts within a
smaller part of their common court area.

Thus, in mixed doubles the woman still tends to play the role appropriate to Hera, the helpmate, as she uses the skills of Artemis and
Athena and Hippolyta to support the efforts of her male partner, rein-
forcing his attempts to win the contest rather than threatening his
mastery over their common environment. However, it must be noted
that side-by-side play is now frequently seen in mixed doubles, particularly when both of the partners are superior players. So it would seem
that men who are sure of their own strength and skill are not offended
by displays of strength and skill in their mates — particularly when
these female forces are combined with their own male forces to their
mutual advantage.

Within the category of socially approved events in which the contestant attempts to project her body into or through space, women
display a high degree of muscular strength as well as great skill and
daring. In swimming, they propel themselves through the water with
great speed, but they seldom compete in the longer distances. As
Aphrodite noted, however, the water-supported movements of swimming
display the female body to advantage, and it is noteworthy that the

aesthetically pleasing patterns of synchronized swimming were developed by women, rather than by men. Similarly, women in gymnastics and free exercise have developed their own movement patterns, which emphasize grace and beauty to a far greater extent than do the standard events for men.

Diving, figure-skating, and skiing are also classed as graceful forms of movement, and in these sports personal velocity is greatly facilitated by the use of such manufactured devices as springboards, skates, and skis. The management of the high velocities produced by these devices requires both strength and skill, but it is skill that is emphasized rather than strength.

Today, in the United States, the image of femininity projected by college women and endorsed by their potential mates is a "double image" — with one aspect identified as "woman at work" and the other identified as "woman at home."

As workers, these college women see themselves dealing with the forces of the universe in consequential ways, even as their men do. But neither the men nor the women picture themselves overcoming the resistance of mass, or of other persons, by sheer muscular force of bodily contact. Rather, they are prepared to use their wits in the realm of ideas, and they are adept in the use of lightweight equipment and manufactured devices that call for dexterity and skill rather than strength. On occasion, the men may still feel called upon to demonstrate the age-old conception of masculinity by performing feats of strength; but few college women seek this expression of their own human powers.

As potential wives and mothers, the college women are concerned with expressing their femininity in quite different ways. Recognizing their own biologically-based need for dependence on the male wage-earner, they modify their behavior in ways designed to enhance their own sexual desirability. They may also, on occasion, conceal their own abilities as workers lest the man of their choice might feel belittled by their competence.

Both sides of the image are evidenced in the socially approved list of sports for women. Strength and bodily contact are de-emphasized in favor of skill and grace; force is applied to weightless objects with lightweight implements; and velocity is attained by use of manufactured devices. And there is no serious competition in which women are matched against men. Rather, in those sports in which men and women participate together, they play as partners, with women generally accepting the supporting rather than the dominant role.

   Thus, in our own time, it would seem that the college women of the
United States have found it possible to combine the sexually-based
image of Aphrodite, Hera and Demeter with the personal powers of
Athena, Artemis, and Hippolyta, without doing violence to either,
within the realm of sports competition. Thus, too, the forms of competition they have chosen may be construed as a dramatic formulation
of their conception of the complex roles females may play as consequential forces within the grand design of the universe. Perhaps
Heracles and Pandora might have been dismayed by this interpretation
of what a woman is and what she can do — but let it be said to the
credit of Theseus that he foresaw this picture some three thousand years
ago when he described Hippolyta as everything a man might hope to
find in a woman — and let us remember, too, that the legend of his
love for her has endured, time without end, through the long years
of human history.

Symbolic Forms of Movement: Dance
(With Lois Ellfeldt)

Conference on Movement sponsored by the National Section on Dance — American Association for Health, Physical Education, and Recreation — Greensboro, North Carolina — June, 1961

Published in: *Focus on Dance II, An Interdisciplinary Search for Meaning in Movement.* Washington, D.C.: American Association for Health, Physical Education, and Recreation, 1962.

Is movement meaningful? Dancers believe that it is. An art form is a formulation of meaning; and dancers, as artists, attempt to formulate meaning in movement forms. But what makes a movement form meaningful? How are the meanings of movement expressed and understood? Are tennis-form movements meaningful? Is walking a formulation of meaning in locomotor-form movements?

Our studies are an attempt to answer questions about the meaningfulness of human movement within the philosophical context of the theory of symbolic transformation.

Section 1. Within the context of the theory of symbolic transformation we have tested the hypothesis that movement is a symbolic form.

Some understanding of the major premises of the theory of symbolic transformation, particularly as it refers to presentational or nonverbal forms, is essential to an understanding of our analysis. These may be found in brief form in Chapters 1-4 of Susanne Langer's *Philosophy in a New Key*, which is readily available as a Mentor paperback book, M25. Chapters 8 and 10 are also particularly relevant to our analysis.

Very briefly, this theory identifies the mind in operational terms as a process that "makes sense" out of sensory perceptions. The function of the mind, as distinguished from the brain, is to symbolize reality-as-perceived-through-the-senses. Human thought is a process of establishing relationships among these symbolic formulations of experiential reality. Human activities, i.e., activities characterized by human thought, are the expressions of the meanings men find in the thoughts that symbolize their intellectual-emotional comprehension of reality.

As a logically developed theory of epistemology, the theory of symbolic transformation identifies the conditions which appear to govern this operational process of transforming sensory percepts into concepts or symbolic forms of experience. Our studies are an attempt to determine to what extent this process appears to operate in the area of man's movement experiences.

Our initial concern has been with "movement in general" as the generic form out of which specialized forms of movement must develop. The problem of differentiating among the specifics must wait upon the identification of the nature of their common generic source.

Section 2. Movement experiences are observed as dynamic, somatic patterns created by body masses in motion. We have called this visually perceivable form of the movement experience a KINESTRUCT.

As an observer watches another person move he does not see the countless details of the movement. He sees a dynamic pattern created by the changing relationships among the body segments. This dynamic, somatic pattern establishes the identity of the movement as distinguished from other similar or different movements. We have called this dynamic, somatic patterned manifestation of movement which is perceivable as a visual form a *kinestruct*. (*Kine* is the root of Greek words referring to movement; the concept of form or structure is suggested by the syllable *struct*.) A kinestruct, then, is defined as a visually perceivable dynamic form constructed by body masses in motion.

Section 3. The visually perceived KINESTRUCT is susceptible to meaningful interpretation by the observer. It can be identified as a symbolic form. We have called this symbolic form a KINESYMBOL or a KINESYMBOLIC FORM.

A symbolic form is a formulation of meaning. Its meaning may be "factual"; which is to say that the form denotes or identifies something. Its meaning may be "conventional"; which is to say that the form is a sign for something. What a form denotes or signifies can usually be expressed in words, man's most obvious vehicle for conveying meanings. Words are verbal symbols. Because they can be arranged syntactically in the form of speech or discourse, they are called discursive symbols. The factual and conventional meanings of these verbal symbols can usually be identified with little difficulty, but the connotations a word may have for a person are often too subtle for verbal identification.

Similarly, a symbolic form of the presentational order formulates meanings at several levels. What a picture denotes or signifies can usually be stated in words. But a picture also has connotations or meanings that can not be fully verbalized. These connotative elements of meaning are "in" the picture as a presentational form, and the mind of the observer deals with these meanings in their own symbolic form even though his tongue cannot give expression to the thoughts in his mind.

The observer who sees a kinestruct can usually "tell in words" what it denotes in terms of "what the person is doing." He can also identify a gesture as a sign and say what it signifies. But words fail him when he tries to describe what is commonly called "the quality of movement" as he sees it in the kinestruct. This "quality" is meaningful to him; he can read it or read into it significant interpretations; but he can not fully translate those interpretations into language or discourse. Like a picture, a kinestruct formulates its connotations in its own terms, and the essential meaningfulness of those connotations is contained in the form as such.

We may, therefore, identify the kinestruct as a symbolic form. To identify this form in terms of its unique components, we have called it a *kinesymbolic form* or a *kinesymbol*.

Section 4. Movement experiences are perceived by the mover as dynamic, sensory patterns created by the kinesthetic sensations elicited by the stimulation of sensory receptors that

occurs during the act of moving. We have called this kines-thetically perceivable form of the movement experience a **KINECEPT**.

Except under special circumstances a mover does not see his own kinestructs. His perception of the reality of his own movements is kinesthetic; and what he perceives is "the feel of the movement." Innumerable sensory events are occurring as the proprioceptive nerve endings are stimulated during movement, but the mover does not appear to be aware of these as separate events. Neither does he appear to be aware of the afferent and efferent neural interactions that make it possible for him to "make movements" of various kinds. He seems to "feel" the movement as a whole; and he "makes it" as a whole. When he focuses his attention on some part of the movement, e.g. the action of the hand, he still "feels" the movement of the part as a whole.

Kinesthesis is analogous to seeing or hearing. Man perceives a picture or a sight or a sound as an organized form. He is not aware of the countless individual sources of visual or auditory stimulation. He can "look harder" or "listen more intently" — which is to say he can focus his attention on some part of what is perceptually available to him — but he cannot sort out the separate sensory events of that perception. He "sees what he sees" and "hears what he hears" as organized perceptual patterns or forms, and he is not aware of the efferent neural interactions that make this organized perception of sight and sound possible.

Similarly, man "feels what he moves" as an organized, dynamic pattern of sensation, or a perceptual form. Combining the concepts of movement and perception, we have called this perceptual form of movement a *kinecept*. A kinecept is defined as a dynamic, perceptual form that incorporates *all* sensory perceptions associated with a kinestruct during the act of creating it.

Section 5. **The kinesthetically perceived KINECEPT is susceptible to meaningful interpretation by the mover. It can be identified as a symbolic form. We have called this symbolic form, too, a KINESYMBOLIC FORM or KINESYMBOL.**

A kinecept may denote something or signify something to the mover. What it denotes, in terms of the movement the mover is making, can usually be "told in words." The mover knows what he means when he makes a gesture or a movement sign; and that meaning can also be verbalized. But the mover is baffled when he attempts to verbalize about "the quality" of his own movements. He is aware of these qualitative differences in his various movements; he can voluntarily alter the quality of his movements. It is also apparent that at times the quality of his movements is related to the intellectual-emotional quality of his "mood." But these connotative, qualitative differences that he perceives as differences in the form of the kinecept can not be verbalized. Like the connotations of the kinestruct, the connotations of the kinecept are inherent in its unique perceptual form. The kinecept may, therefore, also be identified as a symbolic form — a kinesymbolic form or a kinesymbol.

Section 6. The meaning of the KINECEPT is expressed by the KINESTRUCT in KINESYMBOLIC FORM.

The kinestruct and the kinecept have both been identified as kinesymbolic forms. What is the relationship between them? The relationship is similar to that between a picture composed of bits of pigment and the artist's mental conceptualization of the meaning the picture was created to express. The important difference between the picture and the kinestruct is that different physical elements were employed in "making" them. The painter uses pigments; the mover uses his body as a physical object which can be arranged to express meaning in symbolic form.

When a painter finishes arranging his pigments, the symbolic form he has created has become an independent symbolic form, in the sense that it *re*presents the artist's meaning to anyone who looks at it, and it does this without reference to the artist as a person. But the somatic elements of a kinestruct can not be separated from the mover's physical being. His being is an essential component of the kinestruct. As he creates a kinestruct, the interaction between the efferent and afferent neurones at the site of muscle action is so intimate that the kinestruct and the kinecept may be said to "create each other" out of the mover's intent; and neither can "outlive" the other in tangible form. Accordingly there is no tangible *re*presentational form created by the mover. Both the kinestruct and the kinecept are strictly *present*ational forms, each serving to express the meaning of the mover in the moment of their perceivable existence as somatic and sensory realities.

For the mover, the meaning of the movement is conceptualized in the kinesymbolic form of the kinecept. His overt movement is a kinesymbolic expression of that meaning in the form of a kinestruct.

The meanings the mover expresses and the meanings understood by the observer are probably never identical. Each person interprets symbolic forms within his own mental frame of reference. The difficulties in kinesymbolic communication are no different from those inherent in all other forms of attempted communication between human beings.

Section 8. Movement has "intellectual content." Movement experiences may therefore be said to be potentially "educational" experiences, and may appropriately be identified as "subject matter" in educational curricula.

The kinestruct and the kinecept have been identified as kinesymbolic forms. It has been shown that man's movements are intellectually-emotionally meaningful to him, and that he expresses those meanings by moving. As presentational symbolic forms, kinesymbolic forms have been shown to be comparable with the presentational symbolic forms of music and the graphic arts. Movement experiences, or "movement education," would therefore appear to be a "school subject" area comparable with music education and art education in terms of potential contribution to the "fabric of meaning" (Langer) that is identified as liberal education.

Note: In discussing our theory we often encounter the objection that we have not shown *how* kinesthetic neural impulses can be or are transformed into thoughts, concepts, or meanings; and we have not shown *how* the idea of a movement can be or is translated into neural impulses in the motor nerves. Neither have we shown how the proprioceptors "know" what muscle fibers are under tension, or how the feedback system of proprioception operates to coordinate these tension changes to produce the "desired" movement. We have not overlooked this problem! We are keenly aware that these "mind" and "body" relationships have not been established. But neither have the relationships between the mental and physical manifestations of man as a human being been established in terms of scientifically demonstrable "fact" in any area of man's experiences. Our problem as it relates to the kinestruct-kinecept-kinesymbol relationship is just one of the many sub-problems of the nature of man's mind.

Athletics in the Studio

Originally developed as lecture for graduate class in "Theories of Movement," University of Southern California, 1958

Published in: *Journal of Health, Physical Education, and Recreation,* April, 1959.

The movement of a skilled athlete as he throws a ball is beautiful, but it is not dance. The same movement pattern performed by a dancer shows equal skill, but it is not effective in throwing a ball. Yet the athlete and the dancer have the same physical structure; they create the same general pattern of movement; and they both exhibit disciplined control in coordinating the complexity of neuromuscular functioning as they conquer the elements of space, time, and mass. Where, then, does the difference lie? What is the essential difference between "sports movement" and "dance movement"?

During a recent workshop in movement education an attempt was made to get at this difference experimentally. Each group selected a familiar sports activity and then created a "dance" out of the movements, the floor patterns, the interaction between performers, and the meanings implicit in the sports situation. As they did this, they discovered that the essential difference between sports movement and dance movement could be identified in terms of the different purposes of the performers. They also discovered some possibilities for bridging the gulf between "sports persons" and "dance persons" by establishing a line of communication between them.

Take, for example, the lay-up shot in basketball. What is the athlete's purpose? It is specific and clearly defined. He wants to make a specific ball drop through a given basket. His reasons for wanting to do this may be very complex and his emotional involvement in the act may be intense, but at the moment of action these must be submerged so he can focus on his immediate, tangible and primary purpose. Since the action of the ball is governed by the laws of space, time, mass, he must convert his body into an efficient mechanism for imparting velocity and direction to an external mass, adapting each phase of his movement to the requirements imposed by the physical properties of the specific elements involved. He steps just so far; he leaps just so high; he pushes his arm up with exactly the right velocity; and his fingers release the ball at the precise split-second. He is not concerned with the appearance of the movement pattern he creates; he does not care "how it looks." The beauty of his efficient coordination is a by-product, an outcome of his mastery of the physical properties of all elements in the situation.

The dancer must also deal with the realities of space, time, and mass, but his movements are structured by a different purpose. The dancer's purpose is to create an illusion of putting a ball through a hoop by moving in such a way that he conveys a nonverbal comment about what it means to an athlete to "make a basket." Thus, the dancer's purpose is to interpret reality. He does this by intensifying certain significant elements in the movement pattern at the expense of other elements. Every major phase of the total pattern can still be identified — the step, the leap, the up-pushing arm, the release, and the descent. But the dancer's movements are not a replica of the athlete's real attempt to govern the motion of a real ball. The dancer's movements are "stylized" to epitomize the universal elements in *all* lay-up shots. As he abstracts the movement pattern from the limitations of the real game situation, the dancer is no longer bound by the athlete's necessity for adjusting his movements to the actual weight of the ball or the fixed height of the basket. The dancer can extend or diminish his movements at will to emphasize the significant meanings he finds in them. His step can be a giant's stride which conveys the exhilarating feeling of being able to overcome the space that separates him from his objective. His leap can be an extravagant leap which carries his body up, up, up until it appears to defy man's bondage to the law of gravity. His pushing arm can extend and hold its extension as it seems to propel a greater-than-life-size ball far into the spacious universe that extends above the hoop of circumstances into which it must descend.

The dancer's movements may be extravagant, but they are never unpremeditated. Every change in tension is carefully planned to heighten the illusion the dancer is creating, to emphasize the space between the floor and the dancer's body, to lead the eye of the observer upward to the space above the reaching hand. And the essence of the dancer's technique is to make his tremendous effort seem so effortless that the observer sees only the illusion without awareness of the mechanisms used to create it.

Both the actual lay-up shot and the illusion of the lay-up shot are triumphs of neuro-muscular control and technique so well practiced that it can be forgotten at the moment of action; but neither the performances nor the performers are readily interchangeable. The athlete trains himself to respond instantly to each change in a rapidly shifting and unpredictable situation; the dancer spends hours exploring every nuance of the stylized movements which will best represent the universal elements in the pattern. The athlete's movements are governed always by the real properties of the elements of space, time, and mass with which he is dealing at the moment; the dancer's space and time are limited only by his personal limitations of body mass. The athlete strives to develop mechanical efficiency in which the effects of emotionality are minimized; the dancer spends energy extravagantly to maximize the performer's emotional involvement in the activity. Small wonder, then, that the athlete is dismayed when asked to perform "dance movement," while the dancer appears awkward when confronted with the requirements of "sports movement."

The dancer's primary purpose in moving is to convey something of "what it means" in terms of "how it feels," both kinesthetically and emotionally, to conquer space, time, and mass. This is the feeling that gives meaning to the athlete's preoccupation with otherwise meaningless balls and baskets; but it is a meaning the athlete *must not think about* while he is conquering specific units of mass, space, and time lest he interfere with the complex integration of the neuromuscular functioning through which he accomplishes his purpose. Putting the athlete in the dance studio, then, is like asking a business man to write a poem about his business, while putting the dancer on the basketball court is like asking a poet to write a straightforward, concise business letter. Neither will do well in the new situation because the central focus of his training has been on the antithesis of the abilities required for the new assignment.

Does this mean that the gulf between "sports persons" and "dance persons" cannot be spanned? It may be noted that Wallace Stevens and T. S. Eliot achieved success in both poetry and business, but such doubly-gifted persons are few in number. In movement, the athlete's art and the dancer's art each demands its own peculiar abilities, and the persistent practice required to perfect either art may well condition the performer in such ways that performance in the other becomes more difficult. But this problem of dual performance need not prohibit communication based on mutual appreciation of each other's purposes and the ways in which they are achieved. One line of communication between the dancer and the athlete might be established through the creative adaptation of sports motifs to dance performance as suggested by the example given.

By participation in sports, either real or vicarious, the dancer can enlarge his understanding of the meanings and emotional values inherent in man's use of movement to master specific elements in his environment. Through experience in dance, either as a performer or an observer, the athlete may increase his own satisfactions in movement by expanding his comprehension of the need which drives him to conquer space, time, and mass as represented by balls, bats, and running tracks. In turn, increased understanding by both groups of performers can help establish a bridge of meaningful communication across the gulf of differences in *purpose* which will always separate the form of movement called sports from the movement form identified as dance.

The Search for Meaning in Movement
(With Lois Ellfeldt)

Philosophy Section — Western Society for Physical Education of College Women — Asilomar, California — November, 1961

Published in: *New Insights, Report of the 37th Annual Conference of the Western Society for Physical Education of College Women, 1961.*

We have called this paper "The Search for Meaning in Movement" rather than "The Meaning in Movement" because we want to say more about the intellectual landmarks that have guided us to our present position than we do about the theory that incorporates our present point of view. We think this approach has the merit of enabling the reader to think along with us as we go, identifying the foundations on which our final arguments rest. It has the disadvantage, however, of limiting the time we may spend discussing the theory when we reach our conclusions. But so be it.

We have been interested in the significance of movement for many years, but the spark that ignited our present train of thought was the reading of Susanne K. Langer's *Philosophy in a New Key*, some half-dozen years ago. This book has little to say about movement; it is a discussion of the theory of symbolic forms which was developed some forty years ago by the German philosopher, Ernst Cassirer. Quite by chance we were reading this book at the same time; but it was hardly by chance that we underlined the same paragraphs, made squiggly lines in the same margins, and marked *cf. Mvt.* and *cf. Kinesthesis* on the same pages.

Eventually we committed ourselves to a systematic exploration of these intriguing ideas. Since both of us may be described as "people who move," our weekly conversations, arguments, and discussions gave us a physical workout as well as a mental one, for every time we said: "Now, take movement. . . . ." we had to illustrate the thought. This exercise kept us physically fit as we worked our way through Cassirer's *Essay on Man,* and sustained us as we ploughed our way through his earlier three volume work, *The Theory of Symbolic Forms,* which — fortunately for us — is available in English translation.

But while philosophers may deal with concepts that can not be treated by the techniques of science, they must always look to science for the facts that support their conclusions. So we returned again and again to Sherrington's *Man on His Nature,* the classic that is loved by all physical educators because it has so much to say about the proprioceptors. And then we pushed still farther back in time for the clues we might find in Sherrington's *Integrative Action of the Nervous System.*

As we wrestled with epistemology on the one hand and neurophysiology on the other, trying to bring them together in one theoretical construct, we finally recognized the futility of this approach. We were trying to do what philosophers and physiologists alike have been unable to do since the beginning of human history. We were trying to describe a provable relationship between "the mind" and "the body."

Perhaps I should interrupt my story at this point to refresh your thinking about this age-old problem of the relationship between physical reality and man's ability to comprehend it. Some of the troublesome questions are: What is consciousness? How does man feel sensation? What is sensation? What is perception? What is thought? Where are sensation and perception recorded in the animal brain? Is the mind of man an entity that is distinct from his animal brain? What is the substance of mind? Where is it located? How does it produce thoughts? Where are these thoughts recorded? How do these thoughts activate physical structures, such as muscles? How is thought transformed into speech? How are light waves that strike the eyeball transformed into "something seen"? The questions are endless; but the answers are all the same. As recently as 1960, a symposium of eminent philosophers and scientists agreed that the common answer to all of these questions is: "We do not know." The proceedings of this symposium, published under the title *Dimensions of Mind,* make it clear that there is little likelihood of answering these questions so long as they are asked in the foregoing form.

The classic resolution of this difficulty is to bifurcate man and deal with him dualistically by assigning his physical substance to the scientists and his mental essence to the speculations of metaphysically minded philosophers. This dualism did not seriously disturb the educators of the nineteenth century, who directed their attention solely to the mind; but the dualistic mind-body approach to an understanding of man leaves the twentieth century educators who try to educate "the whole child" standing with a foot in each intellectual camp.

Similarly, the physical trainers of the nineteenth century who were content to focus their efforts on modifying the physical structure and physiological functioning of the biochemically organized body had a firm footing in the strongholds of science. But twentieth century physical educators who claim that they, too, educate "the whole child" must show that the mind is actively involved in the process of movement if they wish to join the ranks of educators.

And so we return to our search. The substance of the mind has not been located, but much is known about the physical structures that must be activated to make thought possible. So we returned to our exploration of neurophysiology. Among the recent books in that field, we found J. C. Eccles' *The Neurophysiological Basis of Mind* both readable and illuminating; and Ragnar Granit's *Receptors and Sensory Perception,* which makes very difficult reading, provided us with detailed information about where the neural structures associated with movement fitted into the total picture. The chapters by Ernest Gellhorn and G. N. Loofbourrow in *Science and Medicine in Exercise and Sports* summarize current knowledge in these areas, and we are grateful for them.

Our neurophysiological explorations were rewarded with the assurance that the sensory nerve fibers that convey the sense of movement are represented in the cortex, and the further assurance that the afferent and efferent neural transmitters associated with movement are analogous in every way with the transmitters associated with seeing, although they appear to be even more complex in terms of afferent-efferent relationships.

So we turned from structure to function, going to the psychological literature on perception to see what it had to say about kinesthesis. We found little there, other than routine recitations of Weber's Law, for few psychologists have shown any serious interest in man's movement senses.

A re-examination of traditional theories of learning did little to facilitate our search. Learning theorists have long relegated movement to the category called "motor learning," and this leads them to treat it as a function of the body rather than as a function of mind. But recent developments in the area of learning theory make us hopeful that movement learning may soon be brought into the fold of "real learning" or "mental learning." Today there is much emphasis on the statement that all learning is perceptual learning, which is to say that man can learn only by perceiving events as sensory phenomena, and that learning proceeds by a process of differentiating and integrating sensory perceptions. Knowledge, therefore, is an organization of perceptions; and learning is a process of organizing percepts into concepts or conceptions of experience. As yet the proponents of perceptual learning have had little to say about the sensory perception of movement, but at least they have provided physical educators with an opportunity to call this indispensable sensory data to their attention.

Among the psychologists interested in perception as the basis of all learning, Gardner Murphy has made the most spectacular intellectual leap. The theme that can be detected in *Human Potentialities* is made explicit in *Development of the Perceptual World*. Here Murphy has suggested that the old questions about the nature of consciousness, perception, and mind can be bypassed by dealing with perception as a *response* to an energistic event rather than as a metaphysically defined essence. Recognizing that the essence or substance of consciousness and mind can not be isolated for study by the techniques of science, he is proposing that we explore the substance-less mind by studying its physical counterpart — the physically observable phenomenon from which we infer that consciousness, sensation, perception, and thought "exist." He therefore treats perception as "the overall activity of the organism that immediately follows or accompanies energistic impingements upon the sense organs" (Bartley, p. 22) but he expands the idea of "activity" to include consciousness.

This rather startling definition has the merit of bringing the phenomenon of perception into the realm of physically observable events that scientists can deal with. In this approach, perception may be defined as "what the organism experiences" in conjunction with the transmission of neural energy by afferent nerves. Thus Murphy is committed to the study of animal and human functional behavior as observable evidence of what the organism is experiencing.

And so psychologist Murphy brings us back to philosophers Cassirer and Langer, for Murphy is only saying in his own way what Cassirer said forty years ago. In *Essay on Man*, Cassirer wrote: "The philosophy of symbolic forms starts from the presupposition that, if there is any definition of the nature or 'essence' of man, this definition can only be understood as a functional one, not as a substantial one." (p. 93) Accordingly, Cassirer directed his efforts toward analyzing "what men do" that identifies them as mindful creatures.

But before we return to Cassirer, Langer, and the theory of symbolic forms, we must acknowledge another enormous debt to Gardner Murphy. He, too, has searched the literature of neurophysiology for clues to the nature of perception and thought, but his insight into the significance of what he found there was far greater than ours. In *Development of a Perceptual World*, after citing the studies by neurophysiologists Hebb, Penfield, and Gellhorn, which we have listed at the end of this paper, Murphy wrote:

> *It is not by accident that both Hebb and Penfield discuss the physiological mechanisms of consciousness and voluntary actions concomitantly.* The physiological mechanisms of consciousness appear to be precisely those required for voluntary actions. (*Italics ours.*) *These mechanisms are indeed complex, but as we read Gellhorn, Hebb, and Penfield, they seem to reduce to the* interchange of impulses *between the hypothalmus, the cortex, and the reticular system of the brain stem. The state of this complex interchange seems to correspond both with consciousness and with voluntary control or behavior.* (p. 305-6)

At first glance, the statement that man's thoughts and his voluntary actions are mediated by the same neural structure is startling; but now that Murphy has pointed this out to us, it seems obvious. How else could it be? How could behavior be *voluntary*, in the sense that it is consciously initiated by the person, if it were not mediated by the same mechanisms that mediate the conscious thought that motivated it? A voluntary action is an expression of the thought that created it. Thought and voluntary behavior are two sides of the same coin of mindful being.

And so again we arrive at Cassirer's early insight, this time by the route of neurophysiology with the assistance of a distinguished psychologist. Voluntary human behavior is the overt expression of human thought. By studying the characteristics of the mindful behavior of men we can describe the nature of the mind in operational terms. This is precisely what Cassirer did four decades ago. He focussed his attention on man's nonanimal behavior as represented by his use of myth, religion, language, art, history and science. The theory of symbolic forms identifies the common element that characterizes all of these mental creations of man — man's ability to deal with his perceptions of reality in the symbolic form of concepts, ideas, and thought, and his basic need to express the meanings he formulated by structuring his sensory perceptions.)

Cassirer developed his theory largely in terms of verbal forms of behavior; Langer extended the theory into the realm of presentational or nonverbal forms. It is within the context of her development of the symbolic or meaningful nature of such nonverbal forms of behavior as creating and listening to music, or creating and looking at pictures, that we have developed our theory about the mindful or meaningful nature of the behavior that may be described as creating and looking at voluntary movement patterns. Langer's most recent book, *Feeling and Form*, greatly extends the theories she developed in *Philosophy in a New Key*, and we have found some of the chapters in her *Problems of Art* helpful in structuring our own thinking about movement.

This is neither the time nor the place to attempt an explication of all of the details and ramifications of the theory of symbolic forms. Essentially, a symbolic form may be described as a formulation of meaning. In its private form, as a thought, concept or idea, it is comprehended only by the person who is thinking it; in its public form, it is an expression of that thought or meaning. This distinction between private and public forms of the same symbol may be seen in the distinction between a word that is thought of and a word that is spoken.

A word is a formulation of meaning; a sentence is a formulation of the relationships between words that convey meaning, and is a formulation of meaning in its own right. But let us speak of words, rather than sentences, to illustrate the powers of a symbolic form.

A word may be a *sign* that *signifies* an event or a relationship that existed, exists, or may exist. Thus the word "water" written on a placard serves as a sign, and the reader of the sign reacts to this symbolic formulation of the meaning of a past or an existing situation, or a situation that may exist in the future.

But a word may do more than signify an event; it may name it or *denote* its essential character. Thus, the word "water" is a symbol that stands for something that may be experienced in many forms, but the word "water" denotes the essential organization of elements that makes water what water is.

The word "water" denotes "water in general," but this word has different connotations for a thirsty man than it does for one who has recently slaked his thirst. Or the word "water" may evoke one response from a man who once clung to a life raft for twenty-four hours and a quite different response from a man who uses SCUBA or swimming as a form of recreation. To change the example, the power of connotation is well illustrated by a word like "black," which has many meanings, ranging from an organization of pigments to an emotional mood.

As physical forms, the sounds created by moving the tongue, lips, and vocal cords are only vibrations of air; as symbolic forms, however, they are meaningful to man because he creates these vibrations of air to formulate his comprehension of reality. Thus, these physical forms are symbolic in the sense that they symbolize "what reality means" to man.

Any physical form may be identified as a symbolic form if it has the power to signify, denote, or connote some element of meaning. Thus a picture is a symbolic formulation of meaning. It is the public expression of the artist's private thought. It may signify a conventional meaning, as a pictured arrow may be drawn to signify a direction. It may denote an event which may be identified as a sunset or a man running. But any picture has subtle connotations, both for the painter who created it and for the viewer who looks at it. The connotational power of pictured forms is well illustrated by the Rorschach ink blots; what the viewer sees "in" them is indicative of his past experiences and the meaning they had for him. In any art gallery, people manifest their ability to respond to the symbolic meanings of pictures by their behavior as they look at them; but the connotations of the picture are not necessarily the same for the viewer as they were for the artist who painted the picture. What the artist meant by the picture and what the picture means to the viewer are functions of the different experiences the artist and viewer have had and the different meanings they have found in those experiences.

The public form of a symbol can always be accounted for in terms of physically describable elements. A spoken word is made of sound waves; a written word is made of ink and paper; a picture is made of pigments and canvas. The private form of a symbol must be described as a thought, a concept, or an idea. Its substance is the meaning that the thinker has formulated by organizing and integrating his sensory perceptions of the physical events he has experienced. That meaning may be born of many kinds of experiences and many different kinds of sensory events; but the private forms of all symbols have the same characteristics, the characteristics we describe as conception or thought, We know these thoughts as they are manifested by our behavior. We express what we think by what we do. We infer the thoughts of others by interpreting the public forms or behavior forms in which they are expressed. But since our inferences are based on our own conceptions of reality, i.e., the meanings we have found in our own sensory experiences, the public form of a symbol may have different connotations for the "viewer" than it does for the person who created it to express his private thoughts.

Against this much too brief discussion of the concepts of signification, denotation, and connotation as the characteristics of symbolic forms, we may now summarize our analysis of the private and public forms of man's voluntary movement behavior.

The public form of man's movement behavior may be likened to a picture. As we observe the movements of other people we do not see the countless details of the movements that correspond to the specific contractions of individual muscle fibers or groups of muscles. We see only the dynamic pattern created by the changing relationships among the body masses. This dynamic, somatic pattern may be seen as a unique form, different in some way from all other movement patterns, but it may also be seen as a general pattern that can be identified as a member of a class of movement patterns that have certain characteristics in common.

As a general pattern, the movement may be identified as a conventional gesture that signifies a meaning such as "Hi!" or "Hello" or "come here" or "look at that object." Thus a conventional gesture has the characteristics of a *sign*. But the general pattern also serves to denote what the person is doing. As we observe it, we know: "He is jumping" or "He is throwing a ball" or "He is rising from his chair." What the general pattern denotes to us can usually be expressed in words; for the power of denotation is the power to name.

But a specific movement pattern always differs from the general pattern of the class of movements to which it belongs in subtle ways. As we recognize these subtle differences, they have implications for us, and we "read into" the movement the meanings that these subtle differences convey to us. A jump may convey the idea of joy or fright; or it may only convey the need to surmount a physical obstacle that is in the jumper's path. It may also convey to the observer information about the emotional mood that is the over-all expression of the mover's relationship to reality as he interprets it at any given time. Thus, the public form of a movement pattern has the power of connotation, as well as the powers of denotation and signification. It may, therefore, be identified as a symbolic form or a formulation of meaning.

The private form of movement behavior is known only to the mover. He knows it as the thought that initiates, creates, or corresponds to the movement act.

Except under special circumstances, the mover does not see the movement pattern he is creating; his knowledge of that pattern is kinesthetic knowledge. He experiences his own movements as "the feeling of movement" conveyed by the intricate network of sensory receptors and nerves that may be called, for convenience, the kinesthetic sensorium. While he is moving, innumerable sensory events are occurring, but he does not seem to experience them as separate events. Neither does he appear to be aware of the afferent and efferent neural interactions that make it possible for him to make movements or create movement patterns in accordance with his conscious intent. Just as he "sees a sight" or "hears a sound" as a whole or organized sensory event, so he perceives his own movements as organizations of sensory data that are perceived as a whole.

The analogy between kinesthetic perception and visual or auditory perception may be pursued further. When man sees a word or a picture or hears a word spoken, he is not aware of the interactions between afferent and efferent neural impulses that make it possible for him to see or hear. If he "looks more closely" or "strains to hear" he may become aware of what he is doing, but he is aware of it in the sense of "making an effort" rather than being aware of the neural events that enable him to make that effort. Even when he focuses his attention directly upon "the act of seeing" or "the act of hearing," he still perceives only the organized perceptual pattern as a whole, and it is the pattern, rather than its elements, that denotes the effort to see or hear.

Similarly, man's intentional movements are an integration of sensory and motor events that cannot be sorted out and experienced as separate elements. When a man wants to move in a certain way, he tries to make or create that movement in the same way that he creates the act of seeing when he wants to read what is written on a page. He knows what he is doing; he is not aware of the neural interactions that enable him to do it.

If a man makes a conventional gesture, he knows that he has made it; and he knows what it signifies, because he made that gesture to convey that meaning. When he attempts to create the movement pattern called jumping, he also knows what he is doing and can state his intentions in words. Since he can not see himself jump, his knowledge of his jumping behavior must be derived from his kinesthetic perceptions of the movement pattern called jumping. It is apparent, therefore, that the kinesthetic or private perceptual form of voluntary movement behavior has the power of denotation. To the mover, the organized whole of the perceptions conveyed by the kinesthetic sensorium denotes the name of the act he has performed.

The variety of responses a mover may make to his own kinesthetically perceived movement patterns is evidence that these perceptions have connotations for him. He likes to move in certain ways; he does not like to move in other ways. He seeks to repeat certain movement patterns, attempting to modify them and make them more like his concept of some generalized patterns; he rejects other movement patterns, and may refuse to perform them or he may evidence reluctance if he is urged to attempt them. Sometimes he can verbalize about these responses, offering some reason for his likes or dislikes; more often he can not fully explain his own responses in words. But these responses are always evidenced in some way by what he does when he thinks about the movement, while he is creating the movement pattern, or after he has created the movement pattern. Since his only knowledge of the movement pattern he creates as such is derived from his kinesthetic perceptions of his own behavior, the kinesthetic form of the movement experience must have the power of connotation.

Since the kinesthetic form of voluntary movement behavior has the powers of signification, denotation and connotation, it may also be identified as a symbolic form or concept which may be interpreted as a formation of the meaning the movement has for the mover.

The relationship between the private and public forms of movement behavior is the same as the relationship between the private and public forms of all symbolic behavior. The public form is the overt expression of the meaning the concept has to the person. Just as men organize elements of sound to express their meanings in words or music, just as men organize bits of pigment to express their meanings in pictures, so men organize muscle fiber contractions to express their meanings in movement form. The act of creating a physically observable form and the concept, thought, or idea of that form, are inseparable. The thought is private; the act and its consequences are its public counterpart.

When a painter has formulated his meaning in pigments, the symbolic form he has created becomes a durable public form that can continue presenting the artist's meaning to the public whether the artist is present or absent. The public form of movement presents the mover's meaning to the public only when the mover is present. The public form the mover creates can not be separated from his physical substance, because it is created out of that substance. But the intimacy of the relationship between the private and public forms of movement does not vitiate the arguments that lead us to identify them as symbolic forms.

Man's movement behavior may therefore be described as mindful behavior in the same way that his other mentally-defined behaviors may be described. Man learns to move in the same way that he learns to read, sing, or paint pictures. He learns by structuring his perceptions of movement into integrated wholes that are meaningful to him as symbolic forms. He creates movement patterns in the same way that he creates patterns of sound or pigment, and he creates them for the same reason — to satisfy his basic human need for formulating reality-as-he-perceives it into elements of meaning that his mindful nature can comprehend.

To summarize: The neurophysiologists who deal with the physical structures involved in thought or intellection have assured us that the afferent and efferent neural transmitters associated with voluntary movement are well-represented in the neural complex of hypothalmus, cortex, and reticular or feedback system of the brain stem through which the processes of thought and voluntary action are both mediated. The psychologists have reaffirmed our belief that all learning is perceptual learning, and that education may be construed as a process of facilitating the integration of selected sensory perceptions of physically definable reality. The philosophers have enabled us to define thought or intellection in operational terms as the symbolic formulation of meaning. And we have shown that man's movement behavior, both in its public and private aspects, exhibits the characteristics of other forms of behavior that are construed as symbolic formulations of human meanings.

We may therefore say with some confidence that voluntary movement experiences have intellectual content. They may, accordingly, be identified as "educational experiences," and what is called "physical education" may appropriately be identified as a "subject-matter area" in the educational curriculum, comparable with music education and art education and all other nonverbal forms of education. And it may be asserted that the movement experiences that are provided in physical education classes are comparable with music experiences and art experiences in terms of their potential contribution to the "fabric of meaning" that educators help children weave out of their perceptions of reality.

REFERENCES

CASSIRER, ERNST. *An Essay on Man*: An Introduction to a Philosophy of Human Culture. New York. Doubleday and Co. Anchor Books A3, 1956. (Also Yale University Press, 1944.)

.... *Die Philosophie der symbolischen Formen*. 3 volumes. Berlin: E. Cassirer, 1923-29. (In English-New Haven: Yale University Press, 1953, 1955, 1957.)

ECCLES, J. C. *The Neurophysiological Basis of Mind*. Oxford: Clarendon Press, 1953.

GRANIT, RAGNAR. *Receptors and Sensory Perception.* New Haven: Yale University Press, 1955.

HOOK, SYDNEY (ed.). *Dimensions of Mind.* New York: New York University Press, 1960.

JOHNSON, WARREN (ed.). *Science and Medicine of Exercise and Sports.* New York: Harpers, 1960.

LANGER, SUSANNE K. *Feeling and Form.* New York: Scribner's, 1953.

............*Philosophy in a New Key.* New York: Mentor Books, Md. 101, 1959. (Also Harvard University Press, 1942.)

.... *Problems of Art.* New York. Scribners, 1957.

MURPHY, GARDNER. *Human Potentialities.* New York: Basic Books, 1958.

SOLLEY, CHARLES M., AND GARDNER MURPHY. *Development of the Perceptual World.* New York: Basic Books, 1960.

SHERRINGTON, CHARLES S. *Man on His Nature.* New York: Doubleday Anchor Books, A15, 1963. (Also Cambridge University Press, 1940.)

.... *The Integrative Action of the Nervous System.* New Haven: Yale University Press, 1947.

References cited by Solley and Murphy:

D. O. HEBB. *The Organization of Behavior.* New York, Wiley, 1949.

W. PENFIELD. "Mechanisms of Voluntary Movement." *Brain,* 77:1-17, 1954.

E. GELLHORN. "Physiological Processes related to Consciousness and Perception." *Brain,* 77:401-415, 1954.

Significant Forms of Movement Behavior

(Some clues to the meanings in physical education activities)

National Conference on Interpretation of Physical Education — Sponsored by the American Association for Health, Physical Education, and Recreation; the College Physical Education Association; the National Association for Physical Education of College Women; the Society of State Directors of Health, Physical Education, and Recreation; and the Athletic Institute. — Kellogg Center for Continuing Education, East Lansing, Michigan — December, 1961

Published in *Report of the National Conference on Interpretation of Physical Education*. Chicago: The Athletic Institute, 1962.

My assignment tonight is to focus our attention on the intellectual-emotional components in the experiences commonly called physical education activities. In the paper called "The Search for Meaning in Movement," which you have in your conference packet, I have indicated the neurophysiological, psychological, and philosophical considerations that support the belief that certain forms of movement may be construed as intellectual-emotional behavior. Tonight I want to extend that idea by dealing with it in more general terms.

During the past decade there has been great intellectual fermentation in every discipline that deals with human behavior. The catalyst in all of these conceptual test tubes has been the recognition that there is an essential qualitative difference between human behavior and animal behavior. Many old concepts based on studies of animal behavior are now being abandoned in favor of concepts based on the identification of man's uniqueness as a symbol-using organism. Today it is widely recognized that the symbolic meanings men find in their experiences, or what they *think* events mean, is far more potent in determining their behavioral responses than events as such. In short, it is now recognized that human behavior is symbol-motivated or thought-motivated behavior, and that the behavior of human beings can be understood only as a symbolic expression of human thought.

It may facilitate our subsequent discussion of man's movement behavior if I take a few moments to summarize the current answers to the questions: What is "thought"? How does man make symbolic sense out of his sensory perceptions? What does the human brain do that the animal brain does not do?

Consciousness may be defined as the ability to perceive sensation. In all animals, consciousness is manifested as response to stimulation. The living organism experiences this response to stimulation as sensation; the observing scientist can only note how the organism behaves in conjunction with the sensory event. Such observations have led to the inference that the organism reacts or responds to the general *form* of the stimulus event rather than to its discrete sensory details; and while there is much debate about how this experience is stored for future reference, it is generally agreed that it is the form of the event-as-a-whole rather than its sensory details that modifies the animal's subsequent responses.

Thus, animal behavior appears to be a response to perceptual forms, and as such it can be described in stimulus-response terms. But human behavior does not conform to the familiar S-R pattern. Human beings do not appear to respond to perceptual forms, as such; rather they seem to respond to *relationship among* perceptual forms. The human brain seems to function by comparing the forms of disparate events; it seems to relate these forms to each other, to integrate them into larger wholes, and to organize them in such a way that some of the *relationships* among these forms can be *abstracted from the organization*. These abstracted relationships have no perceptual equivalents; they are only *concepts* of these relationships or *ideas about* how perceptual forms of experience seem to be related to each other. These concepts of "how events are related to each other" are a man's thoughts about the significance of his experiences; they are the sense he makes out of life by identifying connections between seemingly disparate elements in reality-as-he-perceives-it. The symbolic meanings that he finds in the connection between events may be only abstractions, but they are the effective stimulus for eliciting responses in the human organism. Accordingly, the human behavioral diagram reads: Stimulus — Symbolic Meaning Man Finds in the Stimulus Event — Response.

The scientist uses this human ability to think about relationships between events when he infers that an animal has perceived a sensation. In studying human beings, the processes involved in drawing such inferences are more complex, but they are governed by the same principle. We infer what an event *means* to a human being by first relating our concept of the stimulus event to our conceptions of his observable behavior, and then relating our concept of this relationship to similar conceptual relationships existing in our own thoughts. By this involved process of identifying seemingly relevant relationships, human beings are able to construe each other's behavior as analogs of the meanings they find in their own human thoughts.

In human life as we know it, thought and behavior are the two sides of the coin of human existence. Each implies the other; neither can exist apart from the other. Thus, man has no choice other than "to express his thoughts" in behavioral form. As a human being, he functions organismically by responding to the *sense* he makes out of his sensory experiences. The responses are his human behavior. If his sense-making powers are destroyed, he no longer exists as a *human* being, because his behavior becomes animal behavior. But he is most human, or most clearly distinguished from his animal progenitors — which is to say that he lives most, functions best, and finds life most meaningful — when he is able to express the sense life makes to him in articulate terms.

The human behavior called "speech" — along with its written analog — is the most obvious example of man's ability to express symbolic meanings in coherent and well-articulated terms. In speaking, he uses vocalized sounds to symbolize the connection he finds between a concept of an event and the event, as such. By arranging these verbal symbols in the syntactical order agreed upon by members of his language group, man can also express symbolic relationships among a series of concepts. Thus, a sentence serves to make the relationships among a set of concepts more articulate.

The primary relationships expressed by a sentence can be diagrammed, and one of the great virtues of verbal symbols lies in the fact that the speaker must, in effect, diagram the conceptual relationships within his thoughts and make them articulate in order to think or say them in words. But the necessity for diagramming them in serial order imposes limitations on speech as a way of articulating the sense life makes to any man.

(Much of "what life means" or seems to mean can not be neatly arranged in diagrammatic form.) Man's "feelings about life" are too complex and often too incoherent and disorderly to be arranged in serial order. But these inchoate, half-formed meanings also have their analogs in his behavior. They, too, are symbolic thoughts, and as such they elicit a behavioral response. Because they are vague, incoherent, and amorphous, the behavior they elicit is vague, incoherent, and amorphous, — the kind of behavior we designate as "emotional." These incoherent meanings may be expressed in groans, moans, tears, tics, posturings, contractions of involuntary muscles, giggles, squeals, jumping up and down, twirling about, laughing, crying, and so on through all of the forms of behavior we associate with emotion as distinguished from coherent thought.

These "feelings about life" are derived from such complex and interrelated networks of relationships that they can not be diagrammed for expression in sentence form, but they can often be made more articulate in the larger organizational wholes of nonverbal forms. This is the purpose served by such symbolic forms of human behavior as music, pictures, figures, designs, and dance. These and other nonverbal forms of behavior serve to clarify the conceptual relationships within man's "feelings about life" and make them more articulate by suggesting their similarity to relationships exemplified within other perceptual forms.

Music, for example, makes certain relationships more articulate by showing their analogs in sound, time intervals, and rhythms. A musical march is analagous with a locomotor march because it is constructed out of similar time intervals, with sound used to accent the rhythmic structure. Thus, it makes more articulate the relationships that man vaguely senses in the act of walking. Or we might say that the composer takes a fuzzy, half-formed kind of sense and sharpens the outlines of its structural organization. The effect of making the sense of these relationships more articulate is evidenced, for example, by the difference in the behavior of men shuffling along in disordered ranks and men marching to music.

Picture-making serves the same purpose by exemplifying relationships in color and design; dance exemplifies those relationships in movement.

The artist consciously attempts to clarify and make more articulate the relationships he is depicting, and he uses every artifice at his disposal to make his analogies more explicit. But what the artist makes explicit is only what is implicit in every man's behavioral expression of his feelings about life. Picasso's paintings are only a clarification of Rorschach's ink blots; and a dance is only a more articulate formulation of man's posturings and gestures.

We must, however, not lose sight of the fact that these analogies do not exist in the perceptual forms; they exist only in men's thoughts. Every man's analogies are his own; they are the relationships he has personally abstracted form his own organization of experience. They are his concepts of the relationships among sets of concepts. To the extent that two men abstract similar relationships by comparing similar sets of concepts, the meanings they find in the artist's analogies will be similar; but their "rightness" or "wrongness" can be tested only by determining the extent to which they seem to be in agreement with the meanings found by other men in similar experiences.

The metaphors expressed by nonverbal forms can never be completely restated in words and sentences. Nonverbal forms convey their meanings by suggestion, not by diagram. They do what the poet does when he says: "My love is like a red, red rose"; they do what the lover does when he sends a perfect red rosebud to his beloved; they suggest similarities; they do not define their nature. But to the extent that these suggested similarities are comprehended, they help clarify some aspect of the sense of life and make it more articulate, and thus they serve to make human life more meaningful to human beings.

Now, within the conceptual context of this much too brief and much too dogmatic arrangement of verbal symbols in syntactical order, I want to draw some inferences about the meaning-formulating powers of the nonverbal forms of human behavior we call physical education activities. What I have to say seems to me to be applicable to all forms of movement behavior, including the form we call exercise, but because our time is limited I shall confine my remarks to the activities we call dance and sport.

Since the art forms of dance, like all art forms, represent a conscious attempt to clarify and make more articulate some of the relationships within man's feelings about life, they provide a natural springboard for our examination of the meaning-formulating powers of movement.

Every dance is created out of the interactions between the forces of muscle contraction and the forces of gravity — or we might say the interaction between forces *in* the body of the dancer and forces that *act on* his body. The dance, as such, is a dynamic image of the *resultant* of these interactions between man-made powers and the physical forces of the universe. How is this dynamic image similar to man's feelings about life?

Awareness of this similarity is implied in such statements as: "I was greatly moved by his kindness," or "It was a very moving experience." Our language is rich in metaphors that suggest the similarity between emotional states and the movements we make with our physical bodies; but perhaps one very obvious example will serve to illustrate the relationships referred to in these metaphors.

When a man says: "I feel pushed," he obviously does not mean that actual force is being applied to his body; he is actually saying: "I feel as I would feel *if* force were being applied to my body." He is talking about *virtual* forces, rather than the forces that the physicist might describe. (The dictionary defines *virtual* as meaning: so in *effect* but not in *fact*.) What the man who "feels pushed" is talking about is the effect created by the interaction between himself and the universe, as it *feels* to him. The sense this feeling makes to him is partially expressed by his postures and gestures, which are resultants of the interaction between his own physical forces and the physical forces of the universe.

When a dancer creates a dance about "how it feels to be pushed around by life" he exaggerates these postures and gestures and makes them more explicit. Using the interactions between his own man-made powers and the gravitational powers of the universe in the way that a painter might use bits of pigment, he composes a dynamic image of a set of relationships. The relationships within this image are similar to relationships man senses in the interactions between the *virtual* forces that structure human lives and the *virtual* forces that man can exert to counteract them.

Accordingly, a dance may be construed as a metaphorical statement about *how* a man is both literally and figuratively *moved* by what he describes as "a moving experience." In the terms of the physicist, the dance may be described as the resultant of the interaction between man-made forces and gravitational forces, but it suggests the similarity between these interactions and interactions between man's virtual powers as a human being and the powerful forces that structure his existence.

Similarly, a dance may be an analog of the virtual forces that are felt as the rhythms of human life — the organismic rhythms of circulation and respiration, the rhythms of work and play, the solar rhythms that are symbolized by man's calendar — or it may be an analog of the virtual forces that draw men together or drive them apart. Any relationships that the dancer can identify may be suggested in the metaphors of movement; but whatever a dance is about it is an attempt to point out these relationships, clarify them, and make the sense of them more articulate by restating them in terms of the interaction between man-made forces and the gravitational forces of the universe.

If the dance is to be presented to an audience, the dancer attempts to make these relationships more evident by appearing to exert far more force than he actually can exert against forces far greater than the pull of gravity. Thus, he creates an illusion of interactions between super-forces. The audience perceives the apparent resultant of this interaction as a visual image, and each viewer understands "what it means" by discovering analogies between these visually perceived relationships and relationships within his own organization of feelings about life. Thus, every man's analogies are his own, and no one can say "what a dance *really* means." Like the metaphorical *springboard* I used to propel ideas into this discussion, or like the poet's red, red rose, a dance only suggests possible similarities; it does not diagram them.

To the viewer, the dance is a visual image; to the dancer it is an image perceived kinesthetically. But the principles of analogy by abstraction of relationships apply to all perceptual forms. The sense or meaning that the dance makes to the dancer depends upon his ability to abstract relationships from his own organization of kinesthetic perceptions within the larger organization of all that he has ever experienced.

In the forms of dance that we call folk, square, and social, the dancer is seldom concerned about creating an effect for an audience. He is concerned with the sense he finds in the experience of dancing. The essential relationhips in the dynamic kinesthetic image he is creating are defined by the form of the dance; the sense he makes out of those relationships is the meaning he finds in dancing.

But folk dancing differs from presentational forms of dancing, too, in that it involves more unpredictable elements or elements of chance. In a dance designed for presentation, every movement is carefully worked out in advance to suggest the analogies in the clearest possible terms. But the folk dancer must react instantaneously to the unpredictable forces of other people's movements and personalities within the context of the dance. This need for instantaneous response to both actual and virtual forces makes the folk dance more lifelike in that it bears a greater resemblance to the actual circumstances of life. It therefore has another analogous element that further increases the power all dance has to make the sense of life more articulate by analogy. Correspondingly, it limits the power of folk dance to communicate its analogies to an audience because the visual image is always cluttered up with movements that are irrelevant to the dynamic image of virtual powers that the dance, as such, represents.

Any sports performance may be similarly construed as a dynamic image of virtual powers metaphorically expressed as the resultant of the interaction between the actual forces *in* man and the forces that act *on* him.

The gymnast deals almost exclusively with the action of gravitational forces on his own body. Every stunt or event in gymnastics is a metaphorical re-enactment of the drama of man using his own powers to overcome the forces that act on him. By deliberately putting himself in situations where he will be acted on by forces greater than those he encounters in his daily life, and then demonstrating his ability to overcome those forces, the gymnast makes more articulate his awareness of himself as a powerful being that can, to some extent, overcome the forces that seem to structure his life.

In the individual sports, as exemplified by golf and bowling, man again pits his own personal forces against the forces symbolized by a world of objects, and again and again he acts out the symbolic drama of human powers pitted against the forces of the universe. Every successful swing that he makes serves to make his sense of himself as a powerful being more articulate; but — alas — every failure clarifies his awareness of the limitations of his human powers.

In baseball and softball, the sense of life as the interaction between one man's personal forces and the combined forces of the physical universe and the personal forces of other men is clearly articulated by analogy. One man, armed only with a bat, seeks to overcome both the gravitational forces exemplified by the ball and the resistance offered by nine other men who will use all of their powers to keep him from achieving his objective. Small wonder that a home run brings the audience to its feet with excitement in seeing one man do, in effect, what all men feel that they are continually attempting to do. A one-base hit is satisfying, but less so because the runner must then depend on the efforts of other men to assist him in accomplishing what he has set out to do — and the efforts of other men are always unpredictable!

In team games, the situation is structured to equalize the opposing forces, but the men on each team must "work together" to overcome the opposition. Thus, team play articulates man's sense of interdependence with other men; it also intensifies the element of instantaneous reaction to other men's actions.

But there is a significant difference between what men do within the game situation and what they do to prepare themselves for it. A player developing his skill in dribbling, for example, resembles a dancer

creating a dance. He carefully analyzes the relationships in the interaction between his own forces and the forces symbolized by the ball,
and he experiments again and again with various applications of his
own forces until he finds the relationships that produce the desired
effect. But he is not concerned with creating a dynamic image of virtual
powers that will convey that effect to an audience; he is concerned
with how he may best use his own forces to overcome the forces exemplified by the ball. He is trying to sort out his complex ability to
create force; he is trying to clarify it and make it more articulate. He
will not have time to think about these relationships during the actual
game, but in the game he will use the sense these relationships make
to him as an integral part of his attempt to bring all of the forces he
can command into play as he interacts with his teammates in overcoming the opposition of the opponents as well as the gravitational forces
in the ball. Thus, while his practice periods are analogous with the
process of creating a dance, his performance in the game situation is
more similar to dancing a familiar folk dance.

But I must not linger any longer on these analogies; for my purposes
tonight it is enough to suggest their existence. The specific meanings
I have suggested are not necessarily either "right" or "wrong"; you may
find other analogies that seem to you to be more valid. The only point
I am trying to make is that *man's movement behavior is meaningful
to him as behavior that makes his sense of life more articulate*, and
accordingly it enhances his human quality.

Now to turn to the practical question: What implications does this
concept have for this conference devoted to discovering ways to interpret the significance of physical education to other people?

I am not about to propose that we should flood the popular literature with analyses of physical education type movements as symbolic
images of man's virtual powers. I have presented this concept tonight
only for our professional consumption, and I believe it may take us a
long time to digest it for our own professional nourishment. But I also
believe that we can convey whatever sense that concept makes in the
same way that we convey to each other the sense that any concept makes
— by analogy.

I think it is possible to *suggest* the meanings men find in their movement behavior by showing how they use these behaviors. I think we
can show the significance of knowing how to dance by picturing children dancing, adults dancing, and people of all ages spending time
and money to watch others dance. Similarly, I think we can show the
significance of knowing how to circle a high bar, hit a home run, or
cooperate with others in getting a ball into a basket.

The ideas about this must come from us, because no one knows more about the significance of physical education activities than we do, but we shall need some professional help from those who deal with the visual analogies of motion pictures to make our presentations more clearly meaningful. With such help, I believe we can make some films that will serve to make more articulate to all men the sense all men make out of their own movement experiences; and by studying these films ourselves, I think we, too, can arrive at a better understanding of the significance of physical education.

An Inquiry into the Nature of
Movement as Significant Form

(With Lois Ellfeldt)

World Seminar on Health and Fitness in the Modern World — Rome, Italy — 1960.

Published in: *Health and Fitness in the Modern World.* Chicago: The Athletic Institute and the American College of Sports Medicine, 1961.

Reprinted in: E. C. Davis, *The Philosophic Process in Physical Education,* Philadelphia: Lea and Febiger, 1961.

The observation that man finds significance in his own movements is not original with us. The Olympic arena, which epitomizes one aspect of man's long pursuit of excellence in movement, testifies that man has found significance in that pursuit. Dance has long been recognized as a significant art form in every culture; and even before men had learned how to transform thoughts into words that could be used to discuss their movement experiences, man's prehuman ancestors had discovered that they could formulate their deepest feelings in movement rituals. Our studies have been an attempt to identify the nature of the significance man finds in his own movement experiences and the sources from which that significance is derived.

These studies have been in process for several years, and they have carried us in many directions as we have tried to examine all categories of movement. In the present report, however, we shall consider only the stylized movements that men perform of their own volition when they are not motivated by necessities imposed by either their internal or external environment. This limitation to the kinds of movement experiences commonly identified as sports and dance simplifies our task by allowing us to assume at the outset that such movement experiences are a source of some kind or kinds of meaning that men find significant, basing our assumption on the belief that any experiences that men repeatedly seek of their own volition must be meaningful to them in some way. Even within this limitation of the problem, however, it will be possible in the present report to suggest only the general framework of our approach and to identify only the bare structure of our theory.

The concept of "meaning" implies some form of conceptualization derived from experience, because what men call "meanings" are abstractions of the mind. But since the nature of the mind of man and the processes of human thought are still the most puzzling problems of modern science, we must begin by identifying our basic assumptions about man as an intelligent creature characterized by the ability to think in abstractions.

We took our theoretical point of departure about the nature of human thought from the theory of symbolic transformation as developed by Ernst Cassirer and expanded by Susanne Langer. We do not propose to defend or attempt to validate this theory. That task has been undertaken by minds far abler than ours. Briefly, this theory recognizes that man experiences his life through his senses, and that the neural impulses evoked by appropriate stimulation of sensory receptor organs provide him with primary data about himself and his environment. These impulses are transmitted from receptors to effectors by way of the brain, and while this process of transmission is incredibly complex, the general nature of it has long been recognized. But when the subject being studied is a human being, as distinguished from other animal beings, something happens during the process of transmission that cannot be — or at least has not been so far — explained in physiological terms. The sensory perceptions appear to undergo a transformation which changes them from sensations, as such, to abstractions or nonphysical bits of "thought stuff" that represent or symbolize the experience from which the sensations were derived. These nonphysical bits of "thought," which are symbolic abstractions of direct experience, and the coherent and incoherent relationships among them constitute the elements of human mentality, and provide the basis for man's distinctively human mental-emotional comprehension of reality, as he knows it. In this mental conceptualization of experiential reality he finds the meanings and values that give his life whatever significance it may have to him as a human being.

The most obvious manifestation of the mind's ability to find significance in symbolic abstractions of sensory experience is man's use of words. Here it is evident that sounds have been transformed into symbols that stand for or represent elements of meaning, — and in this international gathering it is evident that the same sound may be invested with many meanings, or that a given meaning may be associated with a variety of sounds! But it is also apparent that man finds meaningful conceptualizations of reality in many sensory forms that cannot be verbalized. A picture may convey more than can be said in a thousand words; the music of a violin may incorporate concepts that can not be sung; and even the aroma of steaming coffee may symbolize a great complex of concepts. Who can say what a handclasp means? Who can describe the taste of salt? Man can conceptualize and react to all of the sensory forms that are relevant in his life. Our own studies are concerned with the relevance of man's reactions to the kinesthetic sensations associated with his own stylized movements.

The conditions that facilitate the transformation of sensations into symbolic abstractions, and the subtleties of the theory concerning these symbolic transformations, are far beyond the scope of this paper. For our purposes here it may be said only that such transformations are most likely to occur when: (1) the sense data are perceived or perceivable in an organized form rather than as random, unrelated, vague sensations; (2) this perceptual form is capable of eliciting a reaction from the person as distinguished from an "action" or physical response by the effector systems; (3) this reaction has sufficient intensity to be recognizable by the person, although it may or may not be consciously recognized; and (4) the recognition of it has sufficient relevance to some aspect of his life to alter in some way his total personal conceptualization of reality.

Within this context, if we assume that movement experiences are a source of essentially unique kinds of meaning, we must asume that they can be conceptualized by the mind. This, in turn, presupposes that the experience was perceived through the senses as an identifiable perceptual form, which in turn presupposes the existence of specialized sensory receptors sufficiently sensitive to differentiate among the details of the experience and sufficiently well-developed to convey those details in organized form. What evidence is there to support these suppositions?

In his early work on the integrative action of the nervous system, Sherrington inferred much about the sensitivity and complex organiza-

tion of the proprioceptors as sensory organs. We are particularly indebted to two of his students, R. Granit of Karolinska Instituet and J. C.
Eccles of Australia for their recent work in confirming much that Sherrington could only hint at. The details of their findings are beyond the
scope of this report, but they may be indicated by Granit's cogent observation that ". . . .muscle is the instrument of action, and so it seems
natural that it should be made to feel the arousal reaction of an animal
aroused." (3:164) Essentially, these neurophysiologists have demonstrated that the sensory organs located at the site of muscle action are
among the most highly developed and sensitive of all of the sensory
receptors. These structures would appear to be quite capable of both
formulating and conveying the "feel of a movement" as a uniquely identifiable sensory form. We must stress, however, that this application of
their findings has been made by us, not by them. In addition to the
proprioceptors, a variety of structures in the eye, the ear, and the skin
also convey the sensation of movement — not ordinarily as separate
sensations, but as elements in the integrated perception of a movement
experience.

A recent review by Ittleson and Cantril has synthesized many
studies of perception as a psychological phenomenon. For our purposes
at the moment, the most important generalization in this review is the
observation that "In studying human perception we have constantly
to bear in mind that it is impossible to have any perception which is
devoid of symbolic content." (5:19) This review contains no specific
references to kinesthetic perception as such — for few indeed are the
psychologists who have ventured into this most intimate area of man's
sensory experiences — but there is nothing in the review that pre-
cludes the extension of its findings to the sensory perceptions evoked
by movement.

For evidence that kinesthetic perceptions evoked reactions of some
kind as distinguished from the physical actions of movement, as such,
and for further evidence that these reactions exhibited degrees of intensity and variations of apparent relevance, we turned to our own
movement experiences and our lifelong observations of the movement
of other people in a wide variety of circumstances. Our early analyses
bogged down in a welter of terminology referring to specialized categories of movement — posture, therapeutics, work, sports, play, athletics, mechanics, dynamics, and dance, to name only the obvious ones.
As we tried to abstract the general from this diversity of specifics, it
soon became apparent that we must run the risk of adding to the
terminological confusion by creating still more words that might be
used to discuss all kinds of movement experiences in general terms.

In deriving and defining these words we refined our own concepts of the nature of man's reactions to his movement experiences and the relevance those reactions had to his total conceptualization of reality.

The most obvious aspect of any movement experience is its physical manifestation. As man moves, his body masses create patterns that may be described as dynamic, somatic forms. To identify this patterned physical whole of a movement event, we used the word *kinestruct*. This combines the root of the Greek words relating to movement with the concept of form or structure. A kinestruct, then, is a dynamic, somatic form constructed by body masses in motion.

How does man create a kinestruct? To Hellebrant we are indebted for the observation that "movements not muscles are represented in the cortex." (4:9) A kinestruct results from the synchronization of changes of tension in countless muscle fibres, but man cannot deliberately isolate the action of any one of these fibres in such a way as to direct its contraction or relaxation. He can only conceptualize the general pattern of the movement as a whole, and attempt to create that pattern. His execution of the kinestruct involves the exquisitely intimate interplay of sensory and motor units, the whole being coordinated at appropriate levels of the brain, but it is not given to the mind of man to comprehend these details while he is executing the movement. He thinks about "wholes" of movement; his mind conceptualizes kinestructs, not the thousands of changes of muscle tension which go into the process of kinestruction.

As one person watches another person move, he, too, is aware only of the whole pattern of the kinestruct or such parts of it as he may focus his attention on. The observation of a kinestruct can and usually does evoke some reaction from the observer. We find some kinestructs pleasing or beautiful or satisfying in some way, and we enjoy looking at them; other kinestructs are distasteful to us. These reactions are highly personalized. The same kinestruct may elicit many different reactions from different observers, and these reactions will have varying degrees of intensity. It would appear then that each observer must be relating what he sees to other elements in his own conceptualization of reality, which is to say that the kinestruct has relevance to him as a symbol or symbolic form.

But except in special circumstances, the mover does not see the kinestruct he is creating, so we must look to another source for the reactions which lead him to repeat some kinestructs and reject others. His own awareness of his movements must come from the sensations evoked in the kinesthetic sensorium by the act of moving. While it is possible, at least theoretically, to isolate the sources from which these sensations are derived — the proprioceptors, the skin, the eye, the ear — in general this does not seem to occur during the movement experience. Like the somatic form of the kinestruct, the "feel of the movement" is perceived as an organized whole. To identify this organized perceptual whole or form we have used the word *kinecept*. A kinecept is defined as a dynamic perceptual form resulting from the integration of all kinesthetic perceptions associated with a kinestruct. A kinecept is the form in which the mover experiences his own movements.

Since the kinecept informs the mover about the kinestruct he is creating, it must be the primary source of whatever reactions the mover has to his own kinestructs. If he seeks to repeat a kinestruct, attempting to modify it and refine it, we may infer that what he has experienced had some kind of significance for him. By the same reasoning, if he makes a selection among a variety of kinestructs, rejecting some, resisting the performance of others, and voluntarily exerting himself to create still others, we may infer that each of these kinestructs had specific elements of relevance within the context of his mental-emotional life. And in many subtle ways we may observe that his reactions to his own kinestructs vary both in kind and intensity.

From these observations of reaction, intensity, and relevance it may be inferred that he has conceptualized what he has experienced, and that this conceptualization had some significance to him. In other words, we may infer that the perceptual form of the movement experience, the kinecept, has been transformed into a conceptual form which symbolizes the significance or the meaning he found in the performance of the kinestruct. To identify this meaningful formulation of the movement experience we have used the word *kinesymbol*. A kinesymbol is defined as a conceptual form that represents or symbolizes the meaning a person finds in his perception of the kinecept of a kinestruct.

The crucial question then becomes: What is the nature of this kinesymbolic concept? Here our reasoning must proceed through analogy with other forms of nonverbal and essentially nonverbalizable concepts. The meanings of music are found in the structured organization of sounds. Pictures and designs are meaningful as structured organizations of visual elements. As it is with other nonverbalizable perceptual forms in which man finds valued meanings that he can not express in words, so we believe it must be with man's perceptions of his own movement experiences. His kinesymbolic conceptualization of kinecepts can not be expressed in the symbols of any other sensory medium. It is not verbal, auditory, visual or anything else but what it is in its own right — a conceptualization of kinesthetic sensation which contains its own kind of human meanings in its own kinesthetic form.

The significance of a kinesymbol may not be consciously formulated by the person; certainly he can not convey its meaning to another person in words; but he gives evidence of finding it meaningful by acting in ways that show how much he values that meaning in the total context of his mental-emotional conceptualization of reality. We may thus identify the kinesymbol as a kinesymbolic formulation of personal experience which is meaningful in its own way, making its own unique contribution to "the intricate web of meaning which is the real fabric of human life." (6:36)

The bare bones of a theory that has many ramifications may now be stated in our own terminology. A movement experience is manifested as a kinestruct. This kinestruct is perceived as a kinecept. Like other perceptual forms, the kinecept is susceptible of transformation into conceptual form, this symbolic form of the sensory data being identified as a kinesymbol. Like other conceptual or symbolic forms, the kinesymbol is an element in human thought. It can be retained by the mind and recalled by the mind. It can be related to other kinds of symbols or ideas or meanings arising from other forms of human experience. Thus human mentality uses kinesymbols in the process of thought in the same way that it uses all other kinds of symbols, incorporating them into the ever-changing organization of concepts, ideas, and meanings that constitute a person's personal interpretation of reality. Kinesymbolic intelligence is one of the significant forms of human intelligence, and kinesymbolic knowledge is one of the significant kinds of human knowledge, making its own unique contribution to man's comprehension of reality by adding to the store of meanings that are the basis of the significance man finds in his human life.

After we had formulated this theory, we were delighted to find that J. P. Guilford and his associates had reached a similar conclusion by following a different line of reasoning. In their attempts to identify the varieties of human intelligence and the channels through which these intelligences become operative, they have identified a number of varieties that appear to operate primarily through the sensory channels of kinesthetic perception.

Up to this point we have been focusing our attention upon what might be called the "pure form" of the kinesymbol. But many different elements of perception are involved in any human experience so the meanings of all symbolic forms are inevitably influenced by other elements in the situations in which the experiences occur. As a person performs similar kinestructs in a variety of situations, his kinesymbolic conceptualization of them may acquire many encrustations of meaning derived from his intellectual-emotional comprehension of other elements in the situation and the situation as a whole. Thus, in time a kinesymbol may become a very complex symbol that incorporates something of the import or meaning of all of the situations in which the kinecept was experienced. Since all kinecepts are perceived within the context of a situation, it seems probable that the meaning of any kinesymbol tends to become very complex. Similar kinestructs may thus have very different intellectual-emotional import as kinesymbols for different people, their meanings being related to all of the reactions, both obvious and subtle, that occurred within the context of many different situations. In time a kinesymbol may accumulate many residual connotations, some of which may be mutually contradictory, and the performance of a given kinestruct may thus elicit conflicting emotions.

In this connection it may be noted that habitual postural kinestructs have long been recognized as kinesymbolic expressions of personality which refect the influence of subconscious drives, motivations, and interpretations of self. It seems probable that the kinesymbolic meaning of all habitual kinestructs involves similar emotional components derived from subconscious associations with many other elements in the person's life experience.

Returning to our basic theory that kinesthetic intelligence is one of the significant forms of human intelligence and that kinesymbolic knowledge makes its own unique contribution to man's comprehension of reality, we should like to close this report by identifying only one of the many implications we see in this theory. For us as educators it provides a basis for identification of the *unique educational component* in the experiences commonly categorized under the term "physical education." Without belittling in any way the physiological, psychological, and social concomitants of man's movement experiences, we value our theory because it identifies structured movement experiences as a source of mental-emotional concepts. As such, they can be truly identified as learning experiences in the kinds of terms commonly used in educational parlance, and thus they can be identified as subject matter suitable for inclusion in the educational curriculum. In this context, physical education — or, as we prefer to call it, "movement education" — can be identified as one of the forms of liberal education, comparable with music and the other nonverbal arts as a source of one of the kinds of meaning that enrich man's comprehension of reality.

REFERENCES

1. CASSIRER, ERNST. *An Essay on Man: An Introduction to a Philosophy of Human Culture.* New York: Doubleday and Co. (Anchor Books A3), 1956.

On SIGNIFICANCE IN SPORT AND DANCE97SIGNIFICANCE IN SPORT AND DANCE   97

2. ECCLES, JOHN CAREW. *The Neurophysiological Basis of Mind.* Oxford: The Clarendon Press, 1953.
3. GRANIT, RAGNAR. *Receptors and Sensory Perception.* New Haven: Yale University Press, 1955.
4. HELLEBRANDT, F. A. "The Physiology of Motor Learning." *Cerebral Palsy Review,* 13:9-14, July-August, 1958.
5. ITTELSON, WILLIAM H., AND HADLEY CANTRIL. *Perception: A Transactional Approach.* New York: Doubleday and Co. (Doubleday Papers in Psychology DPP7), 1954.
6. LANGER, SUSANNE K. *Philosophy in a New Key.* New York: The New American Library (A Mentor Book M25), 1948.
7. SHERRINGTON, CHARLES S. *Man on His Nature.* New York: Doubleday and Co. (Anchor Books A15), 1953.

The Unique Meanings Inherent in
Human Movement

Fall Conference of the Southern District Division of the California
   Association for Health, Physical Education, and Recreation —
   Riverside, California — October, 1959

Published in: *The Physical Educator*, March, 1961.

For some years now all meetings of educators have been centered
around our acute awareness of the fact that we are living in a changing
world, and most of our educational discussions have revolved around
the question: What are we going to do about it?

Of course change is nothing new. Human beings have always lived
in a changing world. If this were not so, we should still be huddling
in our caves trying to digest raw dinosaur meat. Our generation differs
from its predecessors only in that the changes are now occurring more
rapidly, and that we are far more aware of the fact that they will continue to occur.

As men's curiosity has led them to a better understanding of their
own nature and the nature of their world, they have always been forced
to develop new ways of thinking about themselves and their human
problems if they wished to survive. This has always been a painful
process, wracked by controversy born of man's reluctance to relinquish
the feeling of security that comes from reliance on the authorities of
his childhood, but only through this often excruciating process of de-

98

veloping new ways of thinking about ourselves can we achieve whatever advances are made in human understanding during the years of our own maturity.

During the past hundred years, our historical colleagues in education have suffered through three major expansions of educational theory and practice. Now we are on the brink of the next phase of development in educational thought, and — as our ancestors were in their moment of history — we are often sorely troubled and dismayed.

Late in the eighteenth century our forefathers enunciated the basic principles of a new concept of the nature of man. One of the revolutionary tenets of their theory of democracy was that public schools should be established so that all children would have an opportunity for education. At that time, and well into the nineteenth century, this eduactional process rested on a belief in the value of facts and mental training. Educators saw the child's mind as a blank tablet upon which the teacher could inscribe the accepted facts of the day with the indelible ink of mental discipline. Accordingly, the new public education was *fact-centered*, and the educational process was identified as something that was *done to* a child's mind.

Physical activity found its way into this fact-centered program of mental training as something that was *done to* a child's body to make it stop wiggling and squirming and interfering with the disciplining of the mind. On this basis, physical training was accepted in the form of exercises intended to make the child's body healthy, strong, and supple; and all of the arguments for this procedure rested on the facts supplied by the sciences of anatomy and physiology.

Some of these exercises did produce these physical benefits; but when directed by poorly-trained teachers these exercises often degenerated into what was called "jumps and jerks" which produced only "perspiration and peristalsis" — both valuable enough in their own right, but scarcely identifiable as educational outcomes. (It is important that we identify these degenerate forms as we go along because they have greatly influenced both the public image and our own private image of the nature of physical education.)

But as time went on, man learned more about his own nature and the nature of the learning process. Psychologists discovered that the mind was only one aspect of the whole child, and that the whole child went to school and learned through his wholeness. The precepts of educational psychology gradually replaced the techniques of mental discipline, and *child-centered* programs in which the whole child could learn *by doing* gradually replaced the mental training in the 3 R's. Education was now identified as the outcome of something that was *done by* the child.

It was not long before the physical trainers recognized that the whole child was actively doing many things in the gymnasium, too, and that he was presumably learning by doing them. So physical trainers shifted their allegiance from biology to psychology and now called themselves physical educators. This generation of our professional ancestors developed our "theories of play" that rest on the psychological values inherent in the racially old activities of running, throwing, jumping, kicking, and striking. Rallying around the slogan "Education through Physical Education," they identified play as one form of doing through which education might be channelled to the whole child — as indeed it is. However, many teachers were ill-prepared to "teach play," and the physical education period often degenerated into the "ball and whistle" program, and its educational values were frequently called into question.

Whenever their new psychological position was assailed, or their own doubts about its validity troubled them too greatly, physical educators shivered in their new professional boots and beat a hasty retreat to their old position of biological security, from which they proclaimed loudly that, whether it was educational or not, physical activity still did do something to the child's body that was not done by any other subject in the curriculum. And this, of course, is true.

But again the educational scene was shifted as the sociologists pointed out that not even the whole child liveth unto himself alone. As cities became more crowded, it was apparent that human beings had to learn to live together. Influenced by this awareness, educators began to develop *group-centered* programs in which the whole child was viewed as a unit to be fitted into the larger whole of the group, and education was identified as the outcome of the whole child's *doing with others*.

It was soon apparent to physical educators that most of their activities belonged in this category of something done with others, and they soon identified a new set of objectives for their *group-centered* physical activities. In 1951, the Year Book of their national organization was devoted to "Developing Human Relationships Through Health Education, Physical Education and Recreation." This clearly identified physical education as a medium through which children might learn to adjust to the requirements of group living, and certainly there is much merit in this point of view.

However, not all teachers were qualified to utilize the group potential in physical activities, and their classes degenerated into "talkie-walkie" programs, with much more "talkie" than "walkie." Administrators who were hard-pressed to find space for the ever-growing school population sometimes asked why it was necessary to provide large gymnasiums and playing fields to be used for group discussions. And again the physical educators shivered in their new professional boots, and again they fell back to their unassailable nineteenth century biological position, again proclaiming the physical outcomes of physical activity as contributions to health and fitness.

At each stage in the development of educational thought, physical education has tried to move forward; but at each stage we have found it necessary to retreat and fire our old biological guns to ward off both real and imagined attacks made by other educators. We have made good use of our nineteenth century muskets. We have trained them on state legislatures to win many battles for laws and requirements; and recently we have triggered them with evidence that European children are more adept than American children in touching their toes and won for physical fitness a quasi-Cabinet post in our national government. At the moment it appears that the wheel set in motion by the physical trainers of the nineteenth century has come full circle. We are back where we started from a hundred years ago, and the tattered old biological banner of physical fitness is again waving triumphantly from our educational battlements.

Now I want to make it perfectly clear that I have no quarrel with any of our historical objectives when they are honestly interpreted in terms of what can happen within the time and situational limits of a physical education class. I know that physical fitness can be improved through exercise. I believe that the learnings achieved through physical activity are valuable learnings. I recognize that human relationships can be improved through participation in plays and games. But in my opinion the use of the word *through* is the clue to our lack of ability to establish ourselves as anything more than "fringers" in the educational group. I believe that many of the objectives of education can be achieved *through* the medium of physical activity; but in my opinion the word *through* also underlines our own basic uncertainty about the *uniquely educational values* that are inherent in our own kind of subject-matter. The question I am raising is this: Is physical activity really a legitimate form of education in its own right? Or is it merely a *medium through which* something identified as *real* education may be channelled to the child and the group? I believe that it is imperative that we who call ourselves physical educators must be able to give clear and unequivocal answers to those questions in the critical years that lie ahead of us.

At the dawn of the space age all men are confronted with the biggest questions men have ever asked themselves. Peering timidly into the unknown immensity of a spacious universe that shrinks his own world to pinpoint dimensions, man is forced to see himself as only a tiny speck being whirled about in measureless space with millions of other worlds, many of them much larger than his; and as his old certainties about the significance of man as master of the world are shaken, his sense of his own identity is threatened. Confronted with the necessity for developing a *universe-oriented* approach to education, all educators are momentarily confused and uncertain. In our moment of panic we are all trying to find security by turning back to the educational faiths of our fathers. The academicians are comparing our curricula and methods with those of our most threatening space-age competitors, and crying out for more facts and a return to good old-fashioned mental discipline. And physical educators, frightened by the muscular strength of our Russian competitors, are crying out for a return to the security of their old biological fortifications.

Have all of us forgotten the most fundamental lesson of history? Are we really persuaded that yesterday's thinking can provide the solutions for tomorrow's problems? I think not. Man has always been thrown into a state of panic by the thought of changing his ways, and historically he has either recovered his wits and moved forward with his expanding knowledge of his universe or been banished from it by the inexorable process of cultural evolution. Optimistically, I believe that we shall accept the first alternative; and we must accept it if we wish to survive.

Man is a biological-psychological-social creature. Certainly education and physical education must minister to these three aspects of his life. But man is far more than a mere biological-psychological-social organism driven by biochemical tropisms and powered by a set of reflexes that can be conditioned. Man is a *human* being, unique among the species of the earth, whose ability to *think* about his own life drives him to ask questions that no other animal can ask about the meaning of his existence. From our growing psychiatric understanding we know that he literally can not live as a human being without finding satisfying answers to the questions: Who am I? What am I? What is the meaning of my human life?

Now his old certainties have been threatened by his own curiosity about the heavens that his ancestors took for granted, and he is forced to find new answers to his own questions about the significance of his human life. But the questions he is asking are not really the questions of science; they are the basic questions of philosophy. And I believe that education must now move from physics and physical fitness to philosophy if it is going to save the sanity and the substance of the human race.

Yes, the time has come when we must again move on in educational thought, probing more deeply into the nature of man and the nature of the experiences in which he finds the meaning of his life. Man's capacity for finding human meanings in his own, direct, sensory perception of himself and his universe is the hallmark of his uniqueness as a human, rather than an animal, being. In those meanings he finds the unique significance of his own human endeavors — his own unceasing pursuit of excellence — in a universe filled with infinitely diverse forms of life. If education is to minister to the needs of human beings in this ego-destroying age of space, it must become *meaning-centered*, because only as man finds his own human endeavours meaningful to himself can be preserve his own sense of human identity.

The development of a meaning-centered educational philosophy will be a painful process. There is more to be learned today than any one person can ever know, and new knowledge is piling up by the minute. A greater variety of experiences is available to a six-year old child today than was available to its grandfather during a long lifetime. New criteria must be established for determining which of the experiences offered in the name of education are most meaningful and which are merely traditional. As these criteria are applied, there will be many casualties among traditional forms of subject matter. Whether or not the traditionally-entrenched forms of physical education experiences will be among these casualties will depend on our ability to answer these fundamental questions: What *unique* learning experiences does physical education provide? What kinds of meaning are inherent in these learning experiences? What values do these meanings have for human beings? How will they help to sustain man's sense of his own human significance and identity in a world of space?

Perhaps we can begin to move past our long need to justify physical education in terms of concomitant values by examining our own personal preoccupation with movement. Why do intelligent people like us spend many hours in the hot sun batting a tennis ball back and forth across a net? Why do we walk miles on tired feet in pursuit of a golf ball, only to deliberately hit it down the fairway again? Why do we go down into the sweatbox called a handball court and deliberately induce fatigue by hitting a small black ball against a wall? Why do we bounce on trampolines, circle high bars, dive from diving boards into cold water, and stretch our ligaments on the practice bar in the dance studio? On the face of it, these seem to be ridiculous occupa-

tions for intelligent adults like us. But all of us seek them voluntarily; and all of us know that they are for us some of the most meaningful of all of our human endeavours.

Why do we do these things? To become physically fit? To develop
our ability to learn by doing? To improve our human relationships?
Certainly all of these things can and do result from these movement
experiences — but, even more certainly, these are not our basic motivations in seeking those experiences. We do these things for one reason
only. We do them because we find these movement experiences meaningful in their own right.

We play tennis for the same reason that men paint pictures, sing,
play musical instruments, devise and solve algebraic equations, and fly
aeroplanes. We play tennis because it satisfies our human need to use
our human abilities, to experience ourselves as significant, creative,
and, therefore, personalized beings in an impersonal world. We do
these things to intensify, structure, and enhance the sensory perceptions that are our only direct source of information about ourselves
and the world we live in; and these sensory perceptions are the source
of the human meanings we find in our human lives.

Sometimes man tries to express these meanings in words he has
devised to represent them, but many of the sensory experiences that
make our lives meaningful to us can never be expressed in words. Can
you describe such a simple thing as the aroma of coffee? The color of
red? The sound of a concerto? Even as I say these words you have re-
sponded to these concepts in many ways that defy the limits of verbal
communication. The unique nonverbal essence of these sensory experiences has its own unique kind of meaning to you, however, because it
is one meaningful aspect of your personal participation in the process
we call life, and it is one of the ways in which you have established
a personalized relationship with an impersonal world. Similarly, the
meanings we find in moving about the tennis court and dance studio
can not be verbalized, but the very fact that intelligent human beings
go to great trouble to move in these ways is evidence that their sensory
perceptions of these movement experiences are meaningful to them
as highly personalized experiences that involve some element of self-
identification as a significant being in an impersonal universe.

What I am saying is not new. Musicians have long ago persuaded
us that the sensory experience of hearing and making the structured
sounds we call music is a meaningful experience that expands a child's
comprehension of one aspect of his universe. The artists have long ago
convinced us that the sensory experiences related to color, design,
form, and structure are liberalizing experiences that increase the meaningfulness of human life. But we who love so dearly the sensory per-

ception identified as kinesthesia, we who have found some of the most valued meanings of our lives in the perceptions identified with movement, have never spoken out about the unique meanings we know are implicit in our movement experiences. Perhaps now, when the concomitant values achieved through those movement experiences are about to be called into question, we shall at long last proclaim the unique meanings found only in movement.

Interestingly enough — and perhaps to our shame — the basic research that supports this belief in the inherent meaningfulness of kinesthetic perception has not been done by physical educators. It is being done by neurophysiologists and psychologists. Recent studies in neurophysiology have demonstrated that the kinesthetic receptors are second only to the eye and ear in their complexity and in the richness of sensory information they convey. Meanwhile the psychologists who are studying the nature of human intelligence have come to recognize that all varieties of sensory perception are subject to the transforming process of human mentality, and recently they have identified kinesthesis as one of the important sources of the knowledge and understanding that we call intelligence. Perhaps these new findings will give us the encouragement we need to speak out about the meanings we have always known were inherent in our own movement experiences.

The meanings inherent in the sensory experience of moving in purposeful ways are the unique educational contribution made by physical education. The more we enlarge the variety of our movement experiences, the more we add to our personal stock of meanings and understandings, and the richer becomes the texture of what Susan Langer has called "the intricate web of meaning that is the real fabric of human life." The less we move, the less we know about this meaningful area of living, and the fabric of our lives is accordingly impoverished. Our primary job as physical educators is to provide opportunities for children to move in many ways for many reasons so that they may find some of the many satisfactions and meanings that we have found in our own sensory experiences of human movement. Our educational significance rests on our ability to provide challenging and satisfying movement experiences in each class period. Our educational survival depends on our ability to make it crystal clear to ourselves and our fellow-educators that the pursuit of excellence in movement is as significant as man's unceasing pursuit of excellence in any other form of human endeavor based on the use of any and all of his other human abilities.

Recently I heard a lecturer quote Karl Marx' statement that "life is only motions of matter." But the woman sitting next to me fortunately mis-heard him and wrote in her notes a much more profound observation: "Life is motions *that* matter." And of course she was right. The wonder of being human is that we have the ability to make motions that *do* matter to us as human beings. Human movement is motion that matters very much to us human beings, and in that mattering lies the source of the vitality that has sustained us professionally during the long years of our search for our true identity as physical educators or movement educators. As we begin to examine our movement experiences to discover the unique meanings they have for us, I believe we shall also discover that the concommitants we have long cited as objectives have been valid only because we always knew that the basic movement experiences through which they were derived were truly meaningful in their own right.

Just "going through meaningless motions" does not produce physical fitness. Fitness comes from continuing to move past the point of mild fatigue. It was only because those movements were meaningful to us that we continued to hit tennis balls while the perspiration poured from our skins, went on walking after golf balls while our legs ached, and continued leaping and falling in the dance studios until we were so tired we could scarcely walk, — and physical fitness resulted from our meaningful perseverance.

Just "going through meaningless motions" does not produce the learning that comes from doing. An idiot child in China may sit all day transferring a feather from one molasses-smeared hand to the other, but he learns nothing from these motions. It was only because the movements we used in playing basketball were meaningful in their own right that we enjoyed competing in this miniature game of life, exhilarated by winning, but undaunted by losing because the basic meaning of the game itself was found in moving in the specialized ways which structure the game of basketball.

And neither were the values of interaction derived from just "going through meaningless motions" together. Ten children sitting in a circle to transfer feathers from one sticky hand to the other would learn nothing about human relationships. It was only because the movements we used to dance the polka were meaningful that we continued bumping our personalities as well as our bodies against each other and learned something about cooperation as a result of this experience.

In short, all of our beliefs about the physical, psychological, and social values of physical education have always rested on our unspoken belief that the movement experiences that make up the subject matter of physical education were uniquely meaningful in their own right. But

— perhaps because we tend to be kinesthetically gifted rather than verbally gifted — we have failed woefully to convey to our fellow-educators the kinds of meanings that are inherent in the movement experiences we so highly prize. I think the time has come when we must try to do this.

In my opinion, we who call ourselves physical educators will never find our own professional soul until we can give our own uniquely meaningful and therefore educational answer to the question: Why is it desirable for a child to try to stand on his head? Perhaps we can begin to answer this with another question: Why is it desirable for a child to smear finger-paint on sheets of paper? Or, why it is desirable for a child to bang two blocks of wood together in a rhythm band? Why is any form of human endeavour, any form of sensory experience, potentially meaningful?

I believe doing a head stand is educational in the same way and for the same reasons that it is educational to paint pictures and make music. I believe it is good for a child to attempt a head stand in order to find out what it means to him to stand on his head. Standing on your head is a sensory experiencing of yourself in relation to the world in which you live. It is potentially meaningful simply because human beings have the blessed ability to establish their own identity through the meanings they find in their sensory experiences. Surely it will have concomitant values, as all human experiences do, but these concommitants are meaningful only to the extent that the basic experience with which they are associated has unique meaning in its own form and in its own right.

Will recognition of the meanings implicit in our movement experiences materially alter our physical education curriculum? I think not. Our curriculum is made up of the kinds of movement experiences that children have long found meaningful because we have never been able to sell normally intelligent children experiences that were not meaningful to them.

Will it be easy for us to sell this concept of the meaning of human movement to those people we call "the administrators"? No. It will not even be easy for us to incorporate this concept into our own educational creeds. But I believe that we can do what we must do in our own moment of history. And I believe that only as we are able to identify the meanings and values that we, ourselves, so highly prize in our movement experiences can we hope to find a permanent place for physical education in the *meaning-centered* curriculum that will meet man's need for discovering his own identity as a human being in an impersonal universe of space.

The Intricate Web

Fall Conference of the Eastern Association for Physical Education of College Women — Swampscott, Massachusetts — October, 1958

Published in *Report of the Fall Conference of the Eastern Association for Physical Education of College Women,* 1958.

Reprinted in *Pennsylvania Journal of Health, Physical Education and Recreation,* December, 1958.

THE INTRICATE WEB

At the Estes Park Conference we talked about our changing world, about changing concepts of what it means to be a person (female), and the implications of these changes for physical education. These were timely topics. Our work *is* changing; our concepts of the nature of human beings, including females, *are* changing; and certainly physical education is affected by these changes. But these are also timeless topics. Human beings have always lived in a changing world. As our universe has evolved, our small part of it has become increasingly complex, and our understanding of what it means to be a person has continually expanded. And in physical education, as in all areas of human concern, it has always been true that yesterday's thinking is not good enough to solve today's problem.

Since we have an anthropologist with us who is much better qualified than I am to deal with the whole panorama of human evolution,
I shall confine myself to the small part of the picture with which I am
most familiar: the development of educational thought in the United
States during the past hundred years.

Painting this picture in very broad strokes, the evolution of educational theory and practice shows three major stages. In the nineteenth
century, education was *fact-centered*. The purpose of education was to
teach facts, and the child's mind was viewed as a blank tablet upon
which the teacher could inscribe facts with the indelible ink of mental
discipline. In a very real sense, education was something that was
done to a child's mind, and the results could be readily measured by
determining the number of facts the child's mind retained.

But as time went on and man learned more about his own nature,
educators discovered that the *whole child* came to school. They became
enamored of psychology and developed child-centered programs in
which the whole child learned by doing.

Then again the focus shifted as the sociologists pointed out that
human beings live together. The whole child now became a unit that
must be fitted into a group, and in the *group-centered* programs *groups
of whole children learned by doing with others.*

Now at the dawn of the space age, man is confronted by his new
awareness of a universe so vast and ill-defined that no one knows where
the center is, or exactly where the child's mind, the whole child, or
the human group fits in the total pattern. Faced with the necessity for
developing a *universe-oriented* program for human beings living in a
universe they only vaguely understand, educators are confused and uncertain. In a moment of panic they are trying to find security by turning back to the educational faith of their fathers, crying: "Facts. Facts.
We must teach more facts — particularly facts about the physical nature
of this illimitable space which now dominates our lives."

The development of education is paralleled by the evolution of what
we now call physical education. In the nineteenth century physical
training entered the educational halls as something that was *done to
a child's body.* It, too, was *fact-centered* in that the facts of biology
were used to account for the effects the exercise produced on the body.

But when the whole child started coming to school, the physical
trainers abandoned the concept of the mindless body as the general
educators abandoned the disembodied mind. They shifted their allegiance from biology to psychology, and developed "theories of play"
that pointed out the psychological values inherent in games in which
the whole child utilized the racially old movements of running, jump-

ing, throwing and striking. The formal *exercise-centered* program gave
way to the *child-centered* natural program, and to emphasize their new
identity as educators the onetime physical trainers adopted the slogan:
Education through physical education. In this vein they wrote about
physical activity as a *medium through which* the whole child might
acquire an education. Unfortunately the use of the preposition *through*
tended to subtly underline the mind-body dichotomy the slogan was
intended to erase. It suggested that physical education was not *really*
education, but only a channel *through which* real education might be
induced to flow. Testimony of the deep doubts the physical educators
themselves had on this point is the flood of protestations that "physical
education *is* a part of total education" that characterize the professional literature of those years. But whenever the educational value
of physical education was challenged too severely, they retreated to
the security of the past and stood firm on the biological *fact* that physical activity *did something* to the whole child's *body* that was not done
by any other educational discipline.

As general education shifted its focus from the whole child to the
group, physical education also moved into its *group-centered* phase. The
emphasis on the social objectives is evidenced by the title of the
1951 Year Book of AAHPER: Developing Human Relationships through
Health Education, Physical Education, and Recreation. But again that
invidious preposition *through* left physical education outside the
charmed circle of unquestionably *real* education. It was still a "fringer"
of the educational group, and like all "fringers" it was vulnerable and
often in need of defense. So again and again physical educators found
it necessary to fire their biological guns.

These nineteenth century muskets have served us well. Trained on
state legislatures they have won many battles for laws and requirements;
and triggered by evidence that European children were more adept
than American children at touching their toes, they have even won a
quasi-Cabinet post for physical fitness in Washington.

The wheel seems to have come full circle. Now, at the beginning
of the space age, frightened by the possibility of greater muscular
strength in the Russians even as academic educators are frightened by
Russian possession of facts, physical educators have retreated to their
past position of security, and the tattered biological banner of Physical Fitness again waves triumphant from their battlements.

I have great respect for the sciences, both physical and biological.
My bachelor's degree was earned in the physical sciences in the very
institution that set off the first chain-reaction leading to the atomic
age. I was well schooled in biology before I earned my master's degree

in physical education at an institution that put great emphasis on the biological objectives. But my doctorate was earned in human development, and it is my faith in the process of human evolution that now sustains me.

As we stand on our tiny platform in space, reluctantly relinquishing our belief that man is the center of the universe, I do not find it possible to believe that either physics or physical fitness will save the human race — or that portion of it that lives in the USA. Retreat to the past can provide no real escape from today's problems; and yesterday's thinking is not good enough to solve them. Once again we must look to the evolutionary development of man's understanding of his own nature for the clues to the kind of education which will enable man to keep pace with his own expanding knowledge of the physical universe in which he exists.

Man, like all animals, is a biological-psychological-social creature. Certainly education must minister to all three aspects of his life. But man knows that he is more than a biological-psychological-social organism driven by biochemical tropisms and a set of reflexes that can be conditioned. Man knows that he is a *human* being, unique among the species of the earth.

This sense of his own uniqueness has long sustained his ego-centered belief that the world existed for his use and that he was destined to be its master. But now as he peers timidly into unknown immensity of a spacious universe that shrinks his own world to pinpoint dimensions, he sees himself as a tiny speck being whirled about in measureless space with millions of other worlds, and his sense of his own identity is threatened. The big questions he must now face are: What is the significance of my human life as I know it? What is the hallmark of my human uniqueness? What is the meaning of my life? These are not the questions of science. These are the questions of philosophy. And I believe that education must move from physics and physical fitness to philosophy if it is going to save the substance and the sanity of the human race.

Man is more than an animal. As Ernest Cassirer puts it: "Man has discovered a new method of adapting himself to his environment. . .as compared with other animals, man lives not merely in a broader reality; he lives, so to speak, in a new *dimension* of reality." Man has climbed the ladder of evolution to a higher rung from which he is able to comprehend the world in a new way — the way of human thought. But just as the eighteenth century anatomists searched in vain for the substance of the soul, so today's neurophysiologists can find no trace of a physical substance that can be identified as the thoughts of a human mind. Man's physical structure does not differ from the structure of similar animals; but the miracle of humanness is that the physical structure of man is somehow capable of dealing with its sensory experiences in a different *way*. Human mentality is not a thing, it is a *process* that transforms the data of sensory perception into the abstractions of human thought. These abstractions have no physical being, but man can retain these bodiless abstractions of sensory experience as the *idea of the experience*. He can remember them, recall them, compare them, reflect about them, relate them, interpret them, juggle them in many different ways, and even partially communicate them to other human beings. He can even think about the process by which he does this.

This intangible "thought stuff" which has no corporeal substance is the most vital element in his life as a human being. It influences his physiological reactions, his psychological responses, and his social behavior. It can even interfere with the conditioning of his reflexes and nullify some of his biochemical tropisms. It is out of this "thought stuff" that he weaves what Suzanne Langer has so beautifully called "the intricate web of *meaning* which is the real fabric of *human life*."

This capacity for finding meanings is the hallmark of man's uniqueness; in those meanings he must find the unique significance of his life as a *human* being in a universe filled with infinitely diverse forms of life. If education is to minister to the needs of human beings in this ego-destroying age of space, it must become *meaning-centered*, because only in terms of meaning can man discover the significance of his own human identity.

Speech, which is a uniquely human ability, is a way of assigning sounds to meanings. The verbal sound becomes the symbol for the abstraction or concept of the experience it formulates. Man's ability to transform experience into abstractions which can be expressed as verbal sounds has long been recognized. These verbal symbols have been much studied, and most of our approaches to human mentality are based on those studies. But more recently philosophers have been recognizing that the process of human mentality transforms many sensory experiences into *meanings* that can not be adequately expressed in words.

Much that man finds meaningful can not be verbalized. Can you describe the aroma of coffee, the color of red, the form of a design, the sound of a concerto, the feeling of a dance, in words? But the unique essence of each of these sensory experiences is *meaningful*, even though it defies verbal description. Each of these unique, nonverbalizable forms represents, stands for, or symbolizes some meaningful aspect of man's *thoughtful* understanding of himself and his universe.

In short, any sensory experience may be transformed into an abstraction which is an "idea of the experience" because that is the way the human mind functions. All of these abstractions may be retained, recalled, reflected on, related, and "thought about." And this abstraction called thought, which stands for or symbolizes the original sensory experience, has its own meaning — even though that meaning can not be expressed in words. If it could be, man would have no need to compose symphonies, paint pictures, mix perfumes, or dance dances. But each of these nonverbal forms is an "organization of experience" symbolizing something of human knowing and understanding. Many of the most important strands in the fabric of human life are *nonverbal meanings*. And many of the strands are abstractions of sensory experience that man can not communicate — the feelings that constitute his private human knowing and understanding of himself in his world — but these vaguely recognized "organizations of experience" also give color and depth and texture to the human fabric of *meaning*.

But I shall confine my discussion to only one sensory experience — kinesthesia — and limit that discussion to the significance of man's kinesthetic perception of his own movements, because I believe that here is where the clue to the next developmental phase in physical education lies. How man communicates his kinesthetically derived meanings and how other men perceive and interpret his communication are other sides of the story — but these must wait.

My thesis is this:

Human mentality is a process which transforms sensory experience into abstractions or concepts which stand for or symbolize the meaning that sensory perception has to a person.

All sensory perceptions are subject to this process.

Man experiences his own movement as a sensory perception identified as kinesthesia.

Kinesthetic perceptions, being of the same nature as all other sensory perceptions, are subject to the mental process which transforms them into retainable abstractions or concepts which stand for or symbolize the meaning inherent in that perception for the person who experienced it.

Therefore, movement, as such, is a meaningful experience to a human being because the kinesthetic perception of movement supplies one of the strands out of which the fabric of meanings which constitute a human life is woven.

In short, *kinesthetic perception of movement* is one of the sources from which man derives the *meanings* of his life as he carries on the uniquely *human mental process* of *transforming sensory perceptions* into human *thought*.

This is the theory of meaning and movement which Dr. Lois Ellfeldt and I have been trying to develop. At the moment it is only a theory and I have no scientifically validated *facts* to offer you in its support. It was developed by using the methods of philosophy. But while philosophy deals with intangibles, its methods are as rigorous as the methods of science, and so I present to you with no apologies our philosophically developed theory. Perhaps twenty years from now we shall have amassed enough experimentally validated facts to convince even the most scientific-minded fact lover. Perhaps not — but that remains to be seen.

Our theory began as a hunch — as all theories do — which occurred simultaneously in our separate minds while we were both reading Susanne Langer's *Philosophy in a New 'Key'* some years ago. Interestingly enough we both marked the same passages in our paperbacked editions and scribbled almost identical questions and comments in the margins. We talked about this now and then at coffee-time, but we were busy with many things, and so the idea was allowed to lie fallow in our minds. But being a productive idea, it began to germinate and send forth little shoots of thought.

Two years ago Dr. Ellfeldt and I finally settled down to write a book on movement that we had been talking about for a long time. We had a beautiful outline for it — but by then the little idea-germ had sent so many tiny shoots into the ground of our thinking that we could no longer cultivate the familiar ground without taking it into account. So we threw away the outline we had prepared and started over.

We began by asking: "What is movement all about? What are its essential elements? What is its significance in man's life?" But here we encountered new difficulties. Dr. Ellfeldt is a dancer with a strong background in therapeutics or corrective physical education. My own primary interests have been in kinesiology and the area designated as "body mechanics." Both of us know something about sports. So as we tried to analyze "movement" we found ourselves using half-a-dozen different vocabularies, each of which referred to some *specific purpose for moving* rather than to the *elements* which are common to all movement. We were spending so much of our time trying to explain "what I mean" by acting out our ideas or drawing parallel examples from several areas that we finally decided to discard all of these purpose-contaminated vocabularies and develop a new set of verbal symbols to facilitate our communication.

Again we posed the question: "What elements can be identified in *all* movement?" There appeared to be three quite distinct but inter-related elements. Obviously movement is a structural phenomenon. As man moves, a dynamic pattern is constructed in space by the changing positional relationship of the somatic structures. But movement is also a sensory phenomenon. As man moves, this dynamic pattern is perceived as a sensory pattern by the complex kinesthetic sensorium. But human movement is also a meaningful phenomenon. The structural pattern and its accompanying sensory pattern have some significance because they are elements in a response made by a sentient person to some aspect of his external and-or internal environment.

We then tried to express these structural, perceptual, and conceptual elements in new words that owned no allegiance to any specific purpose for moving. We used the Greek word *kinein,* — which means "to move" — as the root. Then we combined it with parts of other words that referred to a structure, perception and conceptualization or thought. The words we devised were:

Kinestruct — which refers to the dynamic somatic form created by the structural masses of the body in motion. To kine-structure means to create a kinestruct.

Kinescept — which refers to the identifiable sensory form created by kinesthetic perception of the kinestruct. To kine-sceptualize means to consciously perceive a kinescept.

Kinesymbol — which refers to the *meaning* or symbolic import the kinescept-kinestruct has for the person within the sociopsychosomatic context of the situation. To *kinesymbolize* means to consciously conceptualize the import or meaning of a kinestruct-kinescept.

We found that the meanings of the words kinestruct and kinescept were reasonably easy to grasp. After all, we had spent our lives dealing with the structural aspects of movement and we had always been aware of the sensory nature of kinesthetic perception as the "feel" of movement. But trying to understand the nature of the word kinesymbol led to much mental anguish!

Again and again we had to remind ourselves that *human mentality* is a *process* which transforms sensory perceptions into abstract forms or symbols. We told each other that while words were verbal symbols, music was a nonverbal auditory symbol and pictures were nonverbal visual symbols, and both the sound of music and the sight of pictures were meaningful because they symbolized or stood for a thought that had meaning even though it could not be put into words.

What then is the *meaning* of a *kinesceptual* form? It is identifiable only as a *kinesymbol* — a meaningful formulation of kinesthetic experience which cannot be translated into any other symbolic form. It is not verbal, visual, or auditory, or anything else but what it is — a formulation of experience perceived kinesthetically. It is a kinesymbol which contains its own unique meaning in its own unique sensory form. And as I mentally swung a golf club to kinesceptualize the "feeling" of a golf swing, and Dr. Ellfeldt mentally leaped into the air and came down in a circular fall to kinesceptualize the "feel" of a movement which she enjoys, we both knew that these kinescepts were kinesymbols standing for experiences which had satisfying *meanings* for us, because we had found these experiences "meaning-full."

A kinesymbolic meaning may be transient or long-lasting. It may be vague or well-formulated. It may be fragmentary or complex. It may symbolize something as functional as locomotion, or as nonutilitarian as standing on your head to feel how it feels to stand on your head instead of your feet. But every human kinestruct-kinescept is potentially meaningful as a kinesymbolic formulation of experience which adds one more trace of *knowing about* ourselves and our world to the intricate web of meaning which is the fabric of human life.

A kinesymbol may be satisfying, as a sound that is heard, a picture that is seen, or an odor that is smelled may be satisfying. It may be dissatisfying and disturbing, as a sound or sight or odor may be "bad" as well as "good." But the fact that we can identify the distinction between "like" and "dislike," between "enjoy" and "annoy," in our kinesceptual experiencing of our kinestructs demonstrates that those kinescepts do have meanings which are implicit in the perception of such. (When I tried to do a mental circular fall, I winced! And when Dr. Ellfeldt mentally swung my golf club she frowned.)

There are movements which we like to do because we enjoy the feel of them; there are movements which we do not like to do because the feel of them is somehow distasteful to us; but satisfying and dissatisfying movements are not the same for all people. But neither do all people find the same satisfactions in various kinds of music. Some people like their art forms angular; others prefer more fluid lines. These likes and dislikes are expressions of the totality of a person and the meanings which make his own life meaningful to him.

Educators have long ago accepted art and music as meaningful non-verbal forms of human experience, and there is general agreement that there is unique educational value in seeing organizations of color and hearing organizations of nonverbal sounds. It is conceded that these experiences enlarge the total mentality of the child by increasing the range of sensory experiences which are meaningful to him as a human — as distinguished from an animal — being.

My thesis is that the sensory experience of movement is as *inherently meaningful* as the sensory perception of color, design, and musical sounds. Kinesymbolization is another of man's unique ways of knowing something about what it means to be a human person in a physical universe.

If we believe that it is good to learn, to know, to experience ourselves in our world in many ways, then we must believe that it is good to move; because by moving — creating kinestructs and experiencing kinescepts — we add significance, import, meaning, knowledge — *kinesymbolic knowledge* — to our total store of "knowing about ourselves in the world," which is the source of the meanings we find in our human lives.

And so the basic assumption of movement education is that there is unique educational value in the kinesceptual experience of moving, which is to say that kinesception of kinestructs is in and of itself a meaningful educational experience.

As we create our kinestructs in many situations, their kinescepts may acquire many encrustations of *added* symbolic meaning, derived from the total intellectual-emotional interpretation *associated with* the situation. Thus the kinesymbol may become a very complex symbol which stands for *all* of the meanings in the situation in which the kinescept was experienced.

As we re-create such kinestructs, their kinescepts will then kinesymbolize for us something of all of those meanings and feelings, and may, in fact, become a symbol in the Freudian sense as well as in the "stand for something" sense. To some extent this probably happens to all of our kinestructs and kinescepts. Certainly habitual posture has emotional significance, as all of us know from trying to persuade someone to change his postural habits. His "habitual posture" feels *right* to an individual because it is a kinesymbol of how he feels about himself.

How many concepts are associated with the simple kinestruct of raising one arm overhead? They range from "Heil, Hitler!" to a child's eagerness to answer a question to "two points" in basketball, to the urgency of a child's need to "leave the room." Each of these associations has its own emotional overtones, and some remnant of the emotions associated with the kinescept are incorporated into the kinesymbolic import of every subsequent arm-raising.

The re-creation of a familiar kinestruct-kinescept is like the actual or mental rehearing of a familiar song. The song "brings back" many feelings and meanings associated with it — and the "Stars and Stripes Forever" evokes feelings quite different from "Let Me Call You Sweetheart," because we associate different situations with the two songs.

In the realm of movement, the significance of associated meanings in determining the "quality" of a kinestruct suggests many fascinating fields for exploration. What happens when the performer who has kicked in a leotard in a dance studio tries to kick in a sweat suit on the football field? And vice versa! What meanings are associated with sustained and percussive movement that make them satisfying or dissatisfying to certain persons — sometimes to the point where they resist doing the dissatisfying kind of movement?

Every kinestruct-kinescept has some associated meanings, because man always moves within the context of a situation. But underlying all of the associated meanings is the kinesymbol in its purest form — the meaning we find in movement for its own sake as a sensory experience which increases our understanding of ourselves because it adds one more trace of *meaning* to the fabric of a human life.

This experience, like all human experiences, has certain concommitant values — which are biological, psychological, and sociological in nature. But if we could clearly identify the *unique* meaning of movement as a kinesymbolic form of human meaningfulness, we would have no need to try to justify physical education (which is and always has been movement education) by scratching around for concommitant values. They would still be there. Muscles would still be strengthened by contracting against resistance. Psychosocial interactions would still occur on the tennis court. Human relationships would still be developed, and we would still have competition. But by *identifying the unique value of movement* as a meaningful and therefore educational experience, we who call ourselves physical educators would be able to stand up proudly in our own educational right, and we could *identify ourselves* as educators who guide *one meaningful form* of educational experience.

I think we shall finally achieve this upright posture when we can give a clear-cut answer to the question: "Why ask a child to stand on its head?" Perhaps we can answer it with another question: "What is educational about listening to a zither?" I believe it is good to stand on your head to find out what it *means* to you to stand on your head.

If you are a person, then standing on your head is a meaningful experience because it contributes something to your total understanding of your nature and the nature of the world; it is therefore an educational experience for the reasons that hearing the organization of sounds produced by plucking a zither is an educational experience.

What does this theory mean in relation to curriculum, methods, and total program for physical education in a space age? That remains to be seen. But I hope it will stimulate your thinking during this conference as we move toward the development of a platform on which man can stand as he continues his never-ending search for the meaning of his own identity as a human being in a spacious universe.

Anyone for Tennis?

Symposium on the Service Program — Joint Meeting of the Western Society for Physical Education of College Women and the Western Division of the College Physical Education Association for Men — Reno, Nevada — October, 1964

As I was grubbling around in my mental files for some ideas about the area of instruction in physical education called "the service program," I found myself remembering a speech I had made some six years ago. In it I had told my women colleagues about a dream that had been disturbing my sleep — a nightmare, really. But in 1958 I did not realize how prophetic this vision would be. Now I am more inclined to think of it as a warning. Be that as it may, four years later that nightmare was happening on my campus — even as it has happened or will happen on yours. So, if the women with long memories will bear with me, I should like to rehearse that nightmare for you now — not as a fantasy, but as one of the facts of life that must be dealt with by all college faculties.

In my nightmare, the university faculty, the administrative officers, the board of regents, some members of the state legislature, representatives of several foundations, and a number of wealthy alumni were assembled in solemn convocation. On the stage, there were three large charts. One was a list of the purposes of higher education in our present moment of history — labelled PHE/PMH. The second was a list of all courses in the present curriculum, with a second column headed C/SUI — or cost per student unit of instruction. The third was a map of the campus with the S/SF ratio of students per square foot marked on each area and building.

The President was speaking: "You all know why we are here. The university is bulging at the seams, and still more students are clamoring for admission. Every department is asking for more courses, and some of you are demanding that new departments and schools be established. Something has to give! We must eliminate all nonessentials; we must establish priorities; and every penny in the budget as well as every square foot of campus space must be used with maximum effectiveness to achieve the purposes of higher education for the optimum number of students. I have, therefore, called you together to serve as a tribunal before which each department may plead its case. Then, together, we shall decide what we shall retain for the future and what must be eliminated in the best interests of higher education as a whole."

As I looked around the auditorium, I saw that the scientists were paying little attention to the President. They were sure they would receive every consideration. In fact, even as they sat there they were studying blueprints for a research laboratory which was the exact size and shape of the tennis courts.

The faculties of the preprofessional and professional schools seemed equally self-assured. They knew there was a need for engineers who could build bigger rockets, lawyers who could settle men's squabbles, doctors who could patch up the wrecks of human life, and business men who could keep the economy running.

The faculty of the School of Education was sweating a bit. They feared that they might lose some courses, but in the long run the school would survive. After all, the children of the population explosion had to be taught by someone.

In the humanities section, there was an air of smugness as the men whispered to each other: "Everyone agrees that liberally educated men must be familiar with the ideas of the past." But they seemed a bit defensive as they added: "And we do have a high S/SF ratio and a low C/SUI. We can crowd hundreds of students into one lecture room, and all we ask for is a few books in the library."

The modern languages were jostling each other for a place under the banner of "Communication for International Understanding." But French and German were being shoved aside by Spanish, Russian, Japanese and Chinese, while men with brown skins were whispering together in Swahili and Hindustani as they tried to elbow their way into the center of the group. In the aisle, gray-haired professors were feebly waving the credentials of classical languages, but no one moved over to give them a seat. After all, the past must make way for the future — even if no student of the future could read the motto of the university.

The coaches sat in the back rows, waving a banner that read: "You Can't Touch Us! We Make Money!" This is not necessarily true, and the coaches knew this — but it is generally believed to be true, so the slogan was at least potentially effective. The reverse side of the banner read: "Remember the Alumni!" The non-coaching staff in physical education was huddled under the coaches' banner — but the director of athletics did not even glance in the direction of the women. Why should he? He scarcely knew them by sight. Anyhow, they were a nuisance — always telephoning him about the use of field space and gymnasiums, always loading down the budget with requisitions for fancy equipment. Everyone knew they thought competition was sinful — and while they spent money like water, they did nothing about earning it on the athletic field. (Some of these same thoughts were going through the controller's mind as he mentally totalled up the requisitions for equipment, clothing, towels — and that laundry bill! Why the total salary budget for classical languages was less than the laundry bill from the women's side of the physical education department.)

As each departmental group considered how it might insure its own present status and possibly enhance it with more courses, more students, more time, and more faculty — and perhaps even a new building, or at least a couple of floors in an air-conditioned high-rise complex — the banner of the athletic department caught many an academic eye. Now *there* was one program the university could do without — those subsidized athletes were a disgrace to the academic standards. But few were disposed to tangle with the President on that issue. The physical education department would be easier pickings. It had the lowest S/SF yield; it occupied a lot of space that could be better used; and it probably had a very high C/SUI. That hockey field occupied by 25 girls in shorts could support a high-rise classroom building that would house 5,000 students per hour — or even a multiple-level parking place for faculty cars. Those acres of tennis courts — what contribution did they make to the PHE/PMH?

At the University of Southern California, a private university that is now paying roughly $10.00 per square foot for the land on which buildings may be erected, we had to answer these questions.

In September, 1962, the University undertook the enormous job of reorganizing the entire curriculum. Every course in existing catalogs was scrapped; and every department was instructed to bring in a new set of curriculum proposals organized as a series of 4-unit courses. Also, the forty-year-old pattern of general education requirements was abandoned, and, with much faculty sweat and some academic blood-shed, a new pattern was established. In the new pattern, only two traditional requirements were retained in their old form — 12 units in a foreign language and 4 units in physical education, with provision for satisfying such requirements by appropriate examinations.

Yes, we won that one. But it was a qualified victory, and in our more soul-searching moments of honesty, we must admit that we won it by default.

I sat on the six-man Steering Committee that hammered out the pattern of general education requirements. Again and again I tried to force other departments to come to terms with the basic issues of higher education. But when my own department was under consideration, I chickened-out. Wilfully and knowingly, I let the Committee commit "the ultimate treason." I let them — yes, I encouraged them — "to do the right thing for the wrong reason."

In my own defense, let it be said that I saw an easy first-round victory coming up, so I decided to take it and play for more time to fight the ultimate battle. The Committee had been through a long series of bitterly fought hearings: every member was showing signs of exhaustion; faculty emotions were at fever pitch; and the committee was under fire from all directions. So I chose to take what I could get without further controversy, hoping to defer discussion of the real issues to some future date when the faculty might be less emotional and more rational.

When the physical education requirement came up for discussion, one Committee member stated that the University probably does have some responsibility for the physical welfare of its students. Another commented that the new dormitories increased the need for campus-centered forms of recreation. Someone else mentioned the fact that these classes could be staffed with graduate teaching assistants at very low cost. Questions related to allotment of building space were not raised, because the Committee had not been asked to consider such questions. The upshot of this weary discussion was a vote to retain the present requirement in physical education, *for the time being*, with only one important change. In the old pattern, the units in physical education had been included in the total of 124 units specified for the bachelor's degree. Now it was tacked on to the total with the invidious word *plus*. The statement now reads: 32 courses, totalling 128 units, *plus* "four physical education *activities* in four different semesters." During the time of transition from the old unit-structured program to the new course-structured program, these "activities" still carry one unit of credit. And the Committee was persuaded that these grade units should still be included in the computation of cumulative grade point averages, *for the time being*. But within the new course-structured program, the position of physical education "activity classes" is still ambiguous, because they do not fit into the 4-unit course concept.

Yes, we won a qualified victory. The service program is still doing business at the same old stand. But the long-term status of these courses is highly ambiguous; and the end is not yet. Now that the new program is under way, there is time for more careful consideration of such ambiguities. Even now, new committees are at work devising criteria to be used in evaluating the new curriculum in the near future. And as the building program moves on at an ever-increasing pace, the issues pertinent to space allotment are becoming more and more pressing.

We have a reasonably good service program at USC. It is well bolstered by skill tests, written examinations, collateral readings, and all of the rest of the academic paraphernalia. And I think most of us believe that what is learned in those courses is as important as the learnings that accrue to other courses in the general education program. But there was no evidence that those who approved the continuance of our courses shared — or understood — our educational convictions. They thought in terms of "exercise" and "recreation" — and to my own shame I did not direct their attention to the basic questions of learning.

Exercise? Yes. Students probably do need it. But it may be well for us to recognize that we have not one shred of evidence to support the contention that students who are required to take 4 classes in "physical education activity" are any more fit than the students who are permitted to elect or bypass such "activity classes." And in this day of isometrics, many of our own colleagues are proclaiming that physical fitness can be developed by a few muscle contractions per day, supplemented by a minute or two of stool-stepping.

Recreation? Yes. Students probably need this, too. But we have no evidence to supoprt the contention that recreation in required physical education "activity classes" is any more refreshing than countless self-chosen forms of recreation which the University may or may not provide.

The essential questions are: "What do students *learn* in a tennis class that they can not do or do not learn in any other course? Why should this learning be included in the list of general education course-learnings required for the bachelor's degree? Is this learning so valuable that space must be alloted to appropriate facilities, even if other forms of learning must be shoved aside to make room for them?"

What can be learned on a tennis court that can not be equally well-learned in some facility with a higher S/SF ratio and a lower C/SUI? The only answer I know is this: On a tennis court, college students can learn to play the game called tennis. In the end, all curricular arguments must revolve around this basic fact. Of course we may argue that many other things may happen in the course of this learning. The students get fresh air, sunshine, and exercise. Boy meets girl, and both experiment in a laboratory of human relationships. They experience competition, cooperation, leadership, followership, and ball-chasership. They interact with other members of a group; they may even learn something about sportsmanship and good citizenship; and so on through the long, long list of objectives we sometimes cite for physical education. But right now we are talking about tennis courts — and there is no objective on that list that can not be equally well achieved elsewhere on campus in less space and at lower cost. The only *unique reason* for alloting building space to tennis courts is to *educate* students in the ideas, skills, and organization of the game of tennis. A game? Yes. But a game that can play an important role in their present and future lives.

Will this argument save our tennis courts? Six years ago I admitted that I could not predict the answer to this question. But I also said that I proposed to fight for our tennis courts on these grounds even up to the final moment when I might be dragged away, kicking and screaming, to the small gymnasium where hordes of students were huddled together doing isometric exercises and stool-stepping. In the clutch, I ducked this issue — because at that moment our tennis courts were not seriously threatened. But the time is not far off when they will be.

Six years ago I also noted that there were three kinds of people on any college faculty: those who make things happen, those who watch things happen, and those who don't know what is going on. I believe that the members of our two organizations belong to the first group. I think we are smart enough to influence the happenings on our own campuses. I believe we are honest enough to discard the emotional conviction that our tennis courts *must* be saved in favor of an attempt to formulate a rational answer to the question: What unique contributions do tennis courts make to the purposes of higher education in our present moment of history? And when we have clarified our own thinking on this point, I think we may be skillful enough to persuade the decision-making bodies on our campuses with our logical, well-reasoned answers.

And so I shall end these remarks with the story of David and Goliath. As you will remember, the Goliath that was threatening David's life was very large and powerful. David had only a slingshot and pebble. But David wasted no time in moaning about the terrible fix he was in. He did not try to stave off the giant by muttering vague clichés about the physical fitness and recreation derived from sling-shooting. Instead, he summoned all of his skill to the task of aiming his pebble at a vital point. And because he had no doubts about what he was doing, or why he was doing it, his aim was true — and he slew the threatening Goliath with one well-placed shot.

As we face our own Goliath of forces now influencing the reorganization of higher education at every level, we may be armed with only a tennis racquet and a rubber ball — but like David we have our own skills. If, like David, we can also concentrate our attention on the vital issue, perhaps we can convince ourselves and our colleagues that a tennis racquet swung by skillful hands can be made to serve the purposes of higher education in our present moment of history. I think we *can* do this. I hope that we *will*.

Part II

On Women and Sport

Women in Action:
The Story of DGWS, 1892-1958

A Pageant presented by the Division for Girls and Women's Sports at
the 60th National Convention of the American Association for
Health, Physical Education, and Recreation — Kansas City, Missouri
— March, 1958

(Music arranged by Catherine Allen, University of Pittsburgh;
properties and back-stage management by Eunice Way, Smith
College)

Introduction

At the sixtieth national convention of the American Association for
Health, Physical Education and Recreation the importance of the contribution being made to the objectives of the Association by the
women interested in sports and athletics was formally recognized by the
creation of a DIVISION FOR GIRLS AND WOMEN'S SPORTS,
headed by a vice-president of the Association.

On this significant occasion it seemed appropriate to review the
historical development of girls and women's sports, and it also seemed
fitting to honor the many women who, both figuratively and literally,
had "carried the ball" through the long years during which the concept
of "desirable practices in sports for girls and women" had been in
process of formulation. These two objectives were accomplished by the

presentation of a pageant in the Sports Arena of the Kansas City Convention Hall on March 31, 1958.

The script for the pageant was based in part on the official publications of the Basketball Committee, the Committee on Women's Athletics, the Section on Women's Athletics, the National Section on Women's Athletics, and the National Section for Girls and Women's Sports. These publications provided the chronological framework for the pageant, but the interpretation of the recorded events was evolved from bits and pieces drawn from the memories of the women who had helped make the historical events happen. Essentially, the facts may be considered reasonably accurate; the interpretations given to those facts are inevitably tempered by human fallibility — of which the largest share must be acknowledged by the writer of the script.

When the pageant was presented, the performers were dressed in historically accurate costumes, assembled from the attics of many homes and the storage rooms of many institutions, including the Smithsonian! The narrator stood at a microphone placed at the side of the stage. The accompanist (accordion) and the prompter were off stage but in sight of the narrator, who gave them their cues by hand-signal as needed. The honored guests were seated in two groups directly in front of the stage on either side of the aisle used for the final procession.

> The cast included:
> Narrator
> Accompanist
> Prompter
> 1893 — Calisthenics girls (2)
> 1918 — World War I military personnel
> 1918 — World War I Red Cross nurse
> 1920 — a suffragette
> 1928 — a sports official
> 1942 — World War II military personnel (4)
> 1942 — Red Cross personnel (2)
> *Sports Performers*
> 1893 — Basketball (2)
> 1922 — Hockey
> Soccer
> Swimming
> Track and Field
> 1924 — Modified Sports
> 1925 — Baseball

1928 — Volleyball
1930 — Winter Activities
1933 — Lacrosse
        Speedball
        Archery
        Golf
        Tennis
1936 — Riding
1937 — Outing Activities
1940 — Fencing
        Badminton
1942 — Bowling

SCENE I — circa 1892 "The Delicate Ceatures"

The story of women and their efforts to discover and define their place in the world is a long story with millions of chapters which have been lived by millions of women, each of whom asked her own questions and found her own answers in her own time. These answers are continually changing and they will continue to change as each generation builds on the hopes, disappointments, aspirations, frustrations, accomplishments and failures of the women who have gone before. This afternoon we shall review only one phase of the story. It deals with the efforts of thousands of woman who have attempted to develop a philosophy, a set of principles, a body of policies, and an ever-changing set of practices related to the participation of girls and women in sports and athletics.

The beginning is lost antiquity. Probably it all began when a little cave girl ran to catch her brother and discovered that it was fun to run. Emulating her brother, she threw a rock into the river and discovered that it was fun to throw — fun to jump — fun to climb — to *compete!* But her father saw her running and competing like a boy and ordered her mother to make her return to the cave, which was the proper place for a girl. Perhaps her mother sighed in her heart, but she did as she had been commanded. The little girl was not so easily daunted. She asked that age-old woman's question — the question we have heard every year of our teaching lives. *"Why?"*

But through the years the women who have known that it was fun for a girl to run and jump and compete, even as boys do, also knew in their own lives that girls are different from boys. They knew that "Why?" was not the proper question. In their wisdom they asked: "How? What? Where? Under what circumstances is it good for girls to play?" And gradually through the years they formulated, reformulated, modified, and remodified their concepts of "Desirable Practices in Sports for Girls and Women."

In 1893 the American Association for the Advancement of Physical Education (which certainly needed advancing) was just eight years old. The concept of physical education as an essential part of education was just beginning to be formulated by American educators. What was then thought of as physical training was a composite of German and Swedish gymnastics with a dash of French from Delsarte to give variety to the apparatus work, calisthenics and posture training. At this eighth meeting of our ancestors, the men were alarmed because women were beginning to climb on the gymnastic apparatus. Dr. Luther Halsey Gulick is speaking:

> *It seems to me that there are physiological reasons why women should not do the kind of apparatus work which is largely done by men, where the weight of the body is supported continuously by the arms. . . .The women — and those who are here who do such work will please excuse me — the women whom I have seen who excelled in apparatus work were, as a class, as I recall them, not the kind of women who seemed to me most womanly. Their shoulders were too heavy; and (I will admit that this is utterly unscientific, but simply from a man's standpoint,) their hips are too small.*

But Dr. Dudley Allen Sargent rose to defend the fair sex:

> *For a long time I shared the objections of a great many persons to heavy gymnastics for women. In my younger days I looked upon woman from perhaps a more romantic point of view than at the present time. They were such delicate creatures, I thought, it was entirely brutish to ask them to circle a bar, or to hold their weight between parallel bars. But accidentally some of them got to work, and I found that they began to develop a considerable degree of efficiency. . . .As far as the movements go, there is nothing in the line of gymnastics which some women cannot do with just as much readiness as some men, and I do not think that, outside of the so-called esthetic standpoint, there are any physiological reasons why women should not do most things that men do.*
> (Bless you, Dr. Sargent!)

And so it all began. Women donned their bifurcated pleated serge garments — and the men have been arguing about us ever since. But stubbornly

> Music: "Bird in a Gilded Cage"
>
> Stage: Enter, 2 girls in 1893 costume. They perform the original "Smith routine."

the girls in blue lifted their dumbbells, swung their Indian clubs, and performed their calisthenic drills. And perhaps to symbolize the fact that in the coming years women were going to turn a lot of old ideas topsy-turvy, they stood on their heads.

> Music: Ends in SQUAWAAAAWK. . . . .
>
> Stage: One girl does head stand while other assists and keeps clothing from being disturbed. Bow and OFF.

Which recalls the classic story of the young lady who announced that she would "stand on her head or bust" — and did both!!

Calisthenics was the order of the day, but quietly and with no fuss the movement toward athletics had begun. In 1895, at the tenth convention of the AAAPE, Clara Baer reported that the girls of Sophie Newcomb College in New Orleans had invented a new game called NEWCOMB. Well, at least it was a start in the right direction! And it *was* the first mention of athletics for women at any physical education convention.

To pay our respects to "the delicate creatures" who were strong enough to challenge the traditions of their times and get us started in the direction of athletics for women:

> Will all women who ever did the Smith routine raise their hands?
> All who ever performed on the parallel bars?
> All who have hung by their hands from stall bars?
> All who have ever played or taught Newcomb?
> All who have ever stood on their heads?

Will those who *still can* stand on their heads please stand on their feet to receive our applause?

SCENE II — 1899-1917. The Basketball Committee

With the passing of the old century and the beginning of the new, there was a spirit of gallantry in the air as women began to get organized to break the stereotype of "the weaker sex" and speed the social evolution through which *females* were finally transformed into people. The girls still did calisthenics.

> Music: "Bird in a Gilded Cage"
>
> Stage: Two calisthenics girls enter and repeat the Smith routine.

But in 1892 James Naismith had nailed two peachbaskets to the walls of the gymnasium at Springfield College, and the history of sports for girls and women began in earnest.

Music: "On Wisconsin"
Stage: Enter two basketball players, passing, dribbling shooting. Their fun turns to roughhouse and they start pushing and shoving each other as the narration continues.

Eline von Borries has noted that:

> *Although actually originated for men, basketball had been taken over almost immediately as a game with possibilities for women. Experience, however, soon proved that modifications needed to be made in an effort to eliminate some of the roughness inherent in the men's game in order to make it suitable for girls and women. Every group or institution playing the game made — and in some cases published — its own adaptation of the rules, resulting in considerable confusion.*

What to do about it? Exactly what we've been doing ever since — appoint a committee.

Stage: Exit all four girls

In 1899 four women began the long attempt to find the *right* rules for the feminine version of basketball: Alice Bertha Foster of Oberlin College, Ethel Perrin of Boston Normal School of Gymnastics, Elizabeth Wright of Radcliffe College, and Senda Berenson of Smith College. In 1901, the first Official Basketball Guide for Women was published in the Spalding Athletic Library Series. This great-great-grandmother of the guides we buy in such profusion each year was edited by Senda Berenson for the next sixteen years, and it was generally referred to as "Spalding's Rules." In 1905 the first permanent basketball committee was organized, with Miss Berenson serving as chairman.

In 1906, at the fifteenth annual convention of what was then called the American Physical Education Association, the first talks on athletics for girls were presented. Mary Butler of Cortland State Normal spoke on "Needs and Dangers of Athletics for Girls in Grammar and Secondary Schools," and Gertrude Dudley of the University of Chicago discussed "The Place of Athletics in Education of College Women." (I hear them now! I should be able to. We've been on those topics for more than fifty years!)

A few years later at the 1912 convention of the Midwest District, Blanche Trilling posted a notice of a meeting "for all interested in athletics for girls and women." Such a crowd came they had to move to a bigger room. . .then a still bigger room. . .and we've been moving to bigger and bigger rooms ever since this first convention meeting devoted solely to athletics for girls and women.

To honor the women who established the first women's rules for what is still our most popular team game for girls:

Will all of the students of Alice Foster, Ethel Perrin, Elizabeth Wright and Senda Berenson please stand?

Will all who knew these women raise their hands?

Will all who played under Spalding's Rules raise their hands?

And now, hands up for everyone who has ever played basketball!

SCENE III — 1917-1927 — The Committee on Women's Athletics

In 1917, World War I absorbed the efforts of women as well as men. Women put on military uniforms.

Music: "Over There"

Stage: Woman in uniform of 1918 marches in, salutes, executes a couple of facings and stands at attention.

They joined the Red Cross.

Music: Continues

Stage: Red Cross nurse enters with triangular bandage which she puts on woman in uniform, then both EXIT.

And in 1920, women became *persons* by an act of Congress which ratified the 19th Amendment.

Music: "Yellow Rose of Texas"

Stage: Suffragette marches across holding "Votes for Women" placard, and EXITS.

In the wave of enthusiasm for *fitness* — which seems to accompany all of our wars — many states passed new laws which recognized that physical education had a legitimate and desirable place in the school curriculum.

At the meeting of the Council of the American Physical Education Association, held on January 6, 1917, President Burdick was authorized to appoint a Committee on Women's Athletics. Again quoting Eline von Borries:

> *The need for such a committee was apparent. . .because of the "insistent and increasing demands coming in from all parts of the country for assistance in solving problems in connection with the athletic activities of girls and women. . .which demonstrated the need for a set of standards based on the limitations, abilities, and needs of the sex" and different from the established rules and standards for men.*

Dr. Burdick appointed Elizabeth Burchenal of New York City, Elizabeth Bates of Brown University, Florence Alden of Baltimore Athletic League, Blanche Trilling of University of Wisconsin, Winifred Tilden of Iowa State College, Maude Cleveland of the University of California, plus two men — Dr. L. R. Burnett of Sargent School and Dr. E. A. Peterson of Cleveland Public Schools. It was not a committee on coeducation — many years were to pass before the Association could entertain *that* concept — but at least it was a coeducational committee!

At the twenty-fourth convention of APEA in April, 1917, the newly created committee presented its first program. Florence Somers spoke on "Standardization of Athletics for Women," and another paper was presented by Augusta L. Patrick of the Newark Public Schools.

By 1922, five specific committees had been named to deal with basketball, hockey, soccer, swimming and track and field.

Music: "Take Me Out to the Ball Game"
Stage: Enter as sport is named, the two basketball girls, a hockey player, a soccer player, a swimmer, and a runner, each performing actions symbolizing the activity.

In 1924, moderate sports, in 1925 baseball, and 1927 athletic games were added.

Music: Continues.
Stage: Baseball player joins group.

But of course some girls were still doing calisthenics, albeit with less enthusiasm.

Music: A few bars of "Bird in a Gilded Cage" as calisthenic girls enter, then into "On Wisconsin"

Stage: The two calisthenic girls walk across stage performing the Smith routine in lackadaisical fashion, looking on wistfully as the athletes form a circle, arms on shoulders, and give nine rahs for "Team, team, team." EXIT all.

The successive Chairmen of the Committee on Women's Athletics were: Elizabeth Burchenal, 1917-21; Blanche Trilling, 1921-25; and Katherine Sibley, 1925-27.

But there were other groups also interested in women athletes, and the Committee on Women's Athletics did not always agree with their practice. In 1922, the Amateur Athletic Union sent a girls' track team to the Paris Olympic Games. There was quite a ruckus about this, and it ended with Mrs. Herbert Hoover's calling a meeting. As a result a new organization was established: The Women's Division of the National Amateur Athletic Federation. Its purposes were to "protect girls from exploitation" and to "establish standards." It was a new organization, but the names are familiar: Blanche Trilling, Elizabeth Burchenal, and Helen McKinstry of Russell Sage College. The story of the Women's Division of NAAF is too long to tell today. It made its own contribution for seventeen years, but it also added to the confusion, and in 1939 it was integrated into our present organization.

Will the students of Miss Burchenal, Miss Trilling, Miss Sibley, and Miss McKinstry please stand?
Will all who knew them raise their hands?
Please stand, too, all who wore a uniform in 1918.
And may we see the hands of all who ever competed in track and field; all hockey players; all swimmers; and all who have played baseball, softball, soccer.
And now the hands of all who have used the privilege of the Nineteenth Amendment and voted regularly!

SCENE IV — 1927-1932 — The Section on Women's Athletics

The years from 1927 to 1932 were confused and confusing years in our nation's history. The big boom. . .the big crash. . ."Happy Days are Here Again". . ."Brother, Can You Spare a Dime." They were years of confusion for women in athletics too. What was our place in the total picture? How could we best exert our influence? Who were we? What were we? And how could we get the men to see it *our* way?

Music: "Yes, We Have No Bananas," followed by "The Music Goes Round and Around"

Stage: Enter all sports participants from previous scene, milling
         around in stage, forming small groups, breaking up, form-
         ing new groups.

In 1927, Florence Somers, who was then chairman of the Women's
Athletic Committee, applied to the APEA to have the *committee* recognized as a *section* in the Association. The debate about whether the
Council of the APEA did or did not officially agree to give the committee section status will probably never be settled. The objection was
that the APEA bylaws called for election of officers of sections on the
floor of the convention — and the Women's Athletic Committee did not
operate that way. The upshot of it all was that the Women's Athletic
Committee began to *function as a section,* apparently in the status of
having been neither officially recognized nor denied.

The women justified their difference in procedure on the grounds
that the "Women's Athletic Section" was *different!* It was a year-round
working body which made rules, edited guides, advised on policies
and programs, and conducted research studies; and it was felt that
this responsibility should be safeguarded by more elaborate election
procedures than the casual election from the floor which then pre-
vailed in Association section meetings. Obviously there was something
to be said on both sides, and it was said with considerable emotion
many times during the next four years.

To give the men their due, they had reason for being confused.
Let Helen Hazelton, who did yeoman service throughout this period,
tell it in her own words:

> *From 1927 to 1930 the original Committee on Women's Ath-*
> *letics called itself the Executive Committee of the Women's Ath-*
> *letic Section. At the meeting of the Women's Athletic Section at*
> *national conventions, two members-at-large were elected by the*
> *Section-at-large to be added to the Executive Committee. One*
> *of these members-at-large was chairman of program at the na-*
> *tional meetings.*
>
> *The Executive Committee, made up of the chairmen of the*
> *activity subcommittees and members-at-large, elected a chair-*
> *man at its annual meeting at Christmas time. This chairman —*
> *while nominally chairman of the Women's Athletic Section, con-*
> *tinued the same sort of work as had always been done by the*
> *committee, and the program-making duties which were annually*
> *the sole responsibility of a Section chairman (in other sections of*
> *APEA) were put in hands of a member-at-large who was elected*

*from the floor at the time of the national meeting of the Women's
Athletic Section. . .This procedure was undemocratic. . .but it
was the only way to maintain the efficiency of the rules-making
committees.*

Do you have that all straight now?

While all of this was going on, perhaps to establish our own official
status, the Official Ratings were established in 1928. Then volleyball
was added to the list, and in 1930, winter activities.

Music: "Glow Worm"
Stage: Enter official, who blows whistle, and milling groups sit
down on floor in orderly circle. Volleyball player, followed
by winter activities girl enter, and circle is enlarged to
make room for them. Then official again blows whistle
and all rise and walk off stage in cohesive group.

But there were *more problems!* The women had money! And to
quote Mabel Lee: "the general run of men who were disposed to quarrel with the women at this time apparently did not know of the treasury." But when they found it out, WOW! "They seized upon this as
still another great irregularity since no other section had a treasury of
its own. The cry immediately was raised that the women should turn
this treasury over to the APEA and the APEA should budget the committee's work. Miss Lee adds: "This gave the women deep concern."

In 1929 a small cruse of oil was poured on the troubled waters when
the American Physical Education Review announced a new feature —
a page devoted to athletics for girls and women!

In 1930-31 the basic problems were ironed out in the process of a
complete reorganization of Association structure, policies and procedures. And in 1931 Miss Lee became the first woman to hold the
office of president of the American Physical Education Association. At
long last the women of the Association had an official voice to speak for
them in high places, and no voice has ever spoken more fervently and
more persistently in behalf of women's athletics than the voice of Mabel
Lee.

Please stand, Mabel Lee, to receive our applause.

Please stand with her, Helen Hazelton, and all of the women who
served during the troubled years of 1927-32.

Stand with them, too, all students of Mabel Lee, Helen Hazelton,
and Florence Somers.

140 ON WOMEN AND SPORT

And now a big whistle of appreciation from everyone who has ever tooted an official's whistle.

SCENE V — 1932-1953 — The National Section on Women's Athletics

By 1932 the depression had become very depressing. Many of us who had jobs were not getting paid; and many well-trained physical educators could find no teaching jobs. But we were getting organized just the same — although not without opposition.

Music: Medley of "Dixie" and "Yankee Doodle"

Stage: Enter all previously mentioned sports performers, each carrying a white cardboard square. With much shuffling about and trying of cards in different positions, right, left, down, up, etc. the performers finally form a pyramid with front line sitting, second line kneeling, third standing, and fourth with hands overhead. Official supervises this scene as narration continues.

In her role as president of APEA, Miss Lee found that:

. . .there were some men who were opposed to there being a Woman's Athletic Section at all, feeling there was no need for such a section. Others felt that the women "busied" themselves too much throughout the year and magnified the importance of their own group. . .Some even resented having a woman president of the Association. . .These men had to be placated. . .at least enough of them to carry a majority vote for the women's plans. If the plans for an NSWA were voted down now, it would be years before the women could ever get favorable action. The time was crucial.

Eventually the plans for a working organization to be known as the National Section on Women's Athletics were presented to the Association, and when the matter came to a vote, Miss Lee writes, "John Brown, Jr. jumped to his feet and launched into an impassioned speech insisting that the women be allowed the plans they desired," noting that if the APEA found the procedures objectionable after they had been tried out, they could later be changed. And so it came to pass that on April 20, 1932, the National Section of Women's Athletics was officially recognized as a working section of the American Physical Education Association.

Music: "Marching Along Together"

Stage: The two basketball players bring in a large NSWA organi-
        zation chart placard and stand in front of pyramid, holding
        it between them. (On reverse side of this placard is an out-
        line map of the United States to be used later.)

The outgoing chairman of the old debatable Section on Women's
Athletics — or was it the Committee on Women's Athletics? — at any
rate, Grace Jones presented the APEA with $200 from the old treasury
saying that she "hoped the women's work would always prove an asset
to the APEA." (And if she held her tongue in her cheek as she said
it, surely no one here will call her to account.)
    And thus began the development of what has been called by some-
one the 0-0-0 Section because it was the most overorganized organization the Association had ever seen. But it was effective overorganiza-
tion that opened the way for widespread participation and commit-
ment by women who believed in its purposes.
    Under the chairmanships of Grace Daviess, Eline von Borries, Elinor
Schroeder, Jane Shurmer and Ruth Atwell, lacrosse, speedball

Music: Continues

Stage: Participants in lacrosse, speedball, archery, golf, tennis,
        riding, fencing, badminton, and bowling enter as named and
        find places in the pyramid.

archery, golf and tennis were added in 1933, riding in 1936, outing activities in 1937, fencing and badminton in 1940, and bowling in 1942.
    In 1936, NSWA instituted the effective use of state representatives,
which carried NSWA into every corner of the USA.

Music: "Stars and Stripes Forever"

Stage: Turn organization chart placard over and bring USA map
        into view.

Just as we were beginning to roll along in fine style, it was 1941.
The bombs fell at Pearl Harbor; and the officials' whistles blew
"Squads right!"

Music: Continues

Stage: Enter four women in military uniforms of 1942, marching
        abreast. Official blows whistle and the standing lines of

pyramid fall in behind them in column of fours and continue marching.

Some of us were in USO or Red Cross, doing the hokey pokey.

Music: "Doing the Hokey Pokey"
Stage: Enter a woman in Red Cross uniform. She leads the front
          line of the pyramid in the hokey pokey.

Some of us were in industry.

Music: Continue "Hokey Pokey" with jerky vibrato.
Stage: Second line of pyramid simulates riveters.

And FITNESS was the watchword.

Music: "Oh, How I Hate to Get Up in the Morning."
Stage: All performers start doing toe touch, Burpee exercise, push
          ups, sit ups, etc. The two calisthenic girls come running
          out and start doing the Smith routine with great enthusiasm.

Wherever NSWA women went, they took their Guides with them, —
into the military services and into industry and recreational programs.
In the far places where Red Cross girls carried on their invaluable
services, they did a little missionary work with schools and women's
groups on the side. And in our schools, thanks to the insistence of the
women physical educators who stayed at home to keep on doing the
essential job of teaching, the girls still played.

Music: "Trojan Marching Song" (Fight On for Old SC)
Stage: All sports performers enact their sport.

In 1945, we all returned to our schools and recreation jobs.

Music: Continues.
Stage: Led by military services, all performers file off the stage.

But life had changed for women and would never be quite the same
again. We were now recognized as an indispensable part of the team,
and the stage was set for further progress.

Under the chairmanships of Alice Shriver, Anna Espenschade, Martha
Gable, Laurie Campbell, and Josephine Fiske we tackled the big job we
had to do in many ways. We installed a paid secretary in the office of

the Association, and she soon became one of the Association consultants. The working agreement with what had become the AAHPER was established in 1951, and the Section took over the publication of its own Guides. Meanwhile the Women's National Officials Rating Committee rolled up its sleeves and moved into industrial recreation, community recreation, and the semiprofessional leagues which were being formed in many areas. These were busy years for NSWA, and the four letters became so much a part of our lives that even now we can not quite get them off of our tongues.

In remembrance of those twenty busy, confused, but highly constructive years:

Will all women who wore a uniform in World War II please stand?

Will the ten women who served as chairmen of the Section during the years 1932 to 1953 please stand?

Will all past and present state and district representatives please raise their hands?

And will our one and only consultant please stand alone while all who have ever written a letter beginning "Dear Rachel Bryant" give her the applause she deserves.

SCENE VI — 1953-1957 — The National Section on Girls and Women's Sports

And it grew and it grew and it grew.

Music: "Yes Sir! That's My Baby"

Stage: Enter all sports performers in close huddle, move to center of stage, then slowly expand huddle until it occupies most of stage. All carry white cards and continue to raise, lower, and move them about as they walk. (On six of the cards, a big letter N,S,G,W,A, or S is drawn on the reverse side of the card, to be used later.)

It took in more activities; it moved down into preadolescence and up to adulthood. Its name no longer described its scope and its function. So committees were appointed and arguments were argued, and in 1953 we changed our name to the National Section for Girls and Women's Sports. But the transition was not easily made, and our tongues slipped many times.

Music: "Mairsy Doats"

Stage: Performers with lettered cards step in front of stage and shuffle back and forth, getting the cards in several different orders. Finally the A card holder throws her card away and the others line up as NSGWS.

Now, altogether, let's get it *right!* N — S — G — W — S.

Music: "Yes Sir, That's My Baby."
Stage: All performers chant N — S — G — W — S, and continue with decreasing volume as they follow the A card holder off stage.

But what's in a name? That which we once called NSWA by any other name could smell as sweet — and have just as many thorns. Yes, we really got organized in 1953. The budget grew: we held the first big workshop in Estes Park; we got out more publications.

Who did it? You and you and you. You who believed that "The one purpose of sports for girls and women is the good of those who play" — you who were willing to implement that belief with energy, time and *action*.

As we ask Chairmen Josephine Fiske, Aileene Lockhart, Grace Fox and Mabel Locke to stand, will all the women who held office in the NSGWS please hold up their hands?
Now the hands of all who went to Estes Park?
And will those who can recite the infield fly rule hold up *both* hands.

SCENE VII — 1957-1958 — The Division for Girls and Women's Sports

And now we have reached the years of our maturity. We have become full partners in the over-all program of the American Association for Health, Physical Education, and Recreation. We have served our apprenticeship as a tentative Division of AAHPER, and before this convention ends we shall be recognized as a full-fledged *Division* of the Association. Our chairman will be a vice-president of the Association, sitting on the board of directors and elected by the representative assembly as a symbol of our expanding participation in all phases of Association concern, our expanding influence in areas other than girls and women's sports, and our expanding understanding of the complexity of the problems women *and men* must work through *together*.

As a Division of AAHPER we women are still marching on with our

Music: "Glory, Glory Halleujah!"
Stage: All sports performers enter, one by one, in the order named. They cross the stage, exit, drop their equipment and pick up hats and brief cases. Re-enter at back of stage and sit on floor in a double circle.

basketballs, our hockey sticks, our soccer balls, our swimming suits, our track and field equipment, our baseballs, our volleyballs, our winter activities, our lacrosse sticks, our speedballs, our archery bows, our golf clubs, our tennis racquets, our riding crops, our fencing foils, our badminton birds, and our bowling balls.

Music: Continues, transposed to minor key
Stage: Performers carry on a silent meeting, with the official serving as chairman.

Carying on, too, with our rule books, our standards, our philosophy, our publications, our official's ratings, our audio-visual aids, our international relations, our public relations, our publications, our research — never forgetting our operating codes and our finances.

Through the years we have done a lot of talking, sitting, talking, letter writing, talking, travelling, talking, and *meeting*. And what have we been

Stage: On hearing word *travelling*, basketball player jumps up and "travels," then sits down in confusion.

meeting about? Only one thing — "the good of those who play."

SCENE VII — Desirable Practices

(There is no break between Scene VI and Scene VII)

Through the years we have been trying to keep up with social evolution, trying to keep up with the girls, trying to determine and establish "Desirable Practices for Girls and Women" in their sports and recreational activities.

Music: Medley made up of snatches of all songs used in previous scenes.

We talked about standards. Is it fair for girls to wear hatpins while playing hockey? How far shall a lady's skirt be allowed to dip on

Stage: Hockey player enacts these questions

the hockey field? Shall we insist on medical examinations for all girls?

Stage: Bowling performer takes pulse, etc. on fencer

Sometimes we had to compromise between reality and what we thought was ideal. We talked about competition. Are we for it? Are we against it?

Stage: Much head shaking, final shoulder shrugging, and slow
         nods of agreement. On competition questions, some nod in
         vigorous assent, others shake their heads in violent disagree-
         ment. Then handshakes all around, which become hand-
         pulls, and finally jerk-aways.

What do we mean by competition? How many statements have we written? But that's all settled now, isn't it? Or is it?

We talked about rules. Shall the overhead shot in basketball count
one point or two? Shall we use the one step, two step, or polka stop?
The single

Stage: Basketball players act out shot from above shoulders, chest,
         below waist, one shooting, other guarding. Continue pan-
         tomine for all basketball questions.

dribble, double dribble, or limited continuous dribble? Shall we play
one court, two court, three court or nine court basketball?

We talked about policy. Shall girls be allowed to play touch
football?

Stage: Soccer and speedball players demonstrate touch foot-
         ball. Horror expressed by many, nods of approval by a few.

We talked about guides. Who shall publish them? About publications.

Stage: Continuous argument, rising to higher pitch with some
         clenched fists and knee pounding at mention of money.

We published the Sportswoman, the Service Bulletin, and fliers by the
thousands.

We talked about money. Ah, yes, our reach has always exceeded our
grasp — but what else is heaven for?

We talked about men.

Stage: Smiles, frowns, nods, headshakes.

We talked about alphabets — apostrophes — ofs, ons, and fors.

Music: "La Cucharacha"

Stage: Prompter hands nearest woman placard reading DIVISION,
         and next three women cards reading ON, FOR, OF. These

three women shove each other around in rhumba rhythm, each trying to stand next to DIVISION. Finally, FOR wins, and OF and ON walk off sadly. Prompter hands next woman a card reading GIRL. She takes her place next to FOR without dispute, as an APOSTROPHE and S jostle each other for the next spot. The APOSTROPHE is finally pushed aside. Next woman adds AND, the next WOMEN, followed by further jostling between APOSTROPHE and the next S. Finally both stay, making WOMEN'S, and then SPORTS joins the line without controversy.

But always, no matter what we argued about, we were genuinely concerned with "the good of those who play." And we shall go on talking about that, no matter what our structure, our squabbles, our name, because this is really the reason for our existence as an organization.

And now, as our performers stand before us showing us our new role as the Division of Girls and Women's Sports, let's give them a big, big hand.

Music: "Glory, Glory Halleluja!" (Major key)
Stage: Sports performers not holding cards join in applause as performers from the earlier scenes pass in review, then all bow, and EXIT.

SCENE IX — Preview of Tomorrow

The players for this final scene are the many women who have given leadership to the cause of "the good of girls who play." Will those of you who are seated in the audience today please stand to receive our applause as some of your specific contributions are mentioned.

Our good friends who spoke for us on the board of directors when we had no official voice of our own — the women who have served as president of the Association: Mabel Lee, Mary Channing Coleman, Agnes Wayman, Margaret Bell, Anne Schley Duggan, Helen Manley, Ruth Evans, Bernice Moss, Ruth Abernathy, and President-elect Pattric Ruth O'Keefe.

Now the many, many women who have served on the national board of directors as vice-presidents of other divisions or as district representatives.

Our first vice-president for Girls and Women's Sports: Mabel Locke.

Our vice-president-elect: Jane Mott.

Now, all of the women who have in their time served as chairman of NSWA or NSGWS.

Then, some of the hardy perennials who have bypassed the chairmanship in their devotion to the many other jobs they have done so well: Bessie Rudd, Elizabeth Beall, Marion Purbeck, Gladys Palmer, Christine White, Marjorie Hillas, Dorothy Beatty. . .and others too numerous to name who are represented by them.

Our own Elsa Schneider, consultant in the Office of Education.

Our own Rachel Bryant, our one and only consultant at AAHPER headquarters.

Now, every woman who has ever served on the legislative board.

Every woman who has ever served on a standing committee.

And all women who have ever served on *any* committee at the national, district, state, or local level since 1899.

These are our leaders! Through their efforts the Women's Basketball Committee became the Committee on Women's Athletics, the Section on Women's Athletics, the National Section on Women's Athletics, the National Section on Girls and Women's Sports, and now the DIVISION FOR GIRLS AND WOMEN'S SPORTS.

Come, then, let us applaud ourselves! And then please be seated. Because there is still a more important group that must be honored: the girls who will build the *future* of the Division for Girls and Women's Sports — the girls who will determine whether we shall continue to grow in wisdom as well as in strength — the girls who are now *students* in our colleges and universities.

Stand, students, so we can see our *tomorrow!*

And now, as we move into the reception room to pay our personal respects to our leaders through the years, it seems appropriate that tomorrow's leaders should stand beside them. Will the students please step to the side aisle and come down to the front, each one offering her arm to one of our honored guests now seated in the front section?

Then, if Mabel Locke and Jane Mott and the members of the executive council will lead the way, followed by our honored guests and their student escorts, the rest of us will fall in behind in whatever order is convenient — for well-organized as we are, we women of the Division for Girls and Women's Sports need no further organization as we celebrate our own history of WOMEN IN ACTION.

Music: "Pomp and Circumstance" as the procession files out.

Where Will You Go From Here?

North Central Regional Conference of the Athletic and Recreation Federation of College Women — Des Moines, Iowa — March, 1964

The theme you have chosen for your conference is the most important question of our time: WHERE DO WE GO FROM HERE? But it is not a new question; it is as old as the human race. It was asked many thousands of years ago by primitive men who huddled around smoky fires in drafty caves; and the answers they gave either moved them into more comfortable habitations — or doomed them to extinction. And so it has been throughout all human history. As men and women have asked this question again and again, their answers have opened up new habitations for the human spirit — or closed the doors on human progress and precipitated human disaster.

WHERE DO WE GO FROM HERE? It is an exciting question, because it suggests a willingness to venture into the unknown in search of new possibilities for human development. It is a courageous question, because it suggests a willingness to accept the risks inherent in any venture into a realm that has not yet been explored and charted. And it is a self-confident question, because it suggests that you have faith in your own ability to make your own decisions and chart your own course of action.

So I count it a very special privilege to have a part in this exciting meeting of courageous and self-confident young women who are willing to take responsibility for their own lives — and for the lives of the other women they are representing at this convention.

In this exciting, courageous, and self-confident meeting you are raising the question of human progress in the specific terms of participation in sports. To a casual observer, it might seem that you have come together to talk about field hockey, — and such a casual observer might well wonder what field hockey has to do with the larger issues of our times. But I am not a casual observer. I am a woman who has played field hockey — and golf and tennis and badminton and softball and basketball. I have spent my life encouraging young women to play these games — encouraging them, too, to learn to skate and swim and dance — and hopefully encouraging them to participate in the larger games of social change and human development. So I know full well that questions about field hockey are never trivial or casual. I know that they are very important questions that reach into every area of your lives as young women who are trying to chart your own course of action in our exciting, confusing, and challenging modern world.

The pioneering women who framed the early pattern of women's competition in field hockey knew this too. Like you, they loved this strenuous game for its own sake, but like you they were only superficially concerned with sticks, balls, and conditions of competition. To them, hockey was only a symbol of the larger game they were playing in the arena of social change; and, like you, they talked about hockey because they were deeply concerned with the very big questions: What abilities do women have? How can they best use these abilities to build a better world for themselves and for all human beings everywhere?

Like you, these early hockey players were involved in many forms of human endeavor. Many of them were deeply involved in the attempt to secure for all women the right to vote, to serve on juries, to participate in the major decisions of their times, and to manage their own financial affairs. Others joined the women who were claiming the right to use their abilities in business and the professions. Still others worked wth the antislavery organizations, while others worked to provide educational opportunities for girls like you.

These early hockey players were a courageous and gallant band — and many of them paid a heavy price for their own bravery. In their own lives they took many risks as they ventured beyond the traditional boundaries of their time into new areas of unexplored territory. And as they claimed that territory for themselves, they laid the foundations of a new world for the women of the United States — and for all women everywhere.

These women opened up new territory for the women of my generation — which is the generation of your grandmothers. In our time, we, too, played the game of field hockey as a part of the larger game of social change. Some of us tripped over our own sticks and stubbed our toes, and then felt so sorry for ourselves that we retired from the game. But some of us did play well, and these better players succeeded in scoring a long list of "firsts" for women. So in our turn we opened up more new areas of participation for your mothers, — and they in turn have established new patterns of participation for you to build on. Most of your mothers are not yet ready to retire from the field, but in their wisdom they know that it is now time to pass the ball to you so you may make your own decisions about how you will try to play the game.

In this convention those decisions will be concerned with the old game called field hockey and the very old organizations called WAA, WRA, and ARFCW. Perhaps the decisions you will make would have shocked even the most daring of those pioneering hockey players — because they succeeded for better than they knew in their attempt to enlarge the scope of women's concerns. And perhaps some of us oldsters will smile at other questions you may argue about — because we have heard women argue those same questions hundreds of times during the past forty years. But no matter what questions you may raise, every debate will have very long, deep roots that will bind it to the past, even as the debates nourish the courage that pushes you toward a hopefully better future.

These roots will nourish your debates, but you will often find yourselves confused by the effect they will have on your thinking — for they are not long straight roots that point directly toward the heart of your concern. They are tangled and twisted roots that have many kinks in them — kinks that were developed as the game of social change has moved forward and backward, and sometimes sidewards across the field. Every player who has ever entered the same has left her imprint on them as she ran and turned and twisted and dodged in her attempt to move the ball toward her chosen goal — or retreated toward the opposite goal set by her opponents.

These tangled and twisted roots are so much a part of your own thinking that you scarcely know they are there. But nonetheless they will influence every debate, put words in your mouth as you argue every question, and sometimes make you contradict yourself twice in the same sentence. And always they will charge your arguments with emotion, — and you may wonder many times why you feel so strongly about a minor point in the game of field hockey. But there is good reason for this emotionality — and it can be the best constructive force in this convention if you are willing to deal with it openly as evidence of your own involvement in the major issues of your own life.

Since I have struggled with these same confused emotions many times during the years I have been playing in the hockey game of social change, perhaps I can make my best contribution to your exciting, courageous, self-confident convention by trying to help you trace the main branches in these emotionally charged roots.

Let's call the first root WOMEN — because that is what we are, and this is the very taproot of our personal identity. We were born female; we shall die female; and in between those two points in time we can never be anything else. Fortunately, most of us find this a very satisfying arrangement.

This femaleness defines the structure of our bodies and most of its functions. It also defines our role in the essential process of bringing new human beings into the world. And in one way or another it affects every aspect of our personal role within the larger social pattern. But during the past two centuries, many women have been asking whether having babies and making a home for them is all there is to "being a woman." And gradually we have begun to define ourselves as persons, citizens, thinkers, workers, and human beings whose abilities branch out from this home-husband-children core in many different directions. Accordingly, every woman among us has two pictures of "what a woman is" — both of which are attractive and appealing, but in different ways and for different reasons.

The old, solid, well-established image, which we share with the women of many centuries, pictures us as fragile and lovely creatures, not only too frail to endure the rigors of life without the protection of a strong masculine arm, but also too incompetent to deal with the practical problems of living.

This image offers us many advantages. In it we see ourselves sheltered, cared for, and shielded from the risks of life, while we fulfill our cherished function of child-bearing with few worries about the kind of world our children will grow up in. This is a comfortable thought — but there are also certain disadvantages in this situation. In order to be protected, we must give our protectors authority over our lives, — and this deprives us of the privilege of exploring our own human potential for growth and achievement. So as we begin to wonder what we are and what we are really able to do, we begin to resist this authoritative-protective arrangement and our interest shifts to the newer image.

This newer image, which is only now being defined, emphasizes our competence as intelligent human beings who are well able to share the risks and challenges of life with our strong male companions. This is an exciting image in which we picture ourselves as able to do anything we may want to do. But as we really involve ourselves in the attempt to translate this vision into the realistic terms of effort and achievement, we find that is not easy to be a full-fledged human being who has accepted responsibility for her own life. In our early attempts we encounter many disappointments and perhaps some resistance — and at this point the comforts afforded by the old authoritative-protective pattern begin to loom large in our thinking.

So we are tempted to turn in our hockey sticks, to surrender the excitement of self-discovery by "playing it safe," and by leaving the big game of social change to our authoritative protectors — and to other women who will take the risks for us. But even as we consider the comforts of this strategic retreat, we resist the thought of surrendering our lives to the authority of our protectors — and we grumble about being confined to the tedium of housekeeping and the limited conversational efforts of small children.

And so we waver back and forth between these two images of our own potentialities — always with one eye fixed on the second deep root labelled MEN.

In your public discussions in this convention, you may never speak of MEN directly — but they will never be far from your thoughts. And in the long run, they will have an enormous influence on every answer you give to your question: WHERE DO WE GO FROM HERE?

I shall not chide you for this concern, because I share it with you. Our world belongs to both sexes, and neither can make the journey into the future alone. So I think you should be thinking about men; I think you should consider their stake in the future, and give it full weight in all of your deliberations. And as you plan your own next steps in the great human venture, you must surely plan them in such a way that you will be helping your male companions move forward with you, rather than holding them back by consigning them to the roles played by their grandfathers.

Every woman who has ever tried to find a larger definition of her own life has been plagued by the fear that men will reject her for her temerity. And certainly every woman who has ever tried to move into new territory has at times met with some opposition from her male companions. But if we look at the facts of history, we will discover that men go right on marrying attractive young women — no matter how venturesome they may be.

Perhaps the most frightened women of all times were the gallant band of courageous wives and spinsters who insisted that women were intellectually able to vote and hold public office. They knew that their efforts to establish this idea would make them unpopular in many quarters —and certainly they did. But the forgotten heroes of that long fight are the husbands who did support their wives in this great controversy, working beside them in a gallant attempt to improve life for both sexes. And when this question of women's competence was finally put to a vote in 1920, we must remember that it was the men who cast the deciding votes for women's suffrage. Perhaps many of these men were reluctant to surrender their own political authority — but there is no evidence that they found these new vote-casting women unacceptable. During the years that followed 1920 there is no evidence of a drop in the marriage rate in the United States.

The same story may be told about the women who attempted to enter the world of business and the professions. Again there was much argumentation; and many hard things were said on both sides; but the attractive young women who demonstrated that they were competent to earn a salary did not lack for suitors. Rather, if the truth be told, men soon discovered that these attractive young wage-earners were much more interesting than their home-bound sisters were — and today there are very few men who are repelled by the fact that the young lady of their choice is able to make a substantial contribution to the joint family budget.

So, too, it has been in the realm of sports. Whatever women have chosen to do as sportswomen has antagonized some men and delighted others. But I noticed that the attractive young women who represented the United States in the Olympic Games in 1960 were not forced to spend their evenings alone for lack of eager masculine escorts.

The truth of the matter is that men have always gone along with the women who were brave enough to venture into new territory. Facetiously, it may be said that they have no other alternative! Men need women, even as we need them — and if they reject the attractive young women of their own times, who else is there for them to marry? More seriously, it seems unlikely that the kind of men you want to marry will choose you only out of desperation. The good men of our times have marched side by side with their women during each venture into new territory that seemed to offer a larger definition of human life. I think they will walk forward with you, too, as you try to answer the big question: WHERE DO WE GO FROM HERE?

Because I believe we must have faith in our men, even as we have faith in ourselves, I have shuddered many times as I have watched attractive young women like you deny that faith. I have seen you on the tennis courts, deliberately hiding your own ability as you turned what might have been an exciting match into a dull game of "let's pretend." Again and again I have watched you insult the fine young man you are playing with by treating him like a child. And I have wept inwardly as I have seen you violate all of the high ideals of sportsmanship by "fixing the score" and "throwing the game."

Are these men that you hope to marry really such childish creatures that they will have a temper tantrum over losing a tennis match? Are they really so stupid that they do not know you are insulting them every time you deliberately muff a shot? Do you think they really want to settle for a meaningless score that was arranged by you? Do you think they really want to spend their lives playing a dull game called "let's pretend"? Do you think they have so little faith in their own abilities that they dare not put them to the realistic test?

The greatest joy any woman can know is the joy of being loved for what she *is*, in all the richness and poverty of her being. Every time we try to "fix the score" in a tennis match by pretending to be less than we are, we rob ourselves of the opportunity to know that joy. And tragically, we rob our playing companions of that same opportunity, by forcing them into the childish game of "let's play pretend."

Only as we are brave enough to *be* what we *are* can we hope that someone will love us in all the fullness of our being. And only as we find the courage to be ourselves can we extend that privilege to other people of either sex. Do you really want to deny that privilege to the young man you hope to marry? Or do you want to share with him the joy of loving and being loved freely, fully, and without need for pretense?

And so I urge you to have faith in the men you hope to marry, even as you have faith in yourself. Men may often behave like petulant children, even as we do. They, too, have their fears; and they, too, have their own pretenses. They, too, have their own conflicts as they waver back and forth between the image bequeathed to them by their grandfathers and the newer image of full-partnership with their marriage companions. In many ways, their conflicts are far more distressing than yours are, and often much harder to resolve. But again and again the kind of men you want to marry have demonstrated that they, too, are able to play well in the big game of human development; and again and again they have moved forward with their women toward a larger vision of life for all people.

The issues raised by the tennis match have much to do with our attitudes toward men, marriage, and ourselves — but perhaps we can see these issues more clearly if we now turn our attention to the third root, labelled SPORT. This strong but very tangled and twisted root reaches down into three thousand years of history. The very early Greeks, who gave us our first organized sports as well as the model for our modern Olympic games, loved sports even as we do, but they recognized very early that every sports contest offers two conflicting possibilities. It can bring out the best in men, and encourage them to move toward their highest human aspirations; or it can bring out the worst in men and degrade them to the level of beasts. These two faces of sport are identified in their dual concepts of "good competition" and "bad competition," — or, as they put it, the "good strife" and "bad strife" in all areas of human life.

Their word for the "good competition" was *cum-petere,* in which the prefix *cum* means *with* or *together,* and the root *petere* means *to strive.* The good competition men found in striving together was a cooperative endeavour in which both contestants were working toward a common purpose that would benefit them both. This purpose was to develop their human abilities to the highest possible excellence, and each contest served this purpose by providing each contestant with an opportunity to test his own best efforts against the opposition offered by the best efforts of his opponent. Thus, the opponents honored each other by offering each other their own best efforts, and both opponents honored their gods by demonstrating the good use they had made of the talents their gods had bestowed upon them.

This good competition of men who honored their gods and honored each other is epitomized in the athletic contests that were held every fourth year in the groves of Olympia as a part of the religious festival in honor of Zeus, the father of the Greek gods. In these contests, all contestants took an oath in which they promised Zeus that they would use all of their abilities to the fullest possible extent — and any contestant who failed to do this was punished by the officials — and it was believed that he would also be punished by the gods for dishonoring them and abusing the gifts they had given him.

So there is no question about the fact that the contestants in this "good competition" went all out in their attempts to win the laurel wreath of victory, but both the winner and the loser in every match profited from the opportunity to test himself against the opposition offered by his opponent. And when the issue was decided, the man who lost the match was not dishonored if he had done his best. Rather he was praised for the worthiness of his performance.

Today you can hear the echo of that old ideal of sportsmanship whenever the winner and loser in a tennis match walk toward each other to shake hands and thank each other for a "good game," and then walk off the court together — not as enemies, but as good friends who have shared an exciting experience together.

What the Greeks called "bad competition" or the "bad strife" excluded this idea of cooperative effort undertaken by men who honored each other as they honored their gods. In bad competition, men were intent on proving their own superiority by using their abilities to beat and destroy and humiliate other men. They treated their opponents as enemies, and gloried in their ability to subdue them and grind their faces in the dust. And so they made of each contest a miniature war in which they used their skillful bodies as weapons of destruction — and then boasted about their ability to ward off all danger by destroying the honor and reputation of their enemies.

Today we hear the echo of that unsportsmanlike pattern of bad competition whenever some one tells us how he *beat* his opponent — or when the opponent feels humiliated by being *beaten* by the other contestant.

In Greece, as elsewhere, these two kinds of competition flourished side by side — and both are still with us today. Good sportsmen play to win because they value their opponent's best efforts even as they value their own; but many contestants are guilty of the unsportsmanlike conduct exemplified by trying to *beat* another person in order to humiliate him and exalt oneself.

The pioneering women who tried to bring field hockey and other sports into the domain of participation for women knew both sides of the competition story. They knew the satisfactions women might well find in opportunities to test their own abilities against the best efforts of worthy and cooperative opponents; but they had also seen much of the degradation of the human spirit that is implicit in bad competition. So they tried to protect young women like you from the degrading effects of bad competition even as they tried to provide the framework within which you might experience the joys of good competition. They did this in two ways — and in their concern for your welfare they were probably much too conservative in their interpretations, even for their own times. First they tried to rule out all sports that involved the thuds and blows of direct body contact, and with them many sports in which there is a display of what they called "brute strength" and muscular power. Then they tried to define the conditions under which girls and women might profitably engage in the milder sports without fear of degrading the feminine image.

These women were, themselves, good competitors, and in every game they ever played they did honor to themselves, their opponents, and their gods by putting forth their own best efforts, — but they were almost morbidly afraid of the word *competition*. They had watched men's athletics turn into a battlefield where everyone was trying to *beat* everyone else — and they did not want this to happen in the newly patterned field of women's sports. But in their anxiety, they missed the important difference between the idea of *playing to beat* and *playing to win*. And so they made a mockery of the very ideals they were trying to establish for women by teaching the girls that it was unladylike to *play to win*.

As one of the young girls who entered sports when this dictum was in force, I can assure you that it confused us no end — because it seemed to take the very heart out of the game. But, as I remember it, as soon as we got out on the basketball court or the hockey field, we forgot this injunction, and contested every point just as vigorously as any group of boys ever did. And on occasion we may even have been guilty of trying to *beat* our opponents or of feeling humiliated when we, ourselves, had been beaten.

In the days when there was a stigma attached to the concept of playing to win, the women who were responsible for our welfare devised the idea of a play day that would permit us to enjoy sports participation with girls from other schools. In these play days, each school group was broken up by giving each girl a colored ribbon and assigning her to a color team made up of girls from every school. As I remember it, we had fun at these play days, and we enjoyed the tea and the sociability — but the better players among us always felt frustrated by the lack of meaningful team play in these color teams made up of strangers. And by the time we got home, few of us could remember which color team we had been on, and we could scarcely remember whether these teams to which we had owed such a brief allegiance had won or lost. So, in general, these play days did little to satisfy our desire for all-out competition with worthy and honored opponents.

The sports days which marked the next step in collegiate competition for women offered a more challenging opportunity. Then we took three or four teams from each school, and each team played as a unit in a sort of round-robin competition of quarter games and half games with teams from other schools. But it was not too long before we were playing "A" teams against "A" teams, and "B" against "B" — and then we began to take these games seriously. I must also confess, however, that we did sometimes get confused about the difference between playing to win and playing to beat — and many girls did use the boy's terminology. However, when these games were over, the girls did shake hands with each other and behave like honored friends as they gathered around the tea table, so my guess is that it was their terminology rather than their ideals that was confused.

But throughout the years of sports days the belief that women did not approve of competition and the parallel belief that ladies do not play to win persisted. Scarcely a week goes by even now when I do not hear both statements — usually from men who are chiding me for holding young women like you back, when I should be urging you forward. I have to admit that there is some merit in this accusation, because both statements have been made again and again in the literature of sports for women. But today I know very few women associated with sports who would subscribe to either statement. Personally, all of the best sportswomen I know are good competitors; and personally I think any game becomes meaningless unless both sides "play to win." And despite all of our long years of confusion about ourselves as sportswomen, I still believe that the real glory of women's sports is derived from the fact that they have striven together to maintain the old Greek ideal of "good competition."

Now in your time this old debate is being identified and brought out into the open by the move toward full-scale varsity type competition for college women. Today, many of our colleges — including my own — have women on their faculties who are called *coaches*, and these women are being paid by the same athletic department that is responsible for the men's varsity teams. Our women's teams are competing in tennis, golf, fencing, swimming, and a number of other sports, — but as yet these competitions have not attracted the large audiences of spectators that attend men's sports events. Nonetheless, we are sending our girls half way across the United States to compete in regional and national tournaments; and I can assure you that these tournament participants do play to win — and personally I take pride in the fact that our girls often do.

WHERE DO WE GO FROM HERE? Shall we try to expand this intercollegiate form of competition? Shall we try to organize conferences and leagues? Shall we start looking for highly-skilled performers and try to induce them to attend our colleges by offering them grants-in-aid called athletic scholarships? Shall we try to develop paying spectators who will support these competitions financially? I can cite examples of some colleges that are saying YES to each of these questions. I can also cite examples of many colleges in which the responsible women are saying NO. And I can cite you the arguments that will support both points of view — because I have had to review them many times.

Even as you will do in this conference, I have found myself moving in both directions simultaneously. I do want every woman to have ample opportunity to test herself against the best efforts of worthy opponents; and I do want every woman I know to have the experience of playing to win in a game that will test her abilities to the utmost. But, like the pioneering women who tried to protect my generation from the evils of competition, I shudder at the thought that the excitement of high level competition might lead women to try to *beat* other women in the cooperative game of human development. I do not want the women who are moving out into a larger arena to degrade themselves — and so the men who chide me may sometimes be right in accusing me of wishing to hold young women back.

But in the long run, my opinion will carry little weight. It will be your decisions that will determine the major features of this new look in women's sports. And those decisions will finally be made in conferences like this one in which young women like you give serious consideration to the question: WHERE DO WE GO FROM HERE?

I do not know what decision you will finally make, but I do know that there will be much argumentation and many hard things said on both sides before you arrive at it, — because that is the process which women and men must always go through as they consider a venture into new territory. So this may well be a very stormy conference — and there may well be many even more tempestuous conferences during the years that lie ahead. I shall not try to calm those troubled waters for you — but perhaps I can use the last few minutes you have given me to try to make your argumentation constructive by comparing it with the game of field hockey.

In hockey there are two teams trying to move toward opposite goals against the opposition they offer each other. Before you can play in this game you must know the answers to these questions: Which team am I on? Who are my teammates? Which goal are we trying to move toward? What are we trying to accomplish? What techniques and tools are available to us as we try to accomplish those objectives within the rules of the game?

Having identified your team, you must then ask: What position am I playing? Am I playing wing, or fullback, or goalie? What should I be doing at any instant in the game? That depends, of course, on your ability to size up the situation as well as on your role. Sometimes you may try to hit the ball forward; sometimes you will get into position to receive the ball. Or you may back up the hitter, ready to pick up the ball if it goes through her stick. Or you may try to block a hit made

by your opponents, or get into a position where you can block if necessary. At times you may have an opportunity to carry the ball — and
then you may be able to dodge and twist and drive right through the
opposition to score a goal — or be blocked in your attempt. But as the
game goes on, you will have to make these decisions for yourself, second
by second, — and then abide by the outcomes of your own actions, right
or wrong.

How will you behave as you play your position? Will you be pleasant
and courteous, even when you are fighting the hardest to take the ball
away from your opponents? Will you recognize that they are equally
sincere in their desire to move toward their own goal? Will you give
due credit to the abilities of your teammates — and the abilities of
your opponents? Will you be able to believe that the progress your
team makes as a team is far more important than the satisfaction you
might find in making some spectacular play of your own?

In the excitement of the game, if you happen to raise your stick too
high, will you accept your penalty without whining? If your opponents succeed in pushing you back toward their goal, will you take
this setback without anger or resentment? Will you forego the childish
desire to punish your opponents for outwitting you, and concentrate
on trying to improve your own skill and tactics so you can recover the
territory you have lost?

If the score gets lopsided, will you be tempted to say: What's the
use of trying any more? Will you sell-out your teammates by conced-
ing the victory to the opposition before the game is over?

And what if the opposing team does win the game? What then?
Can you accept this as a part of the risk that goes with every exciting
game? If you knew that the score had been "fixed" in your favor before
the game started, would you still want to go through the motions of
pretending to play the game?

I know the answers you will give to all of these questions because
you would not be here in this conference if you did not cherish the
ideals of good sportsmanship. And so I am confident of your ability
to be equally good sportswomen as you enter wholeheartedly into the
bigger and more challenging game of human development and social
change.

In the big game, the questions we must answer are the same — but
there is no official guide book to give us the answers. There is no
official set of rules, and no referee to enforce them. In the big
game, the only rules that count are those you make for yourself. Your
opponents have the same privilege and the same responsibility. They
can try to play their own game by any rules they may choose. If they
like, they can trip and kick and dig their elbows into your ribs and

threaten you with their sticks — and there are no official penalties for this unsportsmanlike conduct. You can do these things, too, if you want to — and now and then you may win a point with such tactics. But in the end, the rules you choose for yourself will determine whose game you are playing, and what game you have won or lost.

Because you value yourselves as sportswomen, I believe that you know which game you are playing. I believe you are playing on the team that is moving toward the goal of human dignity and the full development of human potentialities. I believe you are capable of getting into that game that is based on the "good competition" of cooperative effort — and of playing it honestly as you use all of your own best efforts to strive together with those who are moving toward the goal of human freedom. And as you play this great game within the rules that define the conduct of good sportswomen, I believe that you will find in it the satisfaction that comes to those who participate in any challenging game.

The decisions you will make in this conference, however large or small they may be, will help to establish the image of the sportswomen of the future. I do not know what those decisions will be — but I believe that I can predict what that image will be like.

At whatever level they choose to compete in the realm of sports, I believe that our sportswomen of the future will be just as feminine as their great-grandmothers were, but much more attractive and much more interesting to their male companions. I believe they will be just as gracious and as considerate of the needs of other human beings as their mothers have been in their homes and places of employment, but much more certain of their own desirability as women who are competent to deal with the larger affairs of the world. I think they will play the games they choose with even more skill than you do, and I believe that their use of their high-level skills will exemplify their respect for the cooperative nature of good competition. In short, I think they will exemplify even more clearly the kind of behavior that you are now developing for all women — the kind of behavior that may well be called "good sportswomanship."

And as to the men in their lives, I have not the slightest doubt that these new sportswomen of the future will find husbands who will love and respect them for what they are — honest sportswomen who know that a good marriage rests on the satisfactions both men and women may find as they strive together in the "good competition" in which both players use all of their abilities to further each other's human development in an attempt to build a happier habitation for the human spirit.

The "Woman's Look" in Sport

National Athletic and Recreation Federation of College Women —
    Corvallis, Oregon — March, 1959

Whenever a group of people assembles in a conference, we may assume that they have certain common interests they want to discuss. In order to establish a frame of reference for these discussions, they usually invite someone to open the conference by identifying those interests in such a way that the attention of the conference participants is focussed on what they all have in common rather than on personal, regional, or institutional differences. As I see it, that is my assignment this morning.

What are the unifying characteristics of the participants in this conference? First, you are all interested in sport, and probably each of you is a better than average performer in some sport; and second, all of you are young women — and, I might add, very attractive young women. These characteristics affect your lives in many different ways, and they will tend to influence your thinking during this conference. So let's examine the implications of these characterstics before you begin your discussions.

You are all interested in sport, but your interests cover a wide range of sports activities. Some of you like ping pong, which is played on a table in a small room; but others of you like golf, which is played outdoors on a course that covers several acres. Some like to swim and emerge cool and clean; while others prefer tennis which makes you hot and sweaty. Some like bowling, in which you perform alone as you try to overcome an inanimate object; some like riding, performing alone to master the will of a large animal; while others prefer fencing, in which you perform alone in opposition to a human challenger. Some choose badminton, in which partners oppose partners, two against two; while still others find your greatest fun in the team games like basketball in which six people coordinate their effort and strategy to overcome the opposition supplied by six other people engaged in similar cooperative efforts.

What do all of these varied sports activities have in common? One of the best answers has been given by Roger Bannister, the great runner. "Sport is a diversion with no purpose beyond providing a testing ground larger than a chess board, but smaller than life itself." This is what all sports have in common. This is the fascination sports have for all of you.

All sports offer diversion — a change of activity — an involvement in something different from our daily occupations and preoccupations. This diversion may be found in all recreational activities; bridge, for example, can provide intense involvement in a challenging situation quite different from our workaday tasks. But sports offer an added incentive. They involve movement, which provides a change for the body as well as for the mind, and they offer the satisfaction that comes from the feeling of movement as a sensory experience.

But the real fascination of sports is not found in idle diversion. We are drawn to sports because they provide a testing ground on which we determine our own abilities by attempting to overcome the resistance offered by another person, group of persons, or a defined set of circumstances. Competition, itself, is inherent in many life situations; but seldom do we have an opportunity to compete openly, freely, fully, in situations where the purpose of the moment is defined as competition. In sports, during the time of play and within the rules of the game, we are morally committed to use all of our resources against opponents — either persons or things — that are resisting our efforts. In that test, we find out what we can do, and how we react to success, failure, and uncertainty; and this self-testing forces upon us a kind of self-evaluation in specific terms not often provided by other life situations.

The sports testing ground is larger than a chessboard or a bridge table. It involves the whole person, not only her mind and ego, but also her muscles, bones, blood, nerves, blood vessels, heart, endocrine glands, liver, lungs, digestive tract, and every fiber of her being. But this testing ground is still smaller than life itself. It is a segment of life, circumscribed by rules within a limited space for a limited time. In one or two hours, within the limits of the playing field, the outcomes of the test will be decided in clearly definable terms, made explicit in the rules. And when the game is over, neither the success nor the failure will have any really drastic effect on the player's life. When the game is over, it is over — and we can return to the larger game of life refreshed by our brief release from its complexity and confusing imponderables.

Both the significance and the transient nature of sports achievement were recognized in the early Olympic games, when men honored their gods by offering them their best performances of feats of strength and skill. The winner in each event received a wreath of honour, but it was made of the leaves of the laurel tree, that withered in an hour, symbolizing the belief that the significance of all athletic endeavors lies in the striving, in the doing, in the experience itself, and not in the final winning or losing. Outstanding performance in any endeavour was considered to be deserving of recognition, but such recognition was only for the moment. The winning athlete could not "rest on his laurels" forever; when the laurel wreath began to wither, it was time for him to move on to new experiences in the larger arena of life itself.

Any sport can satisfy our need for a diversion and a testing ground larger than a chessboard but smaller than life itself, but what determines our personal choices of specific sports? Individual abilities, yes — but not to so large an extent as we may think, for we are more largely persuaded by the availability of specific activities. If we live where there are mountains, we are more likely to choose skiing than hockey; if horses are a part of our lives, we are more likely to choose riding than swimming. We do not learn to play tennis unless we have access to tennis courts; and we do not become fencers unless someone is available to teach us the fencer's art. Availability of facilities, access to instruction, and opportunities to see skilled performers largely determine what sports we try; and encouragement and some degree of early success influence our desire to continue trying to acquire greater skill. We are influenced, too, by the social significance attached to given sports in the communities in which we live. Ojai, California, is a "tennis town," for example, and so a child living in Ojai is influenced to choose tennis rather than softball because tennis is "the thing to do" in that community. Socioeconomic factors also influence our choices. If our parents belong to a country club, we are more likely to play golf; if our only playground is a vacant lot in a crowded city area, we may find our testing-ground on a roughed-out baseball diamond playing Move-up or One Old Cat.

All of these chance factors are a part of the culture in which you live, but by far the most significant factors in determining your choices within a culture are the time and place of your birth. The customs, mores, beliefs, and general attitudes which identify the culture of any group of people are never static. They change through the years, even as they differ from country to country throughout the world. And this is particularly true with reference to the kinds of choices available to women, especially during the past century.

If you had been born in this country a hundred years ago — about the time of the Civil War — you might have chosen to play croquet, a very lady-like game of croquet, in your whaleboned corset, with your floor-length skirts sweeping the grass, and your hat firmly anchored to your hair by a long hatpin. Only the most daring of you would have ventured into the water, clad in voluminous bathing dresses and long black hose that covered every inch of your bodies, arms, and legs — then discreetly referred to as limbs. Or if you had been born in India — or China — or Russia, you would have grown up with very different attitudes toward sports, even as you would have acquired quite different attitudes toward other aspects of your life, and your personal sports choices, if any, would probably have been quite different.

I have just finished reading a fascinating book called "The Cherished Goal" written by a Russian girl — a very attractive young woman, too. Now in her late twenties, she is one of the world's greatest women shot-putters. She was attracted to the shot-put when she was thirteen years old, and with considerable encouragement from the government she has been able to devote most of her time to developing her skill in this event. Other young women have been similarly encouraged to develop skill in the sprints, distance runs, hurdles, jumps, javelin, discus, and in gymnastic performance on the rings, parallel bars, high bar, and horse. To most of you, such devotion to these particular sports events seems incredible; but if you had been born in Russia, you too might have found your personal testing ground on the running track or in the shot-put circle.

What, then, makes participation in a given sport desirable or undesirable for women? This is just one phase of the larger question: How do we determine what is "right" for girls and women in all areas of their lives? I wish I knew a simple answer to give you!

In general terms, the answer depends upon two things: first, the meaning given to the phrase "being a woman" as it is interpreted in the beliefs, customs, practices, and attitudes prevailing in any given culture at any given time; and second, each woman's personal needs and abilities as she interprets them in relation to the role she accepts within the culture in which she lives.

These are both very complex statements — but women are complex creatures, and cultural change has endowed them with even greater complexity than they naturally possess. Many women have tried to simplify these answers by shifting the burden of interpretation to the men in their lives, rephrasing the question to: "What will the kind of man I want to marry approve of? What choices on my part will he be willing to accept?" Personally, I think this only confuses the issue! History shows us that most of the changes in the lives of women have preceded rather than followed men's acceptance of them. But certainly there is no doubt that our interpretations of what we think men think is a strong factor in our decisions.

However, we also know that men, like women, are capable of changing their attitudes and interpretations through the years. During the past fifty years, many women have done many things their grandfathers would not have approved of — but their male contemporaries still find them attractive, desirable, and feminine. On the other hand, some women have alienated themselves from masculine approval by behaving in ways that men find unattractive. An examination of some of these changes and ways of behaving may give us some clues to what makes sports participation "desirable" or "undesirable" for young women like you, who live in the United States in the second half of the twentieth century.

You have many privileges your grandmothers did not have. You have the right to vote and participate in the political life of your country; you have the privilege of working for money outside of your home by choice as well as from necessity; and general acceptance of the belief that women and girls may enjoy participating in active sports is demonstrated by your conference here, today. These privileges were not acquired suddenly nor by accident. Each one marks the culmination of a long struggle against the traditional belief that the word "person" refers only to men.

When the Constitution of the United States was written, there was no statement in it referring to women. None was needed. Everyone just took it for granted that the rights and privileges guaranteed to persons and citizens belonged only to men, because women were not then considered to be "persons"; they were "only females." And so on a memorable election day in 1872 when Susan B. Anthony challenged this traditional belief by attempting to enter a polling place to cast a vote, she was arrested, tried, and fined for "breaking the law" — solely on the grounds that she was a female. Forty-eight years later, in 1920, the Nineteenth Amendment was added to the Constitution to change this interpretation. It was done in a somewhat backhanded way by stating: "The rights of citizens. . .shall not be denied or abridged on account of sex." The wording was ambiguous, but the implications were crystal clear. Henceforth women were to be accorded the rights of citizens. "Females" had been officially recognized as "persons" by an Act of Congress.

Aside from telling you something about your own historical background, this story illustrates a very important point. In 1872, men believed so firmly that women should not vote that they put a distinguished lady in jail for trying to do so. By 1920, they were sufficiently convinced of the error in previous male beliefs to reluctantly accord women the right to vote and hold office. Today, in 1959, they no longer question our right to vote as persons and citizens; they even chide us at times because we do not fully avail ourselves of our voting privileges. What was considered "wrong" for women in 1872 is not only "right" for women in 1959, it is also considered "desirable."

In the business world, there was no Act of Congress to give official recognition to the fact that women as persons were also competent workers. Women entered man's world of paid employment one by one, each woman having to make her own decision to brave the disapproval she might incur from the men in her life. And so it has been, too, in what was once the man's world of sports. Women athletes did not exchange their trailing skirts and hatpins for white cotton shorts in one dramatic moment of transformation. They edged into sports rather gingerly, moving slowly from one innovation to the next — always with one eye on the men they hoped to marry to see how far they could go without being ostracized.

But as a result of these daring feminine invasions into the once masculine realms of business and sports, beliefs about women and attitudes toward them have undergone many changes during the twentieth century. Today in the United States it is generally recognized that voting, working, and playing are human privileges, not restricted to either sex. But this recognition has not blurred the unchangeable fact that men and women are different *kinds* of human beings. Today the important question is: How should the important differences between men and women modify the behavior of male and female human beings as they vote and work and play? The answer to that question is now being formulated by women like you, as you weigh and evaluate your own behavior in relation to your own interpretation of your role as female human beings.

When women first entered the man's world of paid employment, the only model they had to follow was the one that had been set by men. So in the early days many women believed that the way to succeed was to copy the men's model. They copied men's suits, their shirts, even their neckties — and adopted a frozen-faced brusque manner. But women are *not* men — and when people try to be something they are not, they make themselves ridiculous. They were not even good carbon copies of their models; they were caricatures of the men they tried to imitate. Men did not admire these cartoons of themselves. They ridiculed them and avoided them outside of their offices — but they kept on hiring them because they were useful.

As women got used to being in the man's world which had become a woman's world too, they felt less need to prove that they were "like men" and became more like themselves. They softened their tailored suits into feminine dressmaker models and discarded the stiff collars and neckties. As their manner also softened, they did not revert to tea-table manners or the coyness of flirtation; instead they developed a new way of behaving that was appropriate to the business situation while still being characterized by the feminine qualities of graciousness, pleasantness, and courteous consideration of other people.

In the process of adapting themselves to the business world, women learned two important lessons. They discovered that they could win the respect of men no matter what job they did, as long as they did that job well; and they found to their delight that no matter what job they did, they would still be liked and loved as women as long as they looked and acted like the attractive women they were. Today the "woman's look" is an essential part of the business and professional world; and certainly the fact that a young woman has a job does not make her seem less desirable to the kind of man she hopes to marry!

As the "woman's look" has developed in business, the ways in which the important differences between men and women modify their working lives have become increasingly evident. This is too long a story to tell here, but in general it may be said that women have discovered they are best adapted to certain *kinds* of employment, most of which are now identified as "women's fields." Within those fields, it is evident that most women are not competing *against* men, but rather have found ways to work *with* men in the complex business world, and they have developed working patterns that include their homes, husbands and babies. There are some exceptions to this generalization. Some women have found and will continue to find success, satisfaction, and acceptance in jobs usually performed by men. On the job they compete with men on equal terms, neither asking for favors nor offering them. And, it is significant to note, this does not seem to bar them from happy and successful marriages. But, within the framework of our own culture at the present time, it now appears evident that most working women — which includes most of the women of your generation — will find greater satisfaction and more complete acceptance of themselves as women by choosing their jobs in a "woman's field."

The modern "woman's look" in sports has been compounded out of the same elements of innovation, mistakes, and modifications. Much that was considered "wrong" for grandmother is now "right" for you — and many activities that seemed "undesirable" for your mothers have become so "desirable" that they are taught to you in college.

In athletics, as in business, the early women competitors took men for their models, and a few girls still do. But the girls who dressed like men, walked like men, and shouted and swore like men did not prove that men and women are alike. They only underlined the fact that men and women are different. Most of these caricatures who made a travesty of the very goal they sought — the right to participate in sports — have now vanished. They have been replaced by attractive women wearing feminine clothes that are designed to give them freedom to move. Voluminous bloomers have given way to shorts, and year by year the shorts have become shorter — but they are not men's shorts. Hair has been cut short for convenience — but these short coiffures are not men's hair cuts. Girls shout as they play, but they do not shout in men's voices. Today's feminine athletes play hard and they play to win, but they play like women. They have learned to be gracious in victory and good-humored in defeat, and they have brought to the sports arena the belief that people are more important than scores, and friends more important than trophies. When the game is over, they take their showers, put on fresh make-up, and don their feminine blouses, skirts and sweaters, ready to meet their opponents as the friends they are — friends who have offered them their best efforts on the cooperative testing-ground of competition.

The second lesson women in business had to learn was that they could be respected as workers only if they did the job well. And this, too, has been true in the world of sports. Girls who play awkwardly, fumble the ball, don't know the rules, or try to be "cute" on the playing field are not admired by either women or men. They, too, are caricatures, — cartoons of women as athletes; and men make fun of them both privately and publicly. But girls who play well can become hot, sweaty, and red in the face and still be admired, because skilled performance is always beautiful, and men respect skilled performers.

In sports as in business, women have also discovered that they are more successful in certain types of games and less well adapted to others. Out of the long list of activities in which men participate, women have gradually selected those which seem best suited to the interpretation of what "being a woman" means in the cultural pattern of the United States. They have taken these "women's sports" and modified them to suit their needs, establishing both their own rules and their own feminine standards of competition, which differ from the men's rules and standards in many ways. But just as some exceptional women in business have found satisfaction working in so-called "men's jobs," so we must recognize that women can enjoy putting the shot, hurling the discus, running the high hurdles, and performing gymnastic feats. If they enjoy doing these things and are able to do them well, there is nothing "wrong" about doing them, even though our particular cultural interpretation may not include them in the list of sports considered "desirable" for women.

Within our own "women's sports" and women's pattern of competition, both the range of sports and the intensity of competition have greatly increased during the past twenty years. This expansion has raised many new questions about what practices are "desirable" in feminine competition. The answers to these questions affect the programs of your WAA's, WRA's, and URA's — and much of your discussion at this conference will be concerned with them. But as you debate the questions related to interscholastic competition, national tournaments, and co-recreation, I hope you will find a few moments to consider a much more complicated question that underlies your whole interpretation of yourselves as persons and sportswomen.

I think we are past the point of arguing about whether or not girls should "play to win." Of course they should, for this is the very essence of sportsmanlike conduct — to honor your opponent by offering her your very best efforts in the contest you have agreed to wage, both committed to use all of your resources within the rules of the game. If either contestant does less than this, she is guilty of unsportsmanlike conduct. She is "throwing the game," making a travesty of the spirit of competition by giving her opponent points she has not earned. And what meaning does a score have when one opponent "fixes it" by adding or subtracting points at will? If there are differences in skill, they can be openly recognized at the outset by establishing a handicap — and then both players can enjoy the exhilaration of "going all out," using their best efforts in truly sportsmanlike play.

Good sportswomen know what sportsmanship means, and when they play with other sportswomen, they engage wholeheartedly in the contest. But what happens when they play against men in what we have come to call co-recreation? Do they still play an equally honest game? Or do they confuse the purpose of the game with some private estimate of the effect that winning or losing may have on their male companion-opponent? Do they sometimes argue "if I win the game I may lose the man"? Does this argument justify the unsportsmanlike conduct of "throwing the game" by playing below their own top level skill?

Yes, I know the other side of the question, too. But I think we need to consider two other very important questions first. What kind of a person am I? What kind of a man do I want to marry?

Am I the kind of a person who cheats to accomplish my own purposes? Is dishonesty in such a small thing as a game of tennis a good basis for a lifelong relationship? If this man will accept the thinly veiled insult of being given points he has not earned — if he is such a poor sport that he will sulk if he loses a game — how good a marriage risk is he?

Perhaps you can win your man by pretending to lose the game; but doesn't a marriage founded on pretenses, cheating, and unsportsmanlike conduct rest on very shaky foundations? Pretense in tennis can commit you to a lifetime of "playing pretend" in the hope of being loved for what you are *not* rather than for what you are. So why not take a chance? You may lose a date or two by playing an honest game — but you may also win a good sportsman for a husband — and that kind of man is worth waiting for!

The old belief that men must always excel women in everything rested on the false belief that women were not really people. Today, both men and women know that they are — and they know that sports ability is not restricted to either sex. Perhaps this fact is not yet fully accepted by either men or women — but neither have all people yet accepted the fact that human ability is not limited by race, color, creed, or "previous condition of servitude." Yet everywhere in the world good sportsmen and sportswomen are making important contributions to the development of the attitudes of democracy, not only in sports, but in work and in marriage as well. I think attractive girls like you can well afford whatever risks there may be in playing an honest game in the hope of furthering the development of those attitudes.

I can not promise you a husband who will love you for what you truly are, but I can point out that history shows that most of women's fears about the consequences of behaving like honest persons have proved groundless. Men resisted the idea of women in the business world; but today's successful business women are no less desirable to men seeking a mate than their grandmothers were. So, too, many men resist the *idea* that any woman can excel them in sports; but there is no evidence that good sportswomen lack for suitors. Rather, when they use their sports skills within the framework of truly gracious and womanly behavior, this seems to make them more, rather than less, attractive to the kind of men they want to marry.

There never have been any really easy answers to any of the important questions about human beings and their relationships with each other. Both the questions and the answers have changed many times through the years, and they will continue to change in the years to come. But in conferences like this one, young women like you will help to shape the answers that are most valid for college women living in the United States in the present moment of history — and in part for all women of all countries in the future.

So what is the "woman's look" in sports in your time? As I see it represented in this conference, I believe it has two identifiable aspects linked together in the phrase: She is a good sportswoman. As a good sport, she plays the game well and she plays it as a game, respecting both the rules and the spirit of the game that provide her with a diversion that serves as a testing-ground, larger than a chessboard, but smaller than life itself. As a woman, she looks like a woman, acts like a woman, and has established her own friendly, gracious, honest, and womanly pattern of sports participation. And so she has brought to the world of sport and the world of women a new look — the look of the twentieth century woman who is every inch a person — a sports-loving person — an attractive, feminine person — a lovely person who is lovable, and therefore greatly loved.

Folklore, Fiction, and Fantasy

Biennial Conference of the National Association for Physical Education
of College Women — Excelsior Springs, Missouri — April, 1958

Men have always talked about women — and the words they have
said and written about us are beyond counting — words of praise and
blame, words of sentiment and annoyance, words of fascination and
irritation, and above all words expressing man's confusion about that
noble, tantalizing, frustrating, and indispensable creature — the female
of the species.

In recent years women have begun to talk and write about themselves — and in all truth it must be said that they seem to find themselves just as confusing and contradictory as the men have found them.
But before we get to that we must take a brief look at the male point
of view because it does help to explain much of our present confusion
about ourselves.

Whatever men have said about women through the years, either
flattering or unflattering, the underlying theme has been: "Man's desire is woman's duty." Except in the matriarchal cultures — which have
been few in number — men have always taken it for granted that it
was their right to decide what a woman *should* be. Accordingly, they
set up their own "job specifications" for the task of "being a woman";
and when women failed to meet these specifications the men were

greatly annoyed with them — even though their several sets of specifications were sometimes mutually contradictory.

Perhaps the most comprehensive itemization of what men thought
a woman *should* be is the one found in *Proverbs*, Chapter 31, beginning: "A virtuous woman who shall find? Her price is above rubies."
Virtuous, as used here, has no sexual connotations, but certainly the
woman described would have been worth many fine rubies to any
husband. She had strong arms and willing hands. She sought flax and
wool and spun them into fine garments for her family, made coverings
of silk and purple for herself, and wove belts of fine linen to sell to
the merchants. She brought food from afar, and with the fruits of her
industry she bought a field and with her own hands planted and tended
a vineyard. Her "candle goeth not out at night," but she was still up
before dawn to give meat to her household and feed the poor and needy.
Her industry and thrift promoted her husband's career; her own bearing and demeanor enhanced his reputation; and she spoke always with
wisdom and kindness. Small wonder that her husband as well as her
children rose up and called her blessed. She, herself, looked forward
to her own rejoicing only "in time to come."

Even allowing for poetic license, this is a pretty big order for any
woman. But this was not all. The literature shows that men also desired a quite different creature, one that Shakespeare described as
"a tiger's heart wrapped in a woman's hide" — the hide of the docile
homemaker. According to Sophocles, this paradoxical paragon never
asked questions or argued about anything. He put it bluntly: "Women
should be seen and not heard." (But when they had to speak, as we all
know so well, their voices were ever soft, gentle, and low — an excellent
thing in woman.) Legally, however, it made little difference whether
they spoke or not, because no one listened to them. As Blackstone put
it: "In marriage, the husband and wife are one, and the husband is
that one."

For many centuries men believed that "men have marble, women
waxen minds" — but somehow the marble often failed to make a lasting
impression on the wax. In their own devious ways, even the most
docile helpmeets found ways to outwit their husbands, and the "tiger
hearts" were adept at twisting strong men around their slightest whim.
Men found this irritating, because they simply could not understand
how women managed to get around them — and they expressed this
irritation by attributing to women a long list of sneaky and vengeful
characteristics that take up several columns in the index to Bartlett's
Familiar Quotations. Of course, in their more sentimental moments, they
also called them ministering angels touched with a spark of heavenly

176

ON WOMEN AND SPORT

fire, and many other good and noble things — but I shall spare you that list because you have heard it many times — and at times believed every word of it was true.

The lists of adjectives compiled by women were not recorded for inclusion in Bartlett, but then, as now, they described men in two sets of terms. One set they recited to men's faces — and the men accepted them as true; the other set was mentioned only in the privacy of the ladies' sewing circle — a list of terms men would have found quite incomprehensible.

Human beings being what they are, there was probably some measure of truth in every adjective, good and bad, on all four lists; and, human beings being what they are, we may be sure that love did temper many of the angry words of irritation, just as human compassion gave greater validity to the words of tenderness and admiration. The tragedy of the past lies not in the contradictions in these lists but in the fact that the irritation was intensified and the healing power of love was weakened by the very *nature* of the assumptions that defined all relationships between men and women through the long centuries. Shakespeare put it succinctly: "Such duty as the subject owes his prince, even such a woman oweth to her husband."

A prince may relish authority, but the responsibility that goes with such authority often lies heavy on his shoulders. Humanly he is bound to feel that his authority to discharge that responsibility should never be challenged. Humanly, too, he is impelled to expect not only unquestioning obedience but also gratitude and admiration from the subjects whose lives depend upon his beneficence. For the subjects, the posture of perpetual obeisance is difficult to maintain, and even the most docile do become restive at times — even though the docile one may have no wish to accept the responsibilities that go with freedom. Thus, both the ruler and the ruled must at times feel abused and put-upon, and hostility flowing in subterranean channels must ever erupt in irritation about seemingly trivial matters.

But through the long years of history the prince and subject relationship was not confined to marriage. It was the accepted pattern for all human relationsihps. And it was a seemingly trivial matter — a tax on tea — that produced the eruption that challenged this concept of human authority over the lives of other human beings and established a new concept of human equality among men. In time this new way of life called democracy was extended to include female as well as male human beings. Considering the recency of this tradition-shattering interpretation, it is not surprising that women are confused about what they *are*, what they think they *should* be, and how they may best conduct themselves in this strange new world of human equality.

I have rehearsed our old griefs here not to dwell on them with bitterness, but to recognize the hold these old interpretations still have on our lives. From them we derive the folklore, the fictions, and the fantasies that vitiate our enjoyment of our new-found privileges and hold us back from a realistic attempt to find valid answers to the questions: What *is* a woman? What is her place in the grand design of life envisioned in terms of human equality and human worth?

Folklore embodies all of the traditional *beliefs* of our ancestors. We learned these beliefs from our parents, as they learned them from theirs, long before we were able to reason about them. As children, we accepted them implicitly as a part of all of the other knowledge we were gradually acquiring about "how the world is," and they became an integral part of our thinking about the world and ourselves. Accordingly, any attempt to challenge our folklore upsets us emotionally, because it disturbs the certainties by which we have always lived. Much of our confusion about "what a woman is" or what is *right* for a woman stems from this source.

If the belief being challenged is one that gives us status or special privilege, we become angry at the thought of being denied privileges to which we feel entitled. But if the belief being challenged is one which belittled us, we still cling to it with emotional fervor. Even in our own adulthood, going counter to what our parental authorities considered *right* makes us feel guilty of wrongdoing. This feeling of rightness has nothing to do with fact or logic. It is truly a "feeling," and our resistance to exploring it is far more emotional than rational. Like children who have defied their parents, this guilty feeling makes us angry, defiant, or defensive — attitudes which have characterized many women of our times who have done things their ancestors believed were not *right* for a woman to do.

Nonetheless, folklore can be challenged, as it has been many times, and with what Beatrice Webb has called "the inevitability of gradualness," it can be eventually obliterated from our attitudes.

In 1920, for example, Irene Castle set the world on its ears when she cut off what was then called "woman's crowning glory." This event, which would now pass without comment, was given far more publicity than the Nineteenth Amendment, which was finally ratified that same year. Editors editorialized about it. Preachers preached about it. And in many homes all across the country fathers and husbands were pounding the tables shouting: "No! It isn't *right* for women to cut their hair."

I know. I was sitting at one of those tables. My father, too, said: "You can't go against nature. If the Lord had intended your hair to be short, he would not have made it grow." Like many other girls, I became defiant. I said: "But Daddy, the Lord makes your hair grow, and you cut it off every Saturday night." And I, too, got the unanswerable answer: "That's different. I am a *man*."

In the end, I did what the one who is ruled has always done. I knew I couldn't win by force, so I resorted to strategy.

My hair was so long I could sit on it. The utility of that particular virtue escaped me then, as it escapes me now, but in 1920 this was considered the hallmark of femininity. Instead of sitting on my tresses, however, I made enormous "cootie cages" — in the style of the day — and then came to table nightly with the rest of my hair piled loosely into a crown that was anything but a glory. Truly, I was a sight to behold, and my father finally got tired of beholding it. He capitulated, choosing what must have seemed to him to be the lesser of two evils.

On a memorable Saturday night in 1921, my father, mother, sister and I walked solemnly to the barber shop, the *men's* barber shop. As the cold steel of the scissors slid beneath my ear, I almost panicked, for the horrifying thought could no longer be put off: What if I was wrong and Dad was right? Fortunately, I could see him in the mirror, and as he pulled out his handkerchief and blew his nose with great vigor in the traditional masculine attempt to conceal his emotions, I stiffened my resolve, and my hair fell to the floor in great swatches. Silently my mother bent and gathered my shorn locks together and wrapped them in tissue paper, and silently we all walked home.

After I had laid my cut-off hair in a bureau drawer, my mother got out the curling iron and tried to subdue the cropped ends so I could appear in church the next morning. I did — getting a mixed reception compounded of shrieks of congratulations at my daring, dubious approval, and much head-shaking over my temerity.

In time, people got used to it, and other girls cut their hair, one by one. Two years later my father merely shrugged his shoulders when my sister decided to have her hair cut, too. Fifteen years later my mother followed suit, but only because she thought it might relieve her headaches!

This is the story of all attempts to change traditional beliefs about what is *right* for women. Initially, they meet with tremendous resistance — and well they may because our awkward first attempts often seem disastrous. My first hair cut was atrocious! But as women experimented with short hair through the years, finding new ways to shape and curl their coiffures, they gradually found styles that were more becoming. As they did so, the resistance receded, and in time it was evident that there was no basic connection between a woman's virtue and the length of her hair. And it also became apparent that short hair did not necessarily make any woman "more like a man"; rather it was recognized that women had simply adopted a convenient solution to a common problem and adapted it to their own concept of femininity.

But the emotional hold our folklore has on us persists long after we have identified its fallacies. Significantly, I kept my discarded and useless hair wrapped in tissue paper in a bureau drawer for many years — imperishable evidence that I had once been everything my father thought a woman *should* be. Today, the emotions of women are still cluttered with many such treasured symbols of the past, symbols of our claims to special privileges, symbols that prove that we are what our grandfather believed we were, symbols that demand that we be treated as cherished subjects.

Folklore can usually be identified by our emotional reactions to it, but half-facts are far more slippery because they always have a basic element of truth in them. But it is a truth that holds good only under certain specific conditions as we extend the limited truth to a universally-true generalization.

One of our more pervasive half-fact forms of confusion stems from our tendency to identify *averages* as *norms* or as criteria of normality. This fallacy denies the uniqueness of the individual and his implicit human right to be as he was created.

Take, for example, the half-fact: Men are taller than women. It rests on the fact that the *average* height of men is about four or five inches greater than the *average* of women's heights. But an average is derived from a *range* in which, as we know from daily observation, many women are taller than some men, and conversely. The harm is done when we convert this statistical *average* derived from a *range* of heights into a *norm* — thus making tallness for men and shortness for women a criterion of normality. This leads us to subscribe to the popular belief that normal men *should be* taller than normal women, and thus we stigmatize as sexual oddities all short men and all tall women. This forces short men and tall women to the conclusion that they are not what a normal member of their own sex should be — and the emotional trauma suffered because of this fallacious belief is too well known to need explication here.

This tendency to convert half-facts into universal *shoulds* is the basis of much of our current confusion about the nature of women — and of men. This confusion is compounded by the quizzes in popular periodicals that ask: Are women more illogical? More verbal? Are men mechanically adept? More competitive? The "right" answers, found on the next page, tells us that "research shows" that they are. But what the research really shows is a difference between averages, found within two overlapping ranges of scores that indicate that the traits measured are about equally distributed in the two sexes.

Too, our society tends to encourage the development of these stereotypes. Little boys are given mechanos and erector sets; little girls are given dolls. Thus, "boys in general" tend to become more adept at working with machines, while "girls in general" tend to develop skill in folding diapers. But despite this early encouragement, many boys never learn to fix a leaky faucet, and many girls do learn to take down the carburetors in their own sports cars. Similarly, many girls do not become "good little mothers," while many men are remarkably adept in dealing with small children. (And I have noted, as you have, that some girls are highly competitive! And some men are averse to competition.)

This is not to say that there are *no* significant differences between men and women. There are; and they are important differences that affect every aspect of every woman's (or man's) life. But our uncritical conversion of the half-facts of averages into norms for femaleness and maleness obscure our understanding of these *real* differences, and the significance they have in structuring the roles each woman may play in her lifetime.

Our half-facts tend to support our folklore because our reliance on folklore as the basis of our *shoulds* has led us into these fallacious interpretations. Together, half-fact and folklore serve to perpetuate the stereotypes of masculinity and femininity which represent what our ancestors believed men and women *should* be. Our masculine stereotype embodies the qualities of the ideal and invincible frontiersman; our feminine stereotype portrays his ideal wife, an old-world hausfrau with a strong dash of courtesan. (Both types are satirically portrayed in Al Capp's comic strip of Little Abner and Daisy Mae — with further comment made in the characters of Abner's parents!)

In more serious vein, our acceptance of averages as norms that indicate what a "real man" or a "real woman" should be like has condemned many men and women to an unhappy choice between two grim alternatives. Either they feel that they must try to be something they are not or they must live with a feeling of failure and rejection born of being or doing what a man — or woman — *should not* be or do.

We women justify our attempts to fit ourselves into these old rigid molds on the grounds of necessity. At one level we claim that our hope of marriage depends on our ability to be "as men desire us"; at another level we claim that men rule the world outside the home, and our only hope of success lies in pleasing them. Certainly the price of not conforming to a generally accepted pattern may be very high — but is it higher than the price we pay in clinging to the conviction that we are obligated, at all costs, to keep the favor of *all* men — or at least to not irritate them too much?

Sadly enough, our own fearful pretenses drive men to pretenses that are even more painful — for our skill in pretending only serves to convince them that we will not love *them* if they fail to measure up to the male stereotype we seem to be holding up before them. The pressure this fear of not measuring up to male norms puts on men is far greater than any pressure we women live under, for the masculine stereotype of the absolutely invincible creature who is superior in *all* things is an ideal no human being can possibly attain. We women can always excuse our failures by retreating to the old belief that we really are "the weaker sex." Men can find no such relief from their own self-condemnation.

The logical solution of separating the facts from the half-facts and trying to live honestly with ourselves as we are requires great emotional maturity from both sexes. Human beings being what they are, such objectivity is not easy to attain. But what is the alternative? Do we women want to kneel forever before our princes? There are those who believe that we do, no matter how much our knees may pain us and our necks may ache from the continual strain of looking up in search of loving approval. But we must not overlook the fact that maintaining this awkward posture forces our princes to look down — and their necks, too, may well ache from the continual strain of a bent head. Perhaps if we women could find the faith we need to stand upright so we might communicate with our princes at the eye-to-eye level of human dignity, human worth, and human individuality, we might have fewer irritating headaches — and the men's headaches, too, might be decreased by the privilege of maintaining a fully erect posture.

But are men ready to relinquish the stereotype of male superiority? Some are; many are not. And many women will still choose the bent-knee, bent-neck posture. But many of us in this room have surely reached the age and emotional security that will enable us to risk some male disapproval. Perhaps the finest contribution we can make to democracy is to get off our knees and look our male associates in the face at eye level — not belligerently, not defiantly, but naturally and pleasantly, as befits women of our stature. Certainly we who have established ourselves in a profession once limited to men can afford to take whatever risks our choice may entail — for we have nothing to lose and much to gain by taking the kinks out of our necks. Certainly this will irritate the more neurotic of our male associates whose belief in their own superiority must be nourished by conviction of the inferiority of other people. But what is accomplished by making their neuroses our neuroses? And I am sure, too, that we shall also find that many men will find us easier to deal with as easing the crick in our knees and the kink in our necks takes some of the irritability out of *us*. Equally, I am sure that we will like ourselves much better in the erect posture we have so often recommended to our students.

But we must move on to fiction. The fiction writer begins with a scene or situation which resembles "reality" to the extent that the reader can recognize a world somewhat like his own. Within this world, the writer then creates characters with whom the reader can identify — perhaps much like himself or other people he may know. The story revolves around a problem which the reader recognizes or might conceivably have experienced in his own life. The job of the fiction writer is to solve that problem, — and he must solve it, or create the illusion of having solved it, in a finite segment of time. He does this by tampering with the realities of life. He picks and chooses among the relevant facts, ignoring some, emphasizing others. Then he organizes these selected "facts" into a pattern which seems to provide a solution for the problem by banishing it forever from the lives of his characters.

Of the many pervasive fictions that clutter up women's lives, perhaps none is more damaging than the belief that the grass is always greener on other people's lawns than it is on our own. The argument runs something like this: My own problems make me unhappy. Therefore, people who do not have my problems must be happier than I am. The fictional element is obvious. We reach this conclusion by ignoring *their* problems, thus eliminating them from the story.

The greener-grass fiction takes many forms. In the "good old days" when men were men and women were females, and let's have no nonsense about equality, grandma did not have the problems we do today. Therefore, according to many popular fiction writers, grandma was much happier than we are. This leads to the solution that women find happiness by forsaking the ways of equality and returning to the ways of their grandmothers. It is a wonderful, sweeping solution, which provides the "pat answer" to everything that troubles women and men today. But like all fictions it ignores part of the facts. It ignores the problems that grandma — and grandpa — had, and the complexity of their lives, which were different, but no less complex, than our own. It ignores, too, the fact that the clock of history can not be turned back.

How happy were your own grandmothers and great aunts? Did all of them spend their days singing hymns of joy? Or do you number among your female ancestors — and male ancestors — at least one or two who were cranky, cantankerous, and downright neurotic? I'm sure you do — and equally I am sure that you will find among your ancestors of both sexes some solid, good citizens who did what was required of them in their moment of history — and did it with cheerful countenances.

One of my own great-grandmothers produced 22 children in 21 years! She accomplished this remarkable feat by bearing five pairs of twins. I'm sure she had a full life; certainly it was a productive one — although there *is* an element of excessive repetition in it. I don't know how happy she was, and my guess is that she was probably too busy to ask that question. But I do know that I do not envy her. Probably I have problems which she did not have — but neither do I have to cope with 22 offspring. Another of my great-grandmothers was five feet tall and weighed 290 pounds — but that is another story.

Fiction provides an appealing approach to the problems of our lives. If we could only ignore the facts that make our problems complex, life could be so beautiful! The deluding element in fiction, however, often leads us to subscribe to the illusion of a "better reality," and motivates us to reject the realities in our own human situation, as it is. Accordingly, we refuse to make the effort the human situation demands of those who attempt to deal with real problems in a constructive way.

Our fictions are not always rooted in the past. We have our contemporary ones — such as the belief that "other women" are more fortunate than I am. The homemaker envies the woman who has her own pay check; the woman with the pay check envies the woman who has "nothing to do" all day. And both ignore the dry sandy patches of tedium and the devil-grass of responsibility that mar her neighbor's lawn, while belittling the green grass that grows on her own domain. What both really want is the "better reality" of privilege without price — a fictional reality that is mighty hard to find in any world! And it is interesting to note that our relative evaluation of other women's lives seldom extends to the widow with three children who cleans the floors in our office buildings after we vacate them. "Poor thing! That is *her* misfortune. But her problems must be worked out as best she can resolve them — because that is how life *is*."

Fiction always maintains the semblance of reality. It becomes fantasy when we create an entirely new world out of whole cloth. In fantasy, if we need a little green man with a pointed head, we create him — and if we need to disintegrate him, it is a simple task to create a gun that will blow him to bits. In short, in fantasy we create a world designed to satisfy our own desires and needs. Such fantasies as may be created by a great writer like Ray Bradbury can be delightful reading. So, too, our own fantasies can be equally delightful. But they become disastrous when we begin to *believe* in the world we have created. This is the essence of neurosis — to believe that the world *should* conform to some personal fantasy. The essence of psychosis is to believe that it *does!*

One fantasy we have all heard expounded many times — often on the Career Day we arrange for college women — is: Women today can do anything that men can do. To support this shopworn statement we trot out the fact that some women are now listed in every job classification identified by the Census Bureau. This does demonstrate that one or more women have managed to work in all major job classifications, but even at this level it ignores the facts about women's employment, so beautifully assembled by the National Manpower Commission in the book called *Womanpower*. Essentially, the majority of women now working are employed in areas classified as "women's jobs," and those who are working in areas commonly reserved to men are, in general, performing these men's jobs in their own woman's way. The entire pattern of women's employment, as it has developed during the past fifty years, is almost totally different from the pattern of male employment; and *Womanpower* makes it clear that women are working "like women" in ways that are identified with the female values in their own lives. As women did with short hair cuts, so, too, they have done with the right to work — they have adopted a principle and then adapted it to fit their own female and feminine requirements.

The fantasy that women can do anything men can do is easily extended to the more fantastic statement: Any woman can do anything she wants to. To the girls at Career Day this suggests that I, being a woman, can do anything I would like to do. And after graduation this is readily transformed into the neurotic belief that I *should* be able to do anything I want to do — and any person or condition which prevents me from doing this is therefore *wrong*. But this puts us squarely in the never-never land of neuroticism, verging on the psychotic's belief that he is actually the creator and ruler of the world of fantasy in which he lives.

This fantasy of a world in which a woman *should* be able to do anything she wants to do runs through many of the books that are one long whine, however humorously expressed, about "the dilemma" in which educated women find themselves. This same neurotic strain also confuses many of our current attempts to find valid answers to the democratic questions: What *is* a woman? — and its inevitable counterpart — What *is* a man?

Certainly it is difficult for all of us, complex and fallible human beings that we are, to be objective about ourselves as we try to identify our own common needs, as well as our own uniquely individual potential for contributing to the grand design of human life. It is to our credit that we hold meetings such as this one to try to sort out the facts on which to base our own conclusions about what is appropriate for women in our time. And perhaps it will be helpful to all of us to recognize that our thinking on these questions is never purely rational.

We are the products of our history. Our folklore has a strong hold on our emotions; we are prone to accept half-facts as universal truths because we have so long been accustomed to the stereotypes they describe; we cling to our comforting fictions; and like all ego-motivated individuals we try to evade acceptance of our own human limitations by complaining that the world is not what it should be.

But if we can not immediately change every element of our all-to-human natures, perhaps we can at least recognize our own human predispositions. If we can not wipe out the consequences of our history with one quick wave of the hand, perhaps we can recognize the factors that helped to shape that history. And as we live in our own time — as all human beings have always had to do — perhaps we can recognize that our own behavior will help to write the history of the future.

Our own moment in history will demand its own concessions and its own compromises within the democratic ideal of a freedom in which all persons can stand erect in their own implicit right to be what they are, as they were created. But if we truly believe in this ideal, we can move it a little farther toward reality by trying to exemplify its premises in our own lives. To us, the American women born in the twentieth century, much has been given. Accordingly, much may be demanded of us. May we find the faith we need in ourselves to give freely whatever life may demand. May we give it cheerfully, pleasantly, and objectively — accepting without complaint the "inevitability of gradualness," even as we accept our human fallibility as implicit in the human conditon. And as we move forward together, may we now and then find time to laugh with each other about our own inconsistencies in the healing atmosphere of mutuality engendered by gathering together around a banquet table like this one.

The Education of Women in an Evolving Democracy

Lake Geneva Workshop of the National Association for Physical Education of College Women — Williams Bay, Wisconsin — June, 1956

The meaning of dynamic words like education, women, and democracy is continually changing. At any moment in history our interpretation of them is compounded of folklore, fact, fiction, and faith. Folklore, which has been defined as the traditional beliefs preserved unreflectively among a people, may easily be mistaken for fact. The snail's pace of cultural change may deceive us into believing that the facts of change are only fictions; and the persistence of cultural lags may evoke a cynicism which makes a mockery of faith. Failure to differentiate folklore from fact may convert honest searches for better solution into angry attempts to pin the blame of history on some convenient scapegoat. And inability to reconcile faith with fact can lead to the "magic answers" of fantasy and wishful thinking which vitiate the emotional stamina needed to take the next step forward.

Certainly all of these elements are present in current controversies about education. Without question they complicate our attempts to interpret the concept of democracy at home and abroad. And when we come to talk about women, they shroud every discussion with a pall of confusion within which every statement can easily run into head-on collision with a contradictory belief. Perhaps it will be helpful in clari-

186

ON WOMEN AND SPORT   187

fying some of our discussions at this workshop if we take time to look
at the history out of which these confused attitudes have come.

Our evolving democracy is only 180 years old. It was born during
the closing years of the eighteenth century when a group of men who
valued liberty more than life challenged the authoritarian dictates of
a powerful king. Rallying around the slogans of "no taxation without
representation" and "no government without the consent of the governed," they overthrew their authoritarian ruler and established a new
social order. But as they wrote their Constitution — a statement of faith
in human dignity and human worth which has never been surpassed
— they fell into the subtle trap of orthodoxy. Accepting without question the folklore of their time, they perpetuated in their Constitution
the very inequities against which they, as individuals, had rebelled.
The truth they had proclaimed as self-evident — that all men are created equal — did not apply to men whose skins were black. And the
"unalienable rights" which their Constitution guaranteed were categorically denied to the female half of the population.

Certainly they felt no guilt about their inconsistencies. They believed that black men were not really the same kind of human beings
that white men were. And if Martha Washington had said to the Father
of Our Country, "But Mr. Washington, what about us women?" he
would have been honestly astonished. He might have said: "Don't ask
silly questions, Martha. Everyone knows that a female's place is in her
home where she can be cared for by her husband or her father."

Obviously there was an element of convenience in these beliefs.
They made life easier for white men and they fortified the white male
ego with recognition of its own superior status. (The white males did
not recognize that these beliefs also imposed a heavy strain upon them,
making it necessary for them to continually *be* superior in all things,
trying to prove something for which there was no proof — both being
impossible assignments for any human being.) However, they accepted
their folklore as fact and tried to live with its consequences, because
these beliefs had never been seriously challenged in their time.

But these white males soon encountered difficulties in interpreting
the word "equality" even when they applied it only to themselves,
because all men were not equally endowed with every trait and ability.
Some could do this and others could do that. Duties had to be defined;
laws and rules had to be made; and there was much discontent about
every decision because each decision always ate away a bit of someone's personal freedom to do as he pleased. And this in turn chipped
away at the feeling of male privileged superiority which each of them
had transferred from the group generalization to himself as a person.

Three-quarters of a century later, their inability to agree among themselves about one of these decisions plunged them into war. When the war ended, no one was completely satisfied by the outcome, but as a result of it they did amend their Constitution to include men of every "race, color, and previous condition of servitude" in their still disputed definition of "equality." But they continued to perpetuate the rest of their old orthodoxy by rejecting the first woman's suffrage bill which was introduced in the same decade.

Even the Great Emancipator presumably felt no guilt about refusing Mrs. Lincoln the rights of citizenship. A verse written on the occasion of a friend's wedding expressed this point of view.

> *The woman was not taken*
>   *From Adam's head, we know*
> *To show she must not rule him —*
>   *'Tis evidently so.*
> *The woman she was taken*
>   *From under Adam's arm,*
> *So she must be protected*
>   *From injuries and harm.*

Many women agreed with Mr. Lincoln — and many women still do; but a few did not. Lucretia Mott and Elizabeth Cady Stanton led the first Women's Rights Convention at Seneca Falls, N. Y., in 1848, and during the next three-quarters of a century many valiant women defied the folklore of their time and tried to speed up the slow process of social evolution. Among those pioneers were:

Susan B. Anthony, Carrie Chapman Catt, Dr. Anna Howard Shaw, Ida Husted Harper, and Charlotte Perkins Gilman in the women's suffrage movement; Clara Barton in the Red Cross; Emma Willard, Alice Freeman Palmer, Virginia Gildersleeve, and Aurelia Reinhart in education; Ida M. Tarbell and the adventuresome Nelly Bly in journalism; Jane Adams in social work; the redoubtable Hetty Green in Wall Street; Margaret Sanger and her fight for planned parenthood; Eleanora Sears in sports — and a host of others.

More closely related to many of us are our own professional ancestors: Catherine Beecher, Mrs. Mary Hemenway, Amy Morris Homans, Delphine Hanna, Eliza and Clelia Mosher, Lillian Curtis Drew, Ethel Perrin, Jessie Bancroft, Helen McKinstry, Mary Channing Coleman — and each of us honors still other names we would add to this list.

The lives of all of these women were a protest against the social folklore which was sustained by the legal definitions of their time.

They challenged the belief in a categorical male superiority and dared to invade the territories which men believed were reserved exclusively for males. They were mocked, derided, and sometimes accused of being traitors to their own sex. Their tactics sometimes betrayed the desperation born of repeated rebuffs and defeat. They were aggressive in an age when women were expected to be submissive, and at times their own defensive behavior alienated the very persons who might have been most helpful to them. But they stayed by their guns, and in 1920 their combined efforts were rewarded as the legal bastion of male superiority toppled and fell. The Constitution was amended for the nineteenth time and the definitions of democracy were enlarged by adding the sentence: "The rights of citizens. . .shall not be denied or abridged. . .on account of sex." The women of the United States could no longer be described as "only females." They had been legally defined to be persons.

Most of us women in this room experienced this dramatic transition in our own lives, because all of us who admit to being "past thirty-six" were born females and became persons by legal definition. Consequently we inherited the female orthodoxy of our past tempered by the dedication of the women who had rebelled against it. We became the first generation in a new social order. There will never be another generation quite like us!

There were no precedents to guide our gallant and confused generation. The pioneers had opened up a new territory. It was up to us to blaze the trails in it and establish the outlines of the new settlements. All things considered, I think we did a remarkably good job. We do not always recognize the extent of the territory we have settled because it consists of so many scattered patches — an acre here, a square foot there, each made safer for the members of the next generation of women by some one of us who had the courage to transcend the folklore of our own time and accept the risks entailed in social nonconformity as we explored the democratic premises.

The ratification of two amendments to the Constitution provided a legal basis for "equality," but the gap between legal definition and social interpretation could not be spanned immediately. There were too many questions which still had to be answered in the hearts and lives of men and women. The most fundamental ones were, and still are: What are the common qualities of human beings which give all persons the common worth implied by the word "equality"? How is this universal equality modified by specific individual differences such as skin color, sex, and other native endowments? What kinds of interactions among persons who differ from each other in significant ways are most rewarding in a democratic society?

These questions are not easy to answer, and our patience has been tried many times by our human inability to find universally acceptable designs for all of the intricate human relationships covered by them. Meanwhile, personal convictions and social customs based on the folk-lore of male white superiority still govern many of our attitudes and actions. Many overt and subtle limitations are still imposed upon all nonwhite citizens, and the heritage of an ideology which proclaimed women as "the weaker sex" still influences all relationships between men and women.

Many studies of human behavior have demonstrated that the inter-action between two status differentiated groups is a stereotype. It mat-ters little whether the difference between groups stems from race, sex, religious belief, political philosophy, money, or power, − or who hap-pens to be sitting in the saddle. The "superior" group can be tolerant about the "inferior" group as long as it "keeps its place" − which means the place of inferiority. But the "superior" group turns vicious when the "inferior" group tries to invade the "places" which symbolize their superior status.

As groups and as individuals we women who have been trying to find a place for ourselves in a world once reserved for men have not always recognized this sociological truth. Had we been able to do so, we would have recognized that much of the resistance we have en-countered was not directed against us either as a sex or as individuals − it was only a sociological phenomenon! We might still have resented it, but we might have wasted less of our emotional ammunition by con-tinually firing away at the wrong targets. And we might have been more slow to anger if we had recognized our own propensity for falling into the same subtle sociological trap when we were identified with groups whose categorical "superiority" was defined on some other basis.

For the benefit of our younger members, let me review the general outlines of these stereotyped reactions exhibited by men when women began to invade the male precincts.

Men said: "Women are all right as long as they keep their place." "You can't trust women. They will take advantage of any kindness you show them." Men generalized about women, attributing to the whole sex all of the undesirable characteristics displayed by any of them. Emotional outbursts, incompetency, or inefficiency were described as "acting like women" or "just like a woman." Contrariwise, any behavior of which men approved was considered an exception to the general rule, and was often described in masculine terms. "For a woman, she has done a remarkably good job." "She thinks like a man." And "she is as good as any man when it comes to getting a job done."

As employers, men paid women lower salaries than they paid men doing the same job. Women were promoted only if they were outstandingly superior to the men with whom they were competing for a job — and not always then. Men were willing to let women work *for* them, but their emotional hackles rose when women moved into positions which carried equal status. And when women began to move into positions which gave them authority over men, many men experienced a feeling of humiliation about being "bossed by a woman" which was almost unbearable.

Like any other minority group, women were guilty of the corresponding stereotyped responses. Categorical inferiority always has its privileges as well as its limitations. We resented the limitations but we were loathe to relinquish the privileges. We wanted to be protected and taken care of. We were reluctant to take on major responsibilities, preferring to leave major decision-making to the men. Politically, professionally, educationally, and personally we subscribed to the belittling generalizations about our sex by refusing to utilize the skill of women statesmen, lawyers, physicians, professors, and ministers. (It is significant in this connection that gynecology and obstetrics are still the medical specialties in which women have great difficulty establishing themselves.) We reflected men's scornful attitudes by poking fun at "hen parties" and the "old biddies" in our schools and women's organizations. Privately, each one of us considered herself an exception to the generalizations about women, and we often denied ourselves the support we might have found in mutual association with other "biddies" like ourselves (both young and old) because we did not want the men to identify us with them. Again and again we talked out of both sides of our mouths, proclaiming our "right" to equality with one breath while denying it in the next.

We belittled both ourselves and the men by assuming that they would reject us if we behaved naturally in any situation. We fawned upon them, flattered their egos, and did our best to conceal our own natural ability. Again and again we "threw the game," not only in sports but in all of our dealings with men. This betrayal of our own ego-needs made us caustic, vindictive, and defensive. Unable to face our own self-contempt for refusing to try to win by using all of our abilities, we projected our contempt to the men, accusing them of insisting that we must always let them win. We never gave men a chance to behave like human beings, and yet we were angry with them because they did not do so. And again and again we availed ourselves of

the "minority excuse," attributing every failure to men's determination
to hold us back, never admitting that we might at times have failed
because of our own personal inadequacies.

In short, like every other inferior status group, we tended to accept
a stereotype which had some elements of truth in it and behaved as
if it were universally true for all individuals. We could not admit, even
to ourselves, that many of our difficulties stemmed from our unwilling-
ness to risk the consequences of breaking that stereotype — and yet we
were often angry because the men did not do so.

If I seem to be castigating my own generation, I do so more in
sorrow than in anger. We had so much to gain, and so little to lose
except our own sense of inferiority. Both our lack of understanding and
our human frailty made us behave as insecure human beings always do
when they get caught in a status struggle. We were in the thick of it,
and our wounds were many and painful, so perhaps we may forgive
ourselves for taking them so personally. But we can forgive ourselves
only if we also forgive the men whose behavior has been equally human. And we can accept our own forgiveness only if we put our personal houses in order by examining our own stereotyped behavior in
relation to other minority groups. Certainly we cannot change our own
human nature in one easy lesson; neither can we change the human
nature of everyone around us. But unless we can be realistic about ourselves, we can not deal realistically with the education of other women
in our evolving democracy.

Every status struggle between groups follows the same general patterns, but each specific one is complicated by specific elements related
to the nature of the differences between the two groups. The compli-
cating factor in the evolution of equality for men and women is — of
course — sex. Men and women have come to recognize their common
humanity as persons only in recent years; they have identified each
other as male and female since the beginning of human time. Consequently all of the basic attitudes which govern the behavior between
men and women are related to the biologically defined roles which
they play during their lifetime. Males are fathers; they are also children. They are lovers; they may also be satyrs. The role of husband
is essentially a combination of the other four basic roles. All of the
social behaviors, manners, and attitudes which women display toward
men have their basis in one of these biologically determined roles. We
defer to the father, take orders from him, and expect him to provide
for us; we pamper the child and protect him from his own immaturity;
we seek the lover and we flee from the satyr — even while we are
flattered by either token of recognition of our female desirability.

The corresponding biologically determined roles for women are mother, child, lover, mistress — the role of wife being a legally sanctioned combination of the other four. Mothers are entitled to preferential treatment, but they are also expected to care for their young — even when the young have grown to manhood; children must be protected and directed; lovers must be wooed and cherished; mistresses must be pursued but not always respected. The eternal contradictions in these attitudes are obvious. Women are servants who must be placed on a pedestal; caretakers who must be taken care of; and helpless innocents who are wily as serpents while appearing to be as harmless as doves.

This tragic-comic combination of father-child-lover-satyr-husband and mother-child-lover-mistress-wife attitudes is the basis for man-woman behavior in every situation because it grows out of the basic relationship which makes sex differences significant. I am sure these relationships between men and women were confusing enough in the not-so-good old days when men were men and women were women and let's have no nonsense about equality between them. But our generation has compounded the confusion by exploring new relationships between men and women in which sex has no basic significance. We are working together and playing together as human beings in associations for which there are no social precedents. The only behaviors we had to bring to these essentially *human* relationships were those derived from our sex differences — and to date we have not established any firm mutual agreement about distinguishing between situations in which sex matters and those in which it does not.

This has been particularly trying for those of us who have invaded the male strongholds of business and the professions. The only alternatives which seemed open to us were "to act like a woman" or "to act like a man." The first behavior was often inappropriate to the situation; but we cringed inwardly about the implications of the second. The third alternative was still too new for us to recognize and too little understood by both men and women to seem feasible. We are now beginning to identify the possibilities inherent in a "human" behavior when men and women meet in situations in which sex is essentially inconsequential. In general, the women have taken the lead in exploring the behaviors which are appropriate for these essentially nonsexual human relationships. For many reasons, I think we must continue to do so.

Parallel evidence of this development of "human" behavior patterns is seen in our growing ability to work equitably with persons who differ from us in race and religion. In our colleges and universities, for example, a committee assembled to discuss curriculum matters may include persons of several races, religions, political convictions, and both sexes. We will all be aware of these significant differences among us, but we also recognize that they are not significantly related to the questions we have come together to discuss. Focusing on the problems before us, we interact with each other in terms of our common interest in the curriculum, properly identifying the common bond between us *at that moment*, and displaying behavior appropriate to it. This neither ignores our differences nor emphasizes them; it only indicates that *at that moment in that situation* they are essentially inconsequential.

This development in "human" behavior which is related to a *situation* provides the clues to many of the troublesome questions of democracy. Its potential is enormous. It can free all human relationships by untangling the confusion introduced into them by sex-oriented (or race-oriented, or religion-oriented) behavior which is utterly irrelevant to the common bond which unites two people or a group in a given situation. Business dealings, professional associations, political relationships — all of these can be eased immeasurably by separating that which is consequential from that which is inconsequential in the situation.

Preoccupation with sex-oriented attitudes restricts all personal relationships, making the world a lonelier place for both men and women. They can not enjoy the warm mutuality and shared interest of close friendship with each other without being disturbed by the possible sexual implications in it. But neither can men always trust themselves to be close friends with other men, because this in turn raises doubts about their own sexual adequacy. Friendships between women are even more suspect and tortured by doubt. The only close personal relationship fully approved by a people preoccupied with sexual anxiety is marriage — but marriage, too, is often robbed of real companionship and mutuality because of it.

The promise of a world in which both men and women can differentiate between sex and their other mutual interests is full of hope for both men and women. But even in this promised land, the major share of the joint parental responsibility for producing new citizens will still belong to the women. The consequences of this unchanging biological fact are far-reaching. Its social significance is symbolized by the fact that in our language there is no masculine synonym for the feminine word "housewife."

In our society, no man can be "just a husband." He must also do something which identifies him in the world of men and determines his status in it. Even fatherhood does not justify his personal existence; he must also utilize his other abilities to *earn* a living. He may resent this necessity — and many men do — but there is no socially approved way for him to escape from it except by retreat into real or assumed illness.

The word "housewife," which implies the responsibilities of motherhood but does not always include them, may describe the totality of a woman's existence. By becoming "just a wife," a woman may win exemption from all social necessity for justifying her existence in any other way. She may accept her "living" from her husband's hands without apology, even as she derives her status from the status her husband earns. On her husband's income tax return she may be described as a "dependent," entitled to support, and there is no hint of social disapproval in that description. Legally she is entitled to this dependent status and she may sue her husband if he refuses to support her in accordance with his means. She may claim this support even if she does not do the housekeeping duties that are assumed to be her share in the marital partnership. Actually, she does not even have to live with her husband to be entitled to this support. The fact that she is or was his wife entitles her legally to perpetual care.

Many selfish women have taken unfair advantage of these feminine prerogatives, and awareness of the injustices men have suffered at their hands colors the attitudes many men have toward women. It also influences every woman's attitude toward herself and the opportunities open to her as a person.

The privilege of being cared for is an enticing one. It always has a strong appeal for human beings who find the burden of personal responsibility heavy on their own shoulders. Seeking relief from this burden, many people have relinquished their political freedom and accepted the authoritarian rule of a strong dictator who promises them the certainty of bread in exchange for obedience. This large scale conflict between the human desire for security and the equally human wish for individual autonomy is being waged everywhere throughout the modern world. Politically neither women nor men are exempt from it. But in our own country only women have a realistic opportunity to make a choice between dependence and independence in their personal lives.

All persons, both men and women, need to experience both dependence and independence in their relationships with other human beings if they are to live and grow fully in emotional health. But women's special entitlement to dependence rests upon their special biological necessity reinforced by traditional interpretations of it. Their entitlement to the opportunity to develop their personal abilities in independent thought and action rests upon the premises of democracy. The very real problem which confronts every modern woman is to find the best way to incorporate her special biological necessity into her personal need for freedom to develop and utilize all of her other abilities in democratic sharing with the men upon whom she must also at times depend. In theory this solution is not difficult to find. It is implicit in the concept of behavior appropriate to the situation. But in practice, which is cluttered up by both folklore and wishful thinking as well as by the frailty of male and female egos, it requires a depth of understanding and insight which only a few men and women have yet achieved.

Many of the older members of our generation tended to avoid the necessity for exploring this problem by making a clear-cut choice between dependence and independence, either accepting the conventional marriage of our time or choosing to walk alone. Unless we were fortunate enough to find a husband who was far ahead of his time in understanding our striving to grow by developing our personal abilities, perhaps this was the only realistic solution open to us. Or perhaps it was only our own fears and lack of faith which led us to accept or reject marriage as it was without trying to improve it. The women who were born a little later found it more feasible to attempt to combine personal independence with marital dependence. Their experimental solutions were not always successful, but gradually new patterns of marriage are beginning to emerge. The refinement of those patterns is the major problem confronting the young women who are now in college, and it is to their education we must now turn our attention.

I shall not concern myself at this time with the academic content of curricula. All of us have taught long enough to know that any course content can be directed or perverted to almost any end. The factors which predispose college women toward after-college discontent have little to do with curricula; and they are also factors which we, as women educators, can do much to modify.

While they are on campus, women enjoy a kind of "equality" with men which is not tempered to any large degree by their uniquely female ability to bear children. They attend the same classes, participate in the same discussions, and are rewarded with equally high or higher grades. They are encouraged to look toward the same professional goals and they undergo the same professional preparation. In all student activities except athletics they participate and compete with men on an essentially equal basis, only the highest elective offices still being denied to them. Both subtly and overtly they are encouraged to believe — and we women professors are often the most overt encouragers — that similar opportunities are equally available to them in the adult world. This is an illusion which will be belied both by the persistance of tradition and by the consequences of their female ability to bear children.

Far from being a realistic deterrent to many of their ambitions, on campus their femininity gives them only added social advantages. Men pay for their coffee and their corsages. Gentlemen hold doors open for them and step aside to let them pass through. They are called for and escorted, and never permitted to carry heavy burdens. Under these circumstances it is easy for them to assume that their collegiate equality with men will be translated verbatim into personal equality in their careers as well as their marriages, accompanied by all of the privileges accorded to their femininity with none of the limitations imposed by it. Like the effort required to make their career dreams come true, the realistic consequences of the femaleness which entitles them to these special privileges can be ignored by projecting them into the future.

This easy optimism is the prologue to the flippant, bitter, and satirical articles which the most clever of them — who are also the most disgruntled — will later write about the unfairness of the "drudgery" imposed upon "child bearing animals" and the inadequacies of college curricula which failed to prepare them for either avoiding or enduring their female lot. It also robs many of our finest young women of the real satisfaction they might have found in establishing more realistic goals for their female lives and working toward those goals with realistic effort. And their whining holds back the human enterprise to which their honest efforts might have made a rich contribution.

We, as women educators, can do much to avert these disasters. It is our job to continually evoke in these girls a more healthy attitude of realistic appraisal of the facts of life. Encourage them? Yes. But in our encouragement we must include an awareness of both the reality and the relativity of the adult world they are about to enter. The ability to enjoy each aspect of their lives in turn can be developed only if they can recognize both the fundamental and the fluctuating values to be found in every age and every momentary design for living. If we encourage them to set their expectations in rigid molds, or if we do not challenge their illusions of privilege without price, we shall doom them to discontent. But if we can encourage them to enjoy each moment of living for the unique experience it provides, neither belittling it because it excludes other experiences nor rejecting it because it requires concessions to match its privileges, we can help them develop their own resources for discovering the enduring satisfactions in a changing world.

This is an important assignment. But we have another responsibility which goes far beyond this one. Our gradually evolving democracy is

more than a political philosophy. It embodies a way of life predicated
upon belief in human dignity and human worth. Its most basic premise
is that no person, *as a person,* is one whit more important nor one iota
less important than any other person. It recognizes also that each person
is uniquely different from every other person, and that these differences
are significant in determining the roles which each person may appropriately play at each stage of his life, and the kind of interpersonal
and social interactions which will occur because of them. Every struggle for dominance between individuals or between status-differentiated
groups is an experimental attempt to explore the meanings of these differences and the roles which grow out of them. Each of these struggles
challenges some existing belief and tests it to determine whether it is
rooted in folklore or in fact, in some cherished illusion or in reality.
Each challenge requires both faith and courage, because men and
women resist those who try to rob them of some cherished illusion
or tradition which gives them special privileges. No one can predict
the final outcome of any one of these struggles or the new forms of
personal and social interaction which will come out of them. But out
of them the next stage in the evolution of a democracy develops.

No one is more aware of the hazards and the rewards of these struggles than we women educators who challenged the folklore of our own
time, ran the risks of social nonconformity, suffered the penalties of
uprooting old orthodoxies, and won the privileges of independent
thought and action for the women of the next generation. Our victory
is still incomplete. Much of the old folklore still hampers the interaction between men and women. But we have expanded the concepts
of democracy to an extent that even the most daring of our grandmothers
could not have envisioned.

The day of militant suffragism is past. We no longer have to storm
the barricades. But we do have to help the young women who are coming after us find the meaningful values in the equality we have partially established for them. And we must inculcate in them a willingness to share the blessings of liberty with other beleaguered groups
who are struggling as we once struggled. In short, we must help them
to understand both the meaning and the process of democracy.

We must help every college woman understand that she shares with
every other person a common humanity derived from the mystery of
life which animates a biochemical mass and gives it human meaning.
We must also help her understand that she differs from all other persons in significant ways which make her uniquely herself. She did not
choose these unique endowments, and she merits neither personal credit
nor personal blame for being who or what she is. She may be more

fortunate or less fortunate than certain other persons; but this is not cause for either boasting or apology. Her life was given to her as it is and was; she can only use and develop it as fully as she can. Her unique endowments will determine the roles she may appropriately play at each stage of her life. An evolving culture will both enhance and limit the interpretations of these roles during her moment in history. But these are the circumstances which govern all lives, and all persons are equally susceptible to them.

In the circumstances of her life she will play many roles. In some of them she may have authority, responsibility, and the status which goes with them. But she will also find herself cast in many roles in which the reverse is true. In a sense, she will be a person who has many different hats — each of which symbolizes some degree of status, privilege, and responsibility. Her behavior must be appropriate to the hat she is wearing at any given moment, but she must never confuse the symbolic status conferred by the hat with her own personal importance *as a person.* As a person, her needs and desires can never be either more important or less important than the needs and desires of every human being. But they will always be equally important, because she, too, is a human being.

If we can help her develop this basic understanding about herself and other people, she will also understand the concessions and compromises which people must learn to make to accommodate each others' needs. If we can do this, we need not worry unduly about her ability to cope with the multiple human relationships out of which her life will be compounded. She will have learned to value her own "rights" and responsibilities, and she will similarly value the "rights" and responsibilities of other human beings. And recognizing that she herself is often confused by her own inability to differentiate among folklore, fact, and fiction, she will not be unduly dismayed to find that other people suffer from the same confusion. Patiently she will try to disentangle the effects these illusions of knowledge have on her own attitudes, manner and behavior, and she will be better able to run the risks involved in helping other people expose themselves to the same spirit of free inquiry.

If she can see life steadily and see it whole, we need not be unduly concerned about her post-college adaptation to vocation, community life, marriage, and motherhood. She will be able to fit herself to the requirements of her life according to the circumstances of her time, for she will have discovered that the essence of life is found in living it *as it is,* while sharing its essence with others who are as confused as she is in the mutuality of common — though imperfect — understanding.

Our college women and men live in a society which is shot through with cynicism and riddled with materialism. Many of them learn from their parents the folklore of status snobbery, and there are many campus factors which reinforce these learnings. In trying to counteract them, there are limits to our own ability and our own human frailty. We can not do more than we can do — but we must not do less.

The evolution of a democratic society, in which men and women may find greater satisfaction in being themselves as they walk side by side in a companionship of effort which encompasses their differences even while it enhances their human worth, is still far from fulfillment. I do not believe it will be fully realized during our moment in history. This is not cause for bitterness or discouragement. Rather it intensifies our necessity for approaching the education of both men and women with a kind of realism which is untinged by cynicism, and for instilling in them an idealism which is not marred by illusion.

This week we shall concern ourselves with various specific questions related to the education of women in an evolving democracy. Awareness of the inherent complications in every one of them must make us very wary lest we fall into the subtle traps which have ensnared many of our predecessors. If we seek the childish security which comes from firm reliance upon the authority of an older generation, we may at times be too much disposed toward the perpetuation of traditional orthodoxies. If we allow ourselves to be too much persuaded by personal frustrations we have encountered in our own evolutionary development, we may at times allow cynicism to befuddle the realism with which we must explore the tangled ramifications of every question we ask. And if our eagerness for finding answers leads us to cut the Gordian knot of reality with wishful thinking, our failure to see the internal contradictions in some of our solutions will make a mockery of our faith.

As we discuss, argue — and at times explode — we may take comfort from the fact that despite our human difficulties in interpreting the complex meanings in the concept of equality, we are closer to the achievement of the democratic ideal today than any other people have ever been. But the remaining steps are crucial ones, and we must neither be deluded by thoughts of premature accomplishment of them nor discouraged because they are being taken so slowly with many halts and occasional retreats. The ark of democracy can never be jet-propelled. It can only lumber along creaking and groaning with the stresses imposed upon it by the weight of human frailty. Its progress can never be spectacular, for while it is prodded forward by the desire of the human spirit for freedom it is held back by the reluctance of the human spirit to make the concessions which freedom demands. And each inch of forward progress must be achieved by the individual efforts of courageous men and women like ourselves who can discover in themselves the strength to transcend the limits of traditional orthodoxies and venture into the promised land of democracy by exemplifying the premises of that democracy in their own lives.

We did not choose the components of our own lives nor our moment in history. We can only live the lives we have in our own time — with wonder at much we do not understand, with compassion for ourselves and each other as we struggle with the inconsistencies of our own human spirits, and with human pride in ourselves and each other that we have managed to come as far as we have on the difficult road that leads to democracy.

In the Subjunctive Mood

Midwest Association for Physical Education of College Women—
    Spencer, Indiana — April, 1961
Published in *Ideas, Issues, Action, Report on the Conference of the
    Midwest Association for Physical Education of College Women,*
    1961.

When I received your Program Chairman's invitation, I was pleased
by the prospect of a visit with old friends. But since it is professionally
unwise for a speaker to promise more than she is prepared to deliver,
I had to determine what obligations your invitation imposed on me
before I could accept it. The first sentence read: "We feel that we
need to move beyond the *status quo.*" This statement about your inner
necessity was in the indicative mood, so it required nothing from me but
empathy. But the mood of your next sentence was imperative. I read
it with fear and trembling. "We want you to. . . ." In the context of
the situation this meant "I must give you. . . ." "some positive steps
we could take in the next decade that might clarify the function of
physical education in the higher education of women." My fears retreated; my tremor subsided to its normal amplitude. I did not have
to predict; I did not have to give directions. All I had to do was to
suggest possibilities. Fortunately for me, you, too, were in the subjunctive mood.

Your Chairman's final sentence made my decision easy. She wrote: "And we hope that your address could be controversial and a little unsettling." I thought I could promise you that it might be. And so in the controversial and unsettling mood of subjunctivity that expresses both hope and anxiety, I accepted your invitation.

Long experience has made me familiar with the intellectual terrain in the area of physical education for college women — perhaps too familiar. The clichés of our profession came too readily to my mind. It seemed desirable, therefore, to begin by looking over our own professional fence into the surrounding territory to establish broader perspectives for my thinking.

I looked first at the great pile of books on social change, but I soon discarded them. The verbs of sociology can only be in the indicative mood. Within the limits of their research techniques sociologists may say "thus it was" and "so it is." Grammatically speaking, it is also possible to say "this is how it will be," but experience argues against the use of the future indicative in the writings of sociology.

The crucial events that shape the future have always been unpredictable. The social scientists of the eighteenth century could not know that they were pre-Freudian; those of the nineteenth century could not predict the shift of thought initiated by the theories of Kurt Lewin. As van den Berg puts it: "At the moment when history is being created, everything is uncertain." History may only judge the men who were the authors of its creation; it can not be their mentor.

Man's inherent "inability to build on the certainties of old" (van den Berg) also argues against the use of the imperative mood, although many writers are using it today. These are the writers who would dictate to us what "all men must do. . . .or else." If only it were that simple; if only we could tell which way the world is heading; if only we knew where the next step will take us.

But who knows? A new destroyer, a new liberator, a new idea may be born tomorrow, and all that we believe is true today may be proved false in a blinding flash of power or an illuminating flash of insight. In the shadow of the "if" that all men live under, the only imperative any man can know is his own inner necessity to do what he finds he must do in his own time without foreknowledge of the consequences that may ensue from his doing.

Yesterday and today are indicative; man's inner necessity may be imperative; but tomorrow is always subjunctive. The consequential verbs of the future can only express uncertainty. And so I turned to the fearful-hopeful writers whose future tenses are cast in the subjunctive mood. They do not predict; they issue no commands. They urge us, rather, to obey our own inner necessities, to discover what we may become by being what we are. Their hope is that we may develop our own human potentialities by involving ourselves actively in the creation of a future that can not be predicted because it will be created by our own actions.

These writers do not seek to elaborate the *status quo*. They do not try to extrapolate the present into the future. Their search is for "new emergent qualities" and "new realms of experience" (Murphy) in which we may find new realities. It is a visionary search, but it is not a prophetic one. The sober task they have set for themselves is identical with the task your Chairman assigned to me for this conference. Gardner Murphy describes it as "an attempt at a systematic survey of the kinds of directions which might be taken within the very large areas marked as unknown on the map." In my reading I had found more than a perspective for my thinking; I had found a procedure for attacking the problem.

In the subjunctive mood of hope of these writers, then, let us begin to create our own unknown future by attempting a systematic survey of the kinds of directions which might be taken within the areas marked as unknown on the map of physical education for college women. All I can promise you is that what we may find there may well be controversial and unsettling.

Any search for what is unknown should begin with a re-search of presently available knowledge. Fortunately we are in a better position to conduct this re-search today than we have been at any time in our professional history. On the occasion of the seventy-fifth anniversary of AAHPER the Research Council prepared and published a summary of the contributions physical education appears to have made or probably can make to the lives of human beings. This welcome résumé has been extended by the publication of the monumental *Science and Medicine of Exercise and Sport* edited by Warren Johnson. Together, these publications review more than 2,000 research reports, well-organized under appropriate rubrics. At the risk of doing grave injustice to the wealth of detail in these two publications, I shall attempt to summarize them in terms of the areas they enable us to mark as known on the map of physical education for college women.

For operational purposes I shall define physical education for college women as "that which occurs in or results from our college classes for women who are not majoring in physical education." For convenience I shall refer to this as PECW.

The larger volume, which is commonly referred to as SMES, deals primarily with the physically identifiable aspects of structure and function associated with exercise, including sports. These studies are related to physical education only by inference, because the kinds and intensities of exercise with which they deal seldom occur in physical education classes. The book has even less to do with PECW. Except in the brief chapter by Celeste Ulrich on "Women and Sport," there are few references to the second sex, either in the text or in the bibliographies. Nonetheless, we can not ignore what this text book tells us. Its specific conclusions may be generalized in two statements.

The general effect of the persistent performance of any exercise that the exerciser is capable of performing is to increase his ability to perform more exercise of that kind.

The general effect of the attempt to perform an exercise which the exerciser is not capable of performing at that time is to decrease his ability to perform that kind of exercise.

These generalizations are my own, but they are not new. Hippocrates said much the same thing on the basis of empirical observation. In the days of Sherrington, the mechanisms that seem to be responsible for these effects had been studied. As Dr. Bruno Balke, one of the contributors to SMES, pointed out at the International Seminar on Health and Fitness last summer, there has been no new *principle* discovered in exercise physiology for many decades. In general, research effort has been directed toward identification of the specifics within the outlines of the established general principles.

Then moving from the known to the unknown, Dr. Balke pointed out that what exercise physiologists do *not* know is how to induce people to perform with any degree of persistence the exercises that would produce these known effects.

To what extent even the known effects may be ascribed to PECW, we do not know. The field of physical aspects of persistent and intense exercise for men may be well-plowed, but our own area of the physical aspects of physical education for college women has scarcely been scratched.

Turning to the Research Council publication, let me summarize the conclusions that have been reached in the areas of health, psychosocial development, behavioral change, and skill learning.

As to health — as distinguished from the strength, speed, flexibility, endurance definition of physical fitness — Dr. Fred Hein and Dr. Allan Ryan, both of the American Medical Association, present four cautiously worded conclusions based on an examination of 118 research reports.

Regular exercises can play a significant role in the prevention of obesity — and thereby indirectly influence the greater inci-

dence of degenerative disease and shortened life span associated with this condition.

A high level of physical activity throughout life appears to be one of the factors that act to inhibit the vascular degeneration characteristic of coronary heart disease.

Regular exercise assists in preserving the physical characteristics of youth and delaying the stigmata of aging, and probably exerts a favorable influence upon longevity.

Conditioning the body through regular exercise enables the individual to meet emergencies more effectively, and so serves, in turn, to preserve health and to avoid disability and perhaps even death.

To what extent even these limited conclusions may be extended to PECW we do not know, because no specific research on the health outcomes of PECW is included in their references.

Furthermore, it is noted that

. . .there are many people who apparently enjoy good health and a long life, and who contribute more than their share to community life without taking any more physical exercise than the nature of their work allows.

Not all cigarette smokers die of lung cancer; many athletes die young.

In the area of psychosocial development, the common conclusion reached by Gladys Scott and C. C. Cowell in their independent reviews of 150 studies in these overlapping areas is that psychosocial development is a challenging area for research! As to more specific conclusions, Dr. Scott writes:

. . .little doubt remains. . .that intent to learn, receptivity, and motivation toward learning and participation are conducive to accomplishment and lack thereof is inhibiting.

. . .we may conjecture that [sensory variables] may facilitate learning, provide capacity for better neuromuscular performance, and enrich living in general by making the person more sensitive and responsive to his environment.

And with reference to behavioral change, the situation may be summed by a paraphrase of the conclusion cited from a study by Emery Seymour:

It would seem prudent to exercise caution in ascribing with any degree of certainty behavioral changes, whether desirable or undesirable to PECW.

In the area of skill learning Dorothy Mohr reviewed 218 studies, 32 of which involved college women in some way. The most positive conclusion she draws is:

Skill learning does result from physical activity. The second is that every other hypothesis so far investigated requires more research, since the findings so far are conflicting.

With specific reference to PECW, Dr. Mohr writes:

"Only 23 studies were located to defend the supposition that skill learning takes place in regular physical education programs. This may be one of the most widely accepted hypotheses in the profession. . .[but it] certainly needs a great deal of supportive research evidence.

. . .31 studies were seen to uphold the assumption that specific instruction results in skill learning. These were in widely scattered areas, and it would seem that much more research is needed in each aspect of physical skill learning. . ."

If these diligent synthesizers have done their task well, and I believe they have, the present indicative is for us a most discouraging mood.

If I read our general literature correctly, we have been assuming much for which we have no evidence. We have assumed that the function PECW serves in the lives of college women can be described in terms of physical change, modification of health status, psychosocial-behavioral change, and acquirement of movement skills. After 75 years of research, what evidence do we have to support these assumptions? With you, I would prefer to believe otherwise, but in all honesty I must admit that about all we can really claim on the basis of the evidence is the probability that:

Skill learning can result from physical activity;
Motivation toward learning and participation facilitate skill learning; and
Such learning can probably be further facilitated by instruction.

As Benjamin Franklin long ago observed: "One of the tragedies of life is the murder of a beautiful theory by a gang of brutal facts." For women like us who have devoted our lives to PECW, the conclusions drawn from our survey have tragic implications. But could it be our own doubt about the validity of our assumptions that has made our voices so shrill when our colleagues have questioned the necessity of the physical education requirement? Could it be that this doubt was one of the motivations for this conference?

Am I being controversial? Are some of you feeling a bit unsettled? Or am I the only one who hears the imperative voice of my own inner necessity screaming at me: "But PECW *must* have a vital function in the lives of college women. It *must*. It MUST. IT *MUST!*" Surely such passion indicates that PECW serves some vital need in our own lives — and I have too much respect for our integrity to suggest that our emotion indicates only fear lest our jobs be taken from us.

But what is that vital need? What essential functions have the movement experiences we try to provide in PECW served in our own lives? If the questions we have been asking for many years have elicited no defensible answers, perhaps it is time for us to seek for a "radically new way of conceiving the whole issue" (Murphy), which may suggest new dimensions as well as new areas not even marked as "unknown" on our PECW map because we have not yet even postulated their existence. My obligation to you, as I understand it, is to urge you to take this radical step.

Before we attempt to take it, however, I feel impelled to remind you that a leap into the unknown is a perilous journey. We can learn much about its dangers by remembering the experiences of Soren Kierkegaard, the philosopher who pushed with "fear and trembling" into unknown religious territory. "To venture causes anxiety," he wrote as his fears of religious persecution and his very human fear of losing his job led him to suppress his own writings. But this protective maneuver brought him no peace, because it was a symptom of the "sickness unto death" those writings described. In seeking to escape from one horn of the dilemma of man's uncertainty, he had impaled himself on the other and doomed himself to the slow death of self rejection. The dilemma could be resolved only by obeying his own inner necessity to be what he was, a man whose unconventional thinking established a landmark on the course of philosophic thought. And so he completed our quotation: "To venture causes anxiety; but not to venture is to lose one's self."

"To be or not to be"? That is the question that plagues all men. And as it is with men, so it is with their educational disciplines. It is the underlying question of this conference, indicated by your awareness of a need to move beyond the *status quo*. We have been running on our beaten paths within the enclosure of the *status quo* for a long time. The only large-scale movement within our profession in recent years has seemed to many of us to be a retreat rather than a progression. Our vital spirit has been sickening within us. We know it may be dangerous to desert the security of our old arguments; but some inner necessity of our professional life is driving us to take the risk. We may lose our professional lives and our livelihood if the move we make is a false one, but to many of us it seems that at worst we may only be trading the death in life of professional boredom for the living death of professional nonconformity. But our hope is that we may discover that we have been bored because we have been living only a half-life; and we would like to begin to explore the fuller possibilities of our own nature. And so we must make our attempt.

The hopeful possibility that we might find a clue in our own vital involvement in movement suggests that we begin by directing our attention to the inner necessities that seem to drive *us* to move in what might be called PECW ways. I shall begin by publicly exploring my own motivations, but I think most of you will have little difficulty in putting your feet in my shoes as I do this.

To set the stage: It is five o'clock in the afternoon of a hot and humid day. I am walking uphill on the fairway of the 18th hole of a long golf course. My face and arms are sunburned; sweat oozes stickily from every pore in my body. For four hours I have been walking over uneven terrain pushing and pulling an awkward cart filled with clubs. Approximately 100 times I have stopped to pull a club from the cart and swing it in arcs of varying sizes. At least 300 more times I have stopped and waited while my companions did their swinging. My feet are tired; my legs ache; my back is weary. In short, I am both fatigued and physically uncomfortable. My accomplishment will be measured by the number of times I swung a meaningless club at a meaningless ball to drive it into 18 meaningless holes.

The question I must ask myself is not: What am I doing here? I know *what* I am doing. I am playing golf. The question I must try to answer is: *Why* am I playing golf?

Assuming that I am not an idiot, assuming that I am not a mindless physical mechanism, I must assume that any voluntary decision on my part is made on some meaningful basis. I must conclude, therefore, that I am playing golf because this experience is in some way meaningful to me.

What significance do I find in or attach to this experience? Perhaps it is to improve my physical fitness. This I doubt for two reasons. If I really have a strong drive to develop those familiar components of strength, speed, flexibility and cardiovascular endurance in which we are told the Russians excel, I have chosen a very roundabout method of developing them. Few Russians play golf; they use more effective conditioning techniques. But my second reason for doubting is to me even more convincing. Dr. Balke pointed out that human beings, being only human, seldom inconvenience themselves over an extended period of time to do something they know "might be good for them" — and I, alas, am very human. The vital interests of my life involve little weight-lifting and less running, so I am simply not interested in developing the ability to lift heavier weights or run faster and longer. There is no evidence that developing these abilities would enable me to work longer than sixteen hours at a stretch on jobs of my own choosing, which I am now able to do. As to the specific exercise of golf-playing, I doubt that I have deliberately engaged in it to develop my staying power; rather, I think, it is my ability to stay with a task of my own choosing that enables me to play golf.

Now it is probably true that if I persist in performing golf-playing exercise within the limit of my present abilities I can increase my ability to perform golf-playing exercise. But to say I play golf to enable myself to play more golf only brings us back to the original question. *Why* do I want to play *any* golf?

Of course health is not synonymous with physical fitness. Am I sweating and aching on the golf course to possibly prevent obesity, inhibit vascular degeneration, delay the onset of the stigmata of aging, or give me a margin of safety in time of accident? Possibly my golf-playing *has* done these things for me, but was this my motivation for exposing myself to sunburn, perspiration, and fatigue? Can you honestly say that you go on playing golf — or whatever your favorite fatigue-producing game may be — only because you believe it will keep you from getting fat?

Am I concerned with my psychosocial development as I swing my club? Am I trying to bring about behavioral changes in myself? Probably I could profit from some meddling with my psychosocial-behavioral life — and the experience of playing golf with my companions may bring about some such changes, for better or for worse — but I can not believe I deliberately exposed myself to physical discomfort on a hot and humid day in order to bring about those changes.

The gleam I see in some of your eyes indicates that you think you have me trapped. I have almost run out of alternatives. You are think-ing: "Skill learning can result from physical activity; intent to learn and participation are conducive to skill learning." Aha! This seems to make some sense. I have come to the golf course to learn the skill of golf playing. If you say this, I shall agree with you; but this only brings us back to the original question, which can now be rephrased.

Why does an intelligent woman like me *want* to learn the skill of club-swinging? What significance do I find in that process? As an intellectual-emotional-physical person, what significance do I find in the skilled performance of this physical skill *after* I have learned how to direct my body to perform it?

I have elected to learn a skill that appears to have little if any utilitarian value to me. This suggests the question: What is the purpose of any elective learning? A phrase from Gladys Scott's conclusions suggests the answer. It was "to enrich living." What a happy phrase! The purpose of performance in any art is to enrich living. Have I been so preoccupied with perfecting the skills of my golf art — the *objet d'art*, as it were — that I have overlooked the *object* of the art of being able to perform those skills? Certainly my primary objective in learning the skills of golf is the same as my primary objective in learning to play the piano — to enrich my own life by extending its range of experiences.

How has my life been enriched? What does this enrichment mean to me? I can not tell you in words anymore than I can explain the satisfaction I find in making my own inadequate music on the piano. Gladys Scott conjectures that the enrichment may come from increased sensitivity and responsiveness to my environment. I would go one step farther. I would say that my life is specifically enriched by the significance it finds in the structured sensory perceptions conveyed by the complex kinesthetic sensorium about the nature of this experience — this movement experience — within the context of the golf-playing situation.

But my questions continue. How is it possible for the *mind* to find significance in the perception of bodily movement — or, for that matter, in any kind of sensory perceptions? Aren't we talking about two different kinds of phenomena — the mental and the physical? The mind and the body?

The recent symposium on *Dimensions of Mind* devotes many pages to this question that has troubled the minds (and the bodies?) of men ever since they knew they *had* minds. Many theories and hypotheses are discussed, but perhaps the statement of philosopher Herbert Feigl is the most illuminating. After examining a number of pros and cons he writes: "I conclude that the mind-body problem is not a pseudoproblem." This is comforting; at least our questions are not nonsensical, for they have led us to a real problem with real meaning that is under study. Dr. Feigl goes on: "There are. . .a great many genuine but unanswered questions in psychophysiology, and. . . there is plenty of

work left for philosophers in the logical analysis of the intricate relations between phenomenal and physical terms." We can only agree
with him that "The isues of perception, of reality, and of the mental
and the physical require circumspect, perspicacious and painstaking
analyses." But at least we are in respectable company when we raise
our own specialized version of the mind-body problem.

Serious consideration of the ways in which the perceptions conveyed by the kinesthetic sensorium can enrich — or impoverish — our
mental-physical lives may open up an enormous area of unknown territory on our PECW map. But "circumspect, perspicacious and painstaking analyses" take time, and we shall perhaps be fortunate if we discover only a few faint trails into this territory in the next decade or
two. Gladys Scott has been moving in the direction of her own scientific bent; Valerie Hunt and her associates have oriented their efforts
in a psychiatric direction; Lois Ellfeldt and I have been trying to make
some headway on a number of related fronts at the same time, and our
research techniques are perhaps best described as philosophical. We may
all be following blind alleys. All of us may be dead wrong.

It is not my purpose now to try to convert you to any one of these
approaches, although I think all of them have merit. To channel your
thinking toward the confines of any one stream of thought at this point
would defeat the purpose of this conference by restricting the flow of
your own ideas. Neither is it my purpose to convince you that the sensory
perception area is the only area that may be productive of possible direction for exploratory movement. There may be dozens of others; there probably are. And surely some of you may want to take a look in the unexplored rooms of the more familiar categories. I have used the "significance of sensory perceptions" area to illustrate one empirical process
that might be used at this conference to help you discover why your
inner necessities are so necessitous. You may well find other more rewarding ones — by reason or by accident. At all conferences, you know,
"One's grand flights, one's Sunday baths / One's tootings at the wed-
dings of the soul / Occur as they occur." (Stevens)

We have considered the scientists — both physical and social; we
have listened to the educators — both physical and mental; and we
have heard from the philosophers — both ancient and modern. For our
summary let us turn to the poets, the writers who summarize human
experience by expressing its essence in symbolic form.

"Life consists of propositions about life," wrote Wallace Stevens.
"The human revery is a solitude in which/ We compose these propositions, torn by dreams,/ By the terrible incantations of defeats,/ And

by the fear that defeats and dreams are one." We seek "A new text of the world,/ A scribble of fret and fear and fate,/ From a bravura of the mind,/ A courage of the eye. . ./ The meanings are our own." The text "comes from ourselves, neither from knowing/ Nor from not knowing, yet free from question,/ Because we wanted it so/ And it had to be,/ A text of intelligent men at the center of the unintelligible."

Our conclusions? It may be many years before we shall be able to write them. But perhaps in time we shall be able to say with Stevens what he said as he looked back at his own attempts to find new directions in poetry.

> *Ariel was glad he had written his poems.*
> *They were of a remembered time*
> *Or of something seen that he liked. . .*
> *It was not important that they survive.*
> *What mattered was that they should bear*
> *Some lineament or character,*
> *Some affluence, if only half perceived*
> *In the poverty of their words,*
> *Of the planet of which they were part.*

And so in the subjunctive mood of fearful hope and hopeful fear that is the mood of all thoughtful men who would move forward, let us begin our own search for our own lineaments, which though they may be only half perceived in the poverty of our words, may still bear trace of the affluence of our own character.

ACKNOWLEDGMENTS

The debt we owe to many writers who have stimulated our thinking can never be paid by bibliographical listing. We can only acknowledge our awareness of it.

The publications from which I have made direct quotation are:
The Changing Nature of Man, by J. H. VAN DEN BERG. (Norton, 1961)
Human Potentialities, by GARDNER MURPHY. (Basic Books, 1958)
Dimensions of Mind, edited by SIDNEY HOOK. (New York University Press, 1960)
Science and Medicine of Exercise and Sports, edited by WARREN JOHNSON. (Harper, 1960)
Research Quarterly of AAHPER, Vol. 31, No. 2, Part II. (May, 1960)

The lines of poetry I have used are quoted from *The Collected Poems of Wallace Stevens*. (Alfred A. Knopf, 1954.) They are taken from the poems called:

"Sense of the Slight-of-Hand Man"
"Men Made Out of Words"
"Things of August"
"The Planet on the Table"

The Dimensions of Inner Space

Conference Luncheon — National Association for Physical Education of
College Women — Cincinnati, Ohio — April, 1962

For the past two days we have been exploring our professional dimensions, — but a profession does not exist apart from its members, and
so what we have really been doing is exploring the dimensions of our
own lives. Together, we have discovered that perhaps we are a bit
taller than we knew; together we have seen farther than our individual
eyes have looked; and in the private recesses of our own thoughts we
have heard the rumblings of ideas that we did not know were there.

As Wallace Stevens — the American poet who has written much of
what I shall say this afternoon — puts it:

I measure myself
Against a tall tree,
I find that I am much taller,
With my eye;
And I reach to the shore of the sea
With my ear.
Nevertheless, I dislike
The way the ants crawl
In and out of my shadow. (1)

It is impossible to summarize here all the discoveries we have made about the depth and breadth and length of our own vision — or about the smallness of the ants that disturb its shadow. Rather, let us say that for two days we have been stretching our perceptions of

The impossible, possible philosopher's man,
The man who has had time to think enough,
The central man, the human globe, responsive
As a mirror with a voice, the man of glass,
Who in a million diamonds sums us up. (2)

We have been filled with wonder at the glimpses we have caught of the infinite; but now we must return to the infinitesmal. We must return to the minutiae of our working days — the details we must deal with moment by moment to actualize that vision, however imperfectly, in one college, one department, one class, one human life. And so we must turn from philosophy to human biology to discover how biological bodies actualize their visions — how they seek to transform the infinitesmal into the infinite.

In studying biology we learn that life begins as a speck of protoplasm that is barely distinguishable from billions of other specks. But this microscopic human globe has the power of growth. It has its own inner resources; and by using them to draw from the universe the materials it needs, it grows from a globular speck into a uniquely human being that dares to question the universe of which it is a part.

Like all biological organisms, it grows from the center toward the infinite that lies beyond its present comprehension. In the nerves that implement its awareness of life, this outward reaching is accomplished by the progressive myelinization of the sheaths that enclose the neural substances. As the motor nerves are progressively activated from the spinal center out to the peripheral fingertips, we can follow their course in the progressive differentiation of movements made first by the trunk, then the arms, then the arm segments, the hands, and finally the fine movements of the fingers that the child uses to explore the shapes and sizes and textures of the world.

This progressive activation of the motor nerves is matched step by step by the myelinization of the sensory nerves that convey these discoveries back to the inner spaces of human awareness. Thus, we can follow, too, the progressive development of a child's ability to discriminate among the details of what he sees, hears, tastes, and smells. And we can follow it, too, in his ever-increasing delight in discovering his own body as the source of the movements he makes to explore this fascinating world of knowledge that he is gradually discovering.

For the human globe
Life consists

Of propositions about life. The human
Revery is a solitude in which
We compose these propositions, torn by dreams,
By the terrible incantations of defeats
And by the fear that defeats and dreams are one. (3)

But as we reach toward the outer spaces in which "the knowledge of things" lies "round but unperceived" (4) we bring this newly perceived knowledge back into the inner spaces of our ever-questioning minds, and there we write

A new text of the world,
A scribble of fret and fear and fate,
From a bravura of the mind,
A courage of the eye. . .
A text of intelligent men
At the center of the unintelligible. (5)

— the text of "the essential poem at the center of things, the arias that spiritual fiddlings make."(6)

We do not prove the existence of the poem.
It is something seen and known in lesser poems,
It is the huge, high harmony that sounds
A little and a little, suddenly,
By means of a separate sense. . .
A definition with an illustration, not
Too exactly labelled. . . (7)
Our sense of these things changes and they change,
Not as in metaphor, but in our sense
Of them. . .
It is like a flow of meanings with no speech
And of as many meanings as of men. (8)

In this conference we have been stretching the dimensions of our personal and professional interactions with the universe. We have known our own "fluctuations of certainty, the change of degrees of perception in the scholar's dark." (9) We have made some discoveries, some partial discoveries of new knowledge that lies around us waiting to be perceived. Perhaps we have dreamed of the impossible; perhaps we have been too much fearful of the limits of the possible; but yet

> *If the rejected things, the things denied,*
> *Slid over the western cataract, yet one,*
> *One only, one thing that was firm, even*
> *No greater than a cricket's horn, no more*
> *Than a thought to be rehearsed all day, a speech*
> *Of the self that must sustain itself on speech,*
> *One thing remaining, infallible, would be*
> *Enough. . .*
>
>   *. . .honey in the heart,*
> *Green in the body, out of a petty phrase,*
> *Out of a thing believed, a thing affirmed. (10)*

Like all of us, Wallace Stevens had to search for the meaning of "the thing affirmed" in the objective dimensions of his interaction with the universe as well as in the subjective dimensions of his own thoughts. He was an insurance salesman — president of the Hartford Accident and Indemnity Company. By day he dealt with policies and their beneficiaries, even as we do, but he was able to transform these prosaic materials into "the essential poem at the center of things" that illuminates their hidden meanings.

We, too must deal with objects. We, too, must work with things. The biological organisms that people our classes must be dealt with objectively. But when we gather together to explore the farther reaches of those objective dimensions, we, too, can write our own kind of poetry.

And this, I believe, is what we have been doing at this conference.

> *In spite of the mere objectiveness of things,*
> *Like a cloud-cap in the corner of a looking-glass,*
> *A change of color in the plain poet's mind,*
> *Night and silence disturbed by an interior sound,*
> *The one moonlight, the various universe, intended*
> *So much just to be seen — a purpose, empty*
> *Perhaps, absurd perhaps, but at least a purpose,*
> *Certain and ever more fresh. Ah! Certain, for*
> *Sure. . . . .(11)*

Note: All quotations may be found in *The Collected Poems of Wallace Stevens*. New York: Alfred A. Knopf, 1954. They have been taken from the following poems:

1. Six Significant Landscapes, p. 74.
2. Asides on the Oboe, p. 250.
3. Men Made Out of Words, pp. 355-6.
4. Things of August, p. 493.
5. Things of August, p. 494.
6. A Primitive Like an Orb, p. 440.
7. A Primitive Like an Orb, p. 440-443.
8. Bouquet of Roses in Sunlight, p. 430.
9. Notes Toward a Supreme Fiction, p. 395.
10. The Well Dressed Man with a Beard, p. 247.
11. Note on Moonlight, p. 531.

Part III

On Being a Teacher

Effects and Consequences

Los Angeles Council on Clinical Affiliation in Occupational Therapy —
Los Angeles, California — May, 1958

Published in *American Journal of Occupational Therapy*, November-
December, 1958.

Guiding students through the formal education which qualifies them to enter our own professional ranks is a rewarding undertaking. It is also a highly dangerous one. If we do it well, our profession is benefited by a continual influx of capable and enthusiastic new practitioners; but if we fail in our assignment, the wellsprings of our profession soon run dry. It is desirable, therefore, that we continually examine the effectiveness of our own teaching procedures.

Obviously, the immediate effects of our instruction are manifested in the technical competence our students display in their first professional assignments. But just as the dictionary differentiates between "effect" (the immediate result) and "consequence" (the remote outcome), so must we differentiate between techniques and the consequences of the ways in which those techniques were acquired. For it is in the realm of consequences that the danger of poor professional preparation lies, and the source of that danger is in us.

During a highly critical period in the lives of those who will carry on our professional work we are entrusted with almost absolute authority over them. Because we hold the key to the only door that can admit them to the life work they have chosen, our approval is essential to them. In this situation, our students sometimes confuse means and ends. Winning our immediate approval may at times seem more important to them than their eventual professional growth; and because we, too, are only human. we, too, may at times suffer from this same confusion. In our concern for immediate technical competence we may overlook the consequences of meticulous carrying-out of directions. Our desire to have them "do it right," which of course means "do it exactly as I would do it," may blur our awareness of the consequences of not understanding the basis upon which "my way" rests. Unwittingly we may use our authority to drive them to commit what T. S. Eliot has called "the greatest treason." They may "do the right deed for the wrong reason."

If we allow our students to make winning our approval or avoiding our displeasure their primary motivation, they may become very proficient in using techniques. But if they have no real understanding of the reasons for selecting those techniques, their professional lives are in mortal danger. They are on the way to becoming technical robots whose acts are governed only by the voice of authority — *our* authority. But, as the history of knowledge clearly shows, nothing is more vulnerable than an authority; and any profession manned by technicians whose practices rest solely on authorities of the past is soon reduced to a body of rules and procedures which in fifty years will be fifty years behind the times. We who guide the learning of the professional practitioners of the future must be continually on guard to root out "the cause of this effect,/Or rather say, the cause of this defect,/For this effect defective comes by cause." (Hamlet, II,2)

Certainly our immediate responsibility is to teach students to do the job *our* way — which is the best way we know at the moment, but this is not enough. Progress comes from "someone differing with me — and being right." If we want our profession to move forward instead of backward, we must lay the foundation for such differing. We must teach current practices in such a way that our students will eventually dare to discard them in favor of better techniques which they, themselves, will develop. To plan for our own obsolescence is a difficult assignment for us human beings with our touchy egos. It is tempting to induce our students to pattern themselves after us, to cause them to develop in our own image. It is difficult to give them the freedom they need to develop in their *own* images, which may be far better than ours.

Our own competence must be used to provide a structure which will support them during their early performance of professional tasks, but this structure must be only a temporary scaffolding, not a cage. Even as they lean on it, they must feel free to question its adequacy. "Why?" "What is the general principle?" "On what scientific evidence is this practice based?" Asking and answering these questions will lay the groundwork for their own professional competence.

As they acquire knowledge and understanding, we must allow them to use it. Only by accepting responsibility for making decisions and acting on those decisions can they develop faith in their own judgmen. (Of course we must overrule them if an error in judgment is likely to prove catastrophic, but even then we must be sure they understand the reasons for our intervention.) If we want them to become professional persons, capable of thinking for themselves, they must be permitted to function as a professional persons within the limits of their present knowledge and understanding.

Competence in the performance of currently accepted techniques is necessary, but it is only a means and never an end in itself. "We all need some imaginative stimulus, some not impossible ideal such as may shape vague hope and transform it into effective desire, to carry us year after year, without disgust, through the routine work which is so large a part of life." (Walter Pater) Repetition of a familiar technique is not, in itself, such a lasting stimulus. The tinder which can keep the spark of enthusiasm burning during routine utilization of effective techniques is the belief that there is always a better way to accomplish the same purpose, and that we are capable of finding that better way. It is our job to instill that belief. We must somehow convince them that all knowledge in their professional field does not reside in us, that our understandings are not infallible. In short, we must expose our own vulnerability as authorities to encourage them to dare to differ with us, and perhaps be right.

As a consequence of effective preparation our students should eventually transcend our teaching and accept the responsibility for doing their own thinking and experimenting as they attempt to improve the profession they have accepted as their own. The old authorities should, in time, be forgotten. They should no longer be needed, no longer quoted, because a new generation of authorities will have matured to replace them.

If we do our jobs effectively we shall be forgotten as authorities, but we shall be remembered as we remember our own great teachers — as persons, as co-workers whose concern for our own professional growth was consequential in our lives. Our students will remember us not because we gave them the final answers, but because we insisted that they ask questions; not because we gave them a finished product, but because we entrusted them with the responsibility for improving the product our own lives had helped shape.

If we can find it in ourselves to do our jobs effectively, then we can approach retirement with serenity when our own days of professional responsibility are over, because we will have handed on to the next generation the catalyst which transforms technicians into professional leaders, and we can rest assured that the future of our profession will be safe in their hands.

I Like Being a Teacher!

Most of these ideas were developed initially at a meeting of the Western Society for Physical Education of College Women — Asilomar, California — 1950.

The version presented here is reprinted by permission from the NEA *Journal,* December, 1951.

I am a schoolteacher. I have never quite understood why this simple statement of fact should embarrass my friends, but it seems to. At least they take pains to conceal my profession whenever they hopefully introduce me to anything masculine and under 80.

I am not very cooperative in maintaining the deception, however, and sooner or later my shameful state becomes known. At this point the gallant masculine creature always assures me, "But you don't *look* like a teacher."

A Wonderful Profession

Actually, I am proud to be a teacher. I think teaching is a wonderful profession. I suppose I like teaching primarily because I like people. I like them young and growing and optimistic; and I like them mature, realistic, and still eager.

I like teaching because I prefer ideas to things. The outcomes of my job are not measured in terms of money but in terms of people — how they think, how they act, how they live and enjoy life.

I've taught long enough to see some of the ideas I believe in come alive in action and influence not only the people I've taught, but those they have taught in turn. I find it satisfying to be paid for helping in the development of people.

In the classroom I'm the person who shapes the course of events. The children participate in the planning and I listen as much as I talk, but no one is looking over my shoulder telling me what to do next.

This may surprise you, but I like teaching because I like the salary I get. I know that many are underpaid. And I'll fight for better salaries for teachers as long as I live. But I'll fight on the grounds that we are worth more because we are well-qualified, well-trained professional people doing a professional job, rather than snivelling for a dole.

I like my salary for its regularity, for its tendency to increase throughout the years, and for the security it provides. Comes a depression — and I taught through the big one — I may find my salary lower, in fact I may even have to wait a while for it, but I'll still be working. In war or in peace, in depression or in prosperity, there will always be children; and in America, at least, I believe there will always be schools.

My job provides me with sick leave, provision for lifetime disability if that should occur, with retirement at the end. Not affluence, to be sure, but a kind of security difficult to attain without sacrificing personal freedom.

I like my weekends and the little one-, two-, or 10-day vacations that break up my working year. My business friends ponder how best to spend their precious two weeks' vacation; teachers, as a rule, think in terms of a whole summer of stimulating work and play — albeit usually without pay.

I like teaching because, as a woman, it gives me status of a kind difficult for a woman to attain in other professions. Teaching is traditionally a woman's field, and it is one of the few professions in which women are still the majority group. We have welcomed the men; but we have not had to fight them or ape them in order to hold our place, as have women in many other professional fields. We are respected; we are essential.

Where married women are allowed to teach and have maternity leave, the business of teaching synchronizes well with the business of raising a family. When children are of school age, their school hours and the mother's working hours coincide perfectly. Even vacations coincide, which some mothers consider a mixed blessing.

One of the subtler reasons why I like teaching is because it is essentially a cooperative rather than a competitive profession. We meet, we share, we give freely to each other whatever we may have to offer. We don't patent our ideas or our methods, and we don't try to hide them from each other for fear that someone may do a better job or sell more ideas than we do. Perhaps we do compete for prestige, for recognition of the success of our ideas, but it is a friendly, stimulating competition — not a dog-eat-dog competition for a limited market. We live, for the most part, in a cooperative atmosphere.

Teaching is a friendly profession. All of us who have taught for any length of time count our friends by the hundreds. This, like many of my other blessings, I had always taken for granted until last spring when I spent some time in the hospital. Almost before I was under the bedcovers, the flowers started to come until my end of the room looked like a gangster's funeral. The cards poured in by the handful in each mail delivery, until I became embarrassed when I noticed the somewhat envious glances of the other women in the room.

One day after an especially crowded visiting hour, the lady in the next bed said to me: "You really do have a rich, full life, don't you?" I answered without thinking, "Yes, I do, but you see I've been a teacher for 23 years." Thinking it over later, I realized I had said something quite profound.

A Good Life

As I compare my life with the lives of people I know in other fields, I feel that I have something that many of them envy. Teaching has given me a sense of direction, a sense of my own value in the world, and a sense of continuing growth. Teaching is more than just a way to earn a living, it is a way of life. It is a *good* life, — and I like it.